D1168362

Indiana University
Gary Center Library

# THE RESPONSIBILITIES OF THE CRITIC

BOOKS BY F. O. MATTHIESSEN

*Sarah Orne Jewett*
*Translation: An Elizabethan Art*
*The Achievement of T. S. Eliot*
*American Renaissance*
*Henry James: The Major Phase*
*Russell Cheney: A Record of His Work*
*The James Family*
*From the Heart of Europe*
*Theodore Dreiser*


BOOKS EDITED BY F. O. MATTHIESSEN

*Stories of Writers and Artists* (by Henry James)
*Herman Melville: Selected Poems*
*The American Novels and Stories of Henry James*
*The Notebooks of Henry James*, edited with Kenneth B. Murdock
*The Oxford Book of American Verse*

# THE RESPONSIBILITIES OF THE CRITIC

*Essays and Reviews by* F. O. MATTHIESSEN

SELECTED BY JOHN RACKLIFFE

NEW YORK · OXFORD UNIVERSITY PRESS · 1952

COPYRIGHT 1952 BY OXFORD UNIVERSITY PRESS, INC.

*Copyright material in this book is reprinted by permission of the original publishers and by arrangement with the estate of the late F. O. Matthiessen*

'That True and Human World . . .' copyright 1945 by *Accent.*

'Theodore Spencer, 1902–1949,' *Contemporary Poetry,* vol. x, copyright 1950 by Mary Owings Miller.

'Edwin Arlington Robinson,' 'Study Out the Land,' *American Literature,* copyright 1941, 1944 by Duke University Press.

'Four American Poets, 1944,' 'The Private Poet: Emily Dickinson,' 'Phelps Putnam, 1894–1948,' copyright 1944, 1945, 1949 by *The Kenyon Review.*

'Sarah Orne Jewett,' *American Writers on American Literature,* edited by John Macy, copyright 1931 by Liveright Publishing Corporation.

'Yeats: The Crooked Road,' 'Russell Cheney, 1881–1945,' copyright 1941, 1947 by F. O. Matthiessen.

'Melville as Poet,' *Poets of the Year,* copyright 1944 by New Directions.

'Irving Babbitt,' copyright 1942 by *The New England Quarterly.*

'Van Wyck Brooks,' 'A Classic Study of America: Tocqueville,' 'Essay on Rime,' 'Whitman: His Poetry and Prose,' 'Late-Summer Wine: Wallace Stevens,' 'Selfless Devotion to the Arts: Paul Rosenfeld,' copyright 1944, 1945, 1947, 1948 by The New York Times Company.

'Louis MacNeice,' 'Instances of Critical Method,' 'A New York Childhood,' copyright 1938, 1942, 1943 by *Partisan Review.*

'The Great Tradition: A Counterstatement,' 'Moses Coit Tyler,' 'The Flowering of New England,' copyright 1934, 1936 by The Plimpton Press.

'The Scholarly Profession: Hardin Craig,' copyright 1945 by Saturday Review Associates, Inc.

'William Vaughn Moody,' 'An Excited Debater,' copyright 1931, 1933 by The Southworth Press.

'Music on the Fingerboard: Marshall Schacht,' *Fingerboard,* copyright 1949 by Twayne Publishers, Inc.

'The Responsibilities of the Critic,' copyright 1949 by the Board of Regents, University of Michigan; poem from *Ideas of Order,* copyright 1935, 1936 by Wallace Stevens, reprinted by permission of Alfred A. Knopf, Inc.

'The Alienation of the Writer,' *Changing Patterns in American Civilization,* copyright 1949 by The University of Pennsylvania Press.

'Primarily Language: John Crowe Ransom,' copyright 1948 by The University of the South.

'A Monument to Howells,' 'Sherman and Huneker,' 'Nathaniel Hawthorne,' 'Whitman: Sanguine Confused American,' 'Margaret Fuller as Critic,' 'Mark Twain at Work,' 'Our First National Style,' 'The Innocent Eye: Mount and Homer,' 'Fragmentary and Whole: Williams, Aiken, Tate,' 'Henry James,' 'Henry Adams: The Real Education,' 'Classic Models for Modern Critics,' copyright, 1929, 1930, 1938, 1941, 1942, 1944, 1945, 1948, 1949 by Westbury Publications, Inc.

'New Standards in American Criticism, 1929,' 'Axel's Castle,' 'An Absolute Music: Hart Crane,' 'Thoreau: A Relaxed Chronicle,' copyright 1929, 1931, 1938, 1939 by Yale University Press.

Permission to reprint material was kindly granted by *The Yale Literary Magazine* and by the *Harvard University Gazette* through the courtesy of the Faculty of Arts and Sciences, Harvard University.

PRINTED IN THE UNITED STATES OF AMERICA

PS 121
. M3
c.2

*The true function of scholarship as of society is not to stake out claims on which others must not trespass, but to provide a community of knowledge in which others may share.*

'AMERICAN RENAISSANCE'

*It is the moral qualities of its leading personalities that are perhaps of even greater significance for a generation and for the course of history than purely intellectual accomplishments. Even these latter are, to a far greater degree than is commonly credited, dependent on the stature of character.*

EINSTEIN, 'MADAME CURIE'

16,062

# Contents

*Foreword*

T HE work of F. O. Matthiessen as teacher, scholar, and critic began in the late nineteen-twenties and continued until his death in April 1950. His first book, a treatment of Sarah Orne Jewett, appeared in 1929. His last, a study of the life and writing of Theodore Dreiser, was published posthumously in 1951. During a span of more than twenty years he wrote and edited some dozen volumes. (A full list of these is given opposite the title page.) At the same time he was steadily producing book reviews and critical essays for a variety of magazines, journals, and collective volumes. He also wrote an occasional piece of commentary in the fields of education and politics. This book brings together somewhat more than half of these uncollected articles.

The process of selection has not consisted simply of gathering the best of this work. For, with the exception of a few rather conventional apprentice pieces in the nineteen-twenties, Matthiessen's writing in periodicals was from the very start unusually consistent. His first reviews and articles lack the richness of his later work, but even these seldom fall below an assured level of accomplishment. My chief aim, therefore, has been to choose pieces which would most closely reflect his dominant interests throughout his career. The articles fall into a pattern which in its variety and its coherence parallels the full arc of Matthiessen's working life.

The book is arranged in six sections, of which the first and last are in the nature of prologue and epilogue. The opening selection, 'The Responsibilities of the Critic,' is a lecture delivered at the University of Michigan in the spring of 1949. Here Matthiessen gave perhaps the ripest formulation of some of his fundamental values and aims as a critic. The Hopwood Lecture, though broadly inclusive in its range, is clear in its explicit challenges. The standards it sets forth, earned and put to the test through twenty years of wholehearted commitment, he applied to his own work as rigorously as to the work of fellow critics and cultural historians. They provide an exacting gauge by which his own performance can be measured. To Matthiessen, criticism was not a form of personal expression or personal display, nor a substitute for 'creative' activity. It was the fulfillment of a social duty, confined within the healthy limits of a craft. This book can thus be regarded as an illustration in practice of its opening selection.

The Hopwood Lecture is the only long piece in the book which was originally designed to be spoken before an audience. Informal in organization and in tone, it evokes the flavor of Matthiessen's teaching. The mode of exposition, dictated by an anxiety to achieve full and truthful statement, may on first reading seem jerky or loose-jointed. Some of its broadest statements are immediately followed by a suggestion of counterstatement, a halting qualification, a quick pulling back to avoid partiality, to attain completeness. This particular movement of thought was not only a habit of the mind, it was a trait of character. It reflected Matthiessen's determination to 'see the object as it really is,' clearly, but in all its complexity, with all its ambiguities. The same rhythm determined the structure of *American Renaissance,* it gives body to the lucidity of *Henry James: The Major Phase.* Within the smaller framework of the articles and reviews given here, the mental process has in most cases been trimmed and cleared. The thought has not been oversimplified, but it has reached simplicity. In the Hopwood Lecture an attentive ear, hearing the speaking voice, can still detect the brief hesitations which give to the final affirmation its full solid strength.

The second and third sections consist largely of critical appraisals of the work of the artist. Many of these deal with contemporaries in the art to which Matthiessen gave his most concentrated attention, poetry. The division between 'the awakening function of art' and 'the artist at work' is intended to re-

veal a slight shift in the angle of approach rather than to establish any clear-cut distinction. The articles in the second section
weigh the completed product, the whole career. They constitute in a sense a welcoming of the artist's achievement—a welcome which loses none of its critical balance by being grounded
in generosity and sympathy. The articles in the third section
are directed more closely to the fallible creative process. Some
examine the difficulties and obstacles which beset the artist in
his effort to dominate his material. Others consider the personal
restrictions which narrow his field of action. And here again the
critic's tools lose none of their precision by being handled with
generosity and sympathy.

The grouping in the fourth and fifth sections reveals two
slightly different vantage points from which the work of the
critic and the cultural historian can be viewed. The fourth section, 'The Awareness of the Critic,' treats certain critics and
observers who, surmounting their limitations, have made an authentic and serious contribution. The section ends with a consideration of Paul Rosenfeld, whose selfless devotion to the arts
is invoked also in the Hopwood Lecture.

The fifth section, 'The Effort to Repossess the Past,' comprises
work stemming from an effort which impelled and enriched much
of Matthiessen's professional and personal life. The section
opens with the firm announcement, 'It is time for the history of
American literature to be rewritten.' In this review of Norman
Foerster, which appeared in 1929, Matthiessen found his full
stride. He indeed surveys with assurance the whole territory to
be explored in *American Renaissance*. The remaining articles in
the section are estimates of work done in the field of American
cultural history. Here, on his own ground, Matthiessen's evalu-
ations reach their greatest rigor. Forbearing with experimental
beginners, and duly acknowledging new insights and fresh approaches, he is frequently relentless in scrutinizing work which
seems to him to soften, distort, or evade the precious vitality of
the past. The section ends with a short statement provoked by
the discontinued publication in 1942 of *The Southern Review*,
'An Indispensable Resource,' which manifests Matthiessen's

lasting conviction that the duty of the cultural historian is to
serve the people of his own day.

The final section opens with a credo written in Matthiessen's
senior year at Yale. Printed as a 'leader' editorial, it was his one
contribution to the *Lit* during the academic year 1922–1923.
The writing is young, frequently clumsy. But it does disclose,
fully and with unabashed passion, the dedication that lay at the
heart of his lifework. With a fusion of humility and determination, it pleads and insists that the searching mind be balanced
by the feeling heart. These beliefs remained Matthiessen's
guide. The Yale senior's call for 'self-surrender to an ideal' is
put in words that the mature critic outgrew. But the Yale senior's naked honesty survived—toughened, tempered, unshaken.
This piece of juvenilia, written at the outset of an energetic and
often lonely career, may serve here as a key to that career and
as its confirmation.

The final articles are devoted to three friends who died during the last years of Matthiessen's life. The brief pages on Russell Cheney formed the introduction to Matthiessen's book of
selections from Cheney's paintings and letters. Even out of context they convey some of that book's prevailing tone.

The essay on Phelps Putnam, one of Matthiessen's most thorough and penetrating studies, is at once an act of criticism and
an act of friendship. In essence it is a careful, measured estimate of a minor poet whose career by most standards would be
considered largely a failure. Yet the estimate somehow succeeds
in being also a tribute to the man, a heavily weighted tribute
which in passing gravely questions the society that helped to
form him. Matthiessen always maintained that the man is to be
sought in his work, a view expressed repeatedly in this book.
The approach is at fundamental variance with that which tends
to seek first in the private life the key to the work. The essay on
Putnam is a demonstration of impersonal critical values being
tested under personally arduous conditions. It balances and
quietly lays bare some of the unresolved conflicts which for
Matthiessen gave life its texture and formed its tragedy.

The book closes with two short pieces on Theodore Spencer,

the colleague to whose memory Matthiessen dedicated the *Oxford Book of American Verse*. The present collection begins with the speaking voice—Matthiessen's voice defining the responsibilities of the critic. It ends with the voice of a friend, talking about that devotion which is 'the chief thing . . . in keeping the arts alive.'

The arrangement of this book, made in the endeavor to represent Matthiessen's dominant interests in their true proportions, inevitably obscures one central factor, his growth. Yet a strictly chronological presentation would have been perhaps even more likely to blur the underlying pattern of his total career. The present arrangement emphasizes one unusual aspect of that career—the fact that all Matthiessen's basic positions were taken early. His religious outlook and his political convictions were firmly established by the mid-twenties. His development as critic and scholar can indeed be measured in the consistency with which his ideas, constant in their main outlines, gain body and weight through the years. One notable index to this development—quite aside from the increase in purely technical mastery—lies in the ripening of emotional tone. This paralleled his perpetually acute response to 'the inexorable history of our time.' Even more fundamentally, it reflects the emergence of that quality which he defined, in reviewing the work of a poet, as more 'convincing' than any mere opinions: 'a deeply matured consistent attitude.' In the interplay between his books and the shorter articles collected here, and among these articles themselves, revealing comparisons can be made: the assurance and clarity in the reviews on Norman Foerster and Edmund Wilson, for example, have been enriched and tempered in the later reviews on Katherine Anne Porter, Paul Rosenfeld, and Wallace Stevens.

Considerations of space and proportion have dictated the omission of many articles which, judged by their quality alone, would have been valuable additions. Since the book is centered around literary criticism and cultural history, I have excluded work dealing chiefly with education and politics—two phases of American life that absorbed Matthiessen's attention and ener-

gies.* Fortunately he himself put on the record, in *From the
Heart of Europe,* a candid summation of some of the ideas and
actions which grew out of his persistent self-examination as
teacher and citizen. Readers whose interest in this side of Matthiessen is aroused or disappointed by the present selection
should turn to that book, which he described as 'less a travel
book than a journal of opinions.' Further material will be found
in the Matthiessen Memorial Issue of *Monthly Review,* October
1950, which consists chiefly of essays and statements by friends
and colleagues. The extensive bibliography of Matthiessen's
publications, prepared by C. L. Barber, is indispensable for
anyone who wishes to gain further acquaintance with his work.†

Of several long reviews which grouped the current output of
contemporary poets, I have retained only the major part of one,
the last, under the title 'Four American Poets, 1944.' These multiple reviews of verse contain some of Matthiessen's most alert
critical writing, but their inclusion would have overweighted
this book with material in one field. In the case of many of the
poets, Matthiessen gave later a more rounded, if highly condensed, estimate in his introduction to the *Oxford Book of
American Verse* and in his chapter on recent poetry in the *Literary History of the United States.*

I have omitted almost all reviews of books which themselves
have lost even a passing topical interest. For its representative
value I have given one example, 'An Excited Debater,' a review
from the early 'thirties of a book on the 'liberation' of American
literature. Its inclusion was suggested in part by Matthiessen's
statement outlining his standards for book reviewing, given in

* A full selection of his statements on education might find their focus in a
Harvard-Yale section. It could begin with his lively young evocation of
'three Yale worthies'—James Fenimore Cooper, Alphonso Taft, and Oliver
Wolcott. It would include several later pieces which witness his abiding
loyalty to Yale, his conscientious and independent service to Harvard, and
his anxious concern with American education as a whole. The section could
conclude with the bequest in his will to the Yale University Library: 'Having
given the bulk of my career to Harvard, I should like to leave whatever
little money I have, as a token of gratitude, to my own Alma Mater.'

† A supplement to the bibliography appeared in *Monthly Review* in
September 1952. The memorial issue was published in book form as *F. O.
Matthiessen: A Collective Portrait,* edited by Paul M. Sweezy and Leo
Huberman (Henry Schuman, New York, 1950).

the first section under the title 'The Winter Critic.' There he laments the universal overpraise of mediocrity and looks back with qualified approval to the old-style 'cutting and slashing' of the nineteenth-century quarterlies. Matthiessen's own cutting and slashing, showing the controlled anger of the outraged scholarly conscience, should still afford refreshment. A parallel example is his indignant account of the editorial mauling accorded to the poems of Emily Dickinson.

Several articles originally formed part of larger works. Those on Melville, Marshall Schacht, and Russell Cheney were written as introductions. The characterization of the achievement of Sarah Orne Jewett is taken from a chapter on 'New England Stories.' Most of Matthiessen's later contributions to larger volumes are readily available, among them the prefaces to his two selections from Henry James, and his chapters on Edgar Allan Poe and recent American poetry in the collaborative *Literary History of the United States.*

The titles of selections taken from magazines have in many cases been retained unchanged, though I have modified or substituted titles when those originally used by the magazine seemed inadequate or possibly misleading in the context of this book. In the case of untitled book reviews I have appended a title based on the author or the book or taken from the text of the review.

Two pieces which I have already mentioned are printed from manuscripts found among Matthiessen's papers; I have not discovered any record of their previous publication. The first of these, 'The Winter Critic,' immediately follows the Hopwood Lecture. The standards it urges stem from accumulated years of practicing a trade too often shirked or dishonored, that of the book reviewer. Like the Hopwood Lecture it can serve to measure and illuminate much of the work that follows it. The other article here printed from manuscript is 'An Indispensable Resource.' Written at a time of national crisis and world war, it gave clear warning of some of the dangers then threatening American cultural life. Like many of Matthiessen's political statements omitted from this collection, it has gained, not lost, in cogency.

An editor's foreword is clearly not the place to attempt to es-

timate Matthiessen's contribution as scholar and critic, to define
his place in our cultural history. This book, though necessarily
incomplete, will, I hope, make the task of assessment easier, the
need for it more clear. Though we no longer have the man, we do
have his work. That work can form part of our usable present—
'as we walk into the second half of our menaced century.'

I would like to express my gratitude to those friends of Matthiessen's who have generously given me their help, especially
C. L. Barber and Bettie Barber, Leo Marx, Laurette Murdock,
and Mary Rackliffe. In this book as in much else my greatest
debt is to Paul and Nancy Sweezy.

JOHN RACKLIFFE

*Boston, Massachusetts*
July 12, 1952

# I.  THE RESPONSIBILITIES OF THE CRITIC

# The Responsibilities of the Critic

MY deliberately grave title is in the tradition from Matthew Arnold, my first critical enthusiasm as an undergraduate thirty years ago. But at that very time a new critical movement was rising, the critical movement in which we are living today. T. S. Eliot's first important essay, 'Tradition and the Individual Talent,' was written in 1917, when he was twentynine; and I. A. Richards' first independent and most influential book, *The Principles of Literary Criticism*, came out in 1924, when he was in his early thirties. The talents and principles of those two then young men have been the most pervasive forces upon the criticism of the past quarter-century.

We know now what a revolution they instigated, if one may use such a violent word as revolution in the field of the arts, where all victories fortunately are bloodless, and where what was overthrown remains undestroyed and capable of being rediscovered at the next turn of the wheel of taste. When Eliot was growing up, the tastes and standards of Arnold were still prevailing; and Eliot found himself wholly dissatisfied with Arnold's preoccupation with the spirit of poetry rather than with its form. The form of Eliot's own first poems was deceptively radical, since he was really rejecting the easily flowing forms of the romantics and the Elizabethans for the more intricately weighted forms of the symbolists and the metaphysicals.

When Richards, as a psychologist who believed in the basic importance of the words with which men try to fathom their meanings, began to read Eliot's poems, he encountered the kind of language that proved most compelling to readers just after

This speech was given in May 1949 as the Hopwood Lecture at the University of Michigan.—ED.

the First World War. The immense loosening of speech that had accompanied the rapid expansions in mass education and mass communication had reached the point where, if the artist was again to communicate the richness and denseness of real experience, he must use a language that compelled the reader to slow down, to be concerned once more with the trip rather than with the arrival. As the young English critic T. E. Hulme had been arguing, before he was killed in battle in 1915, poetry must always endeavor thus 'to arrest you . . . to make you continuously see a physical thing, to prevent you gliding through an abstract process.'

What resulted from the joint influence of Eliot and Richards was a criticism that aimed to give the closest possible attention to the text at hand, to both the structure and texture of the language. You are all familiar with the names of its practitioners who, if we confine ourselves to America alone, have already produced a more serious and exacting body of work than we had previously witnessed in this country. To be sure, Richards' most gifted follower was one of his own students at Cambridge, England. William Empson, in his precocious *Seven Types of Ambiguity* (1929), begun when he was still an undergraduate, pushed to its subtle extreme Richards' kind of linguistic analysis. Empson in turn has had a particular vogue here among the critics whom we now associate with the newly founded Kenyon School of Criticism, most notably with John Crowe Ransom, Robert Penn Warren, and Cleanth Brooks. Others whose names are linked with that school, Kenneth Burke, R. P. Blackmur, Allen Tate, Austin Warren, and Yvor Winters, however divergent their methods and emphases, reveal throughout their work how they have had to reckon with Eliot and Richards, whether in concord or belligerence.

The effect of this new movement upon the study of literature in our universities has been by now considerable. Although opposed by both the old guards of philologists and literary historians, most of the critics I have mentioned now hold academic appointments, which may or may not have been good for their work. But their work has thereby become instrumental in the revolt against concentrating exclusively on the past, and against concentrating on literary history instead of on literature. As a result both teachers and students are more capable of close analysis and lively appreciation than they were a generation ago.

But by now we have reached the stage where revolt has begotten its own set of conventions, to use the terms of one of Harvard's great former teachers, John Livingston Lowes. As we watch our own generation producing whole anthologies of criticism devoted to single contemporary authors and more and more detailed books of criticism of criticism, we should realize that we have come to the unnatural point where textual analysis seems to be an end in itself. The so-called little magazines have been essential and valiant outposts of revolt in our time when the magazines of wide circulation, in decline from their standards in the nineteenth century, have abandoned serious discussion of literature almost entirely.

But the little magazines seem now to be giving rise to the conventions and vocabulary of a new scholasticism and to be not always distinguishable from the philological journals which they abhor. The names of the authors may be modern, but the smell is old. The trouble is that the terms of the new criticism, its devices and strategies and semantic exercises, can become as pedantic as any other set of terms if they are not handled as the means to fresh discoveries but as counters in a stale game. In too many recent articles literature seems to be regarded merely as a puzzle to be solved.

This is not to underestimate the great and continuing service performed by the few quarterlies devoted to criticism, or by those even littler magazines that often last only long enough to introduce one or two new talents in poetry or fiction. The important experimental work of our time has again and again been able to secure its first publication only through their pages. This is one of the consequences of what F. R. Leavis, the editor of *Scrutiny*, has called the split between 'mass civilization' and 'minority culture.' But to recognize that phenomenon in our democracy should only be to combat it.

There is potentially a much greater audience in America for the art of literature than the blurb-writers, who often pass for reviewers in the Sunday supplements, would seem to suspect.

The effectiveness of the critics in the little magazines in having by now prepared a wider public for, say, Joyce or Kafka or Eliot, amply testifies to that. But the dilemma for the serious critic in our dangerously split society is that, feeling isolated, he will become serious in the wrong sense, aloof and finally taking an inverted superiority in his isolation. At that point criticism becomes a kind of closed garden.

My views are based on the conviction that the land beyond the garden's walls is more fertile, and that the responsibilities of the critic lie in making renewed contact with that soil. William James used to insist that the first duty of any thinker is to know as much as possible about life in his own time. Such an exhortation may seem too general to be of much use, but it can be grasped more concretely if we envisage the particular responsibilities of the critic in a whole series of awarenesses. These awarenesses may encompass some of the breadth and comprehensiveness which James assumed to be the thinker's goal, and some of the feeling of being drenched with actual life, which he believed to be the thinker's best reward. Much of the ground that we will traverse was also implied to be within the critic's scope by the early work of Eliot and Richards, though some of it has been lost sight of by their followers.

The first awareness for the critic should be of the works of art of our own time. This applies even if he is not primarily a critic of modern literature. One of Eliot's observations which has proved most salutary is that of the inescapable interplay between past and present: that the past is not what is dead, but what is already living; and that the present is continually modifying the past, as the past conditions the present. If one avails himself of the full resources latent in that perception, one is aware that it is not possible to be a good critic of Goethe today without knowing Mann, or of Stendhal or Balzac without knowing Proust, or of Donne or Dryden without knowing Eliot.

The converse is equally true, if less necessary to be argued in the academy. But once outside, particularly in the rapid and rootless life of our cities, the tendency even for practitioners in the arts is to be immersed wholly in the immediate. This is not what James foresaw, since he took for granted the constant meeting-point between what was already known and what was still to be known. But today we can take no tradition for granted, we must keep repossessing the past for ourselves if we are not to lose it altogether. The value in this urgency is that what we manage to retain will really belong to us, and not on authority at second hand. The proper balance, even for the critic who considers his field to be the present, is to bring to the elucidation of that field as much of the art of the past as he can command.

A recently dead critic, Paul Rosenfeld, was a heartening example of this balance. Prolonging in this country the rich cultural life of his German-Jewish forebears, he moved naturally among the arts, and it would never have occurred to him that a critic of contemporary music would try to speak without having all the great composers of the past at his finger tips. But he regarded the work of the present, especially in America, as his particular province, and often said that if our younger composers were to have a sense of possessing any audience, someone must make it his function to listen to them all. In complete modesty and selflessness he took that task upon himself. As his friends knew, Paul Rosenfeld gave himself away to his generation, a very unusual act in our fiercely competitive world, where even our intellectual life seems so often to become poisoned by the habits of our business civilization.

I have cited Rosenfeld because his generous openness to all the arts and his devoted impressions of what he found now seem so foreign to the grimly thin-lipped disciples of a more rigorous analysis. Indeed, one of them, writing currently in *The Hudson Review*, has declared that the recent volume of tribute by Rosenfeld's contemporaries from the 'twenties and 'thirties praised him for a 'thoroughly degraded function.' Such total lack of comprehension is a devastating illustration of what Auden meant by saying that one of the worst symptoms of sterility in our present culture is that of 'intellectuals without love.'

No incapacity could be less fruitful in the presence of the arts. Its recent frequency may be another unhappy by-product of the sort of specialization that leaves the student knowing only his own field. Such self-enclosed knowledge may often mean that he really knows nothing at all. At least it is hard to conceive of a good critic of literature who does not have an alert curiosity about other fields and techniques. Anyone understands his own subject and discipline better if he is aware of some other subject and discipline. To what extent this awareness should lead to mastery will vary greatly with individual aptitude. It does not seem profitable to insist that any given critic should also be expert in linguistic theory or mathematical logic or Marx or Freud, but I can hardly think of a critic today being indifferent to the access of power his mind could gain from a close study of one or more of these.

This does not mean that the misapplication of theory from one field to another is not as big a pitfall as it always was, or that fads don't often outrun facts. But as one instance of valuable cross-fertilization between fields there is cultural anthropology. Utilizing the disciplines of history and sociology, it has proved a particularly stimulating ally to the study of literature in a period when literature itself, in the hands of Joyce and Mann, has been rediscovering the vitality of primitive myth. Through our renewed awareness of folk patterns we now realize that the fertility rites which solemnize the death and rebirth of the year are equally germane to our understanding of *The Waste Land* or *The Winter's Tale* or *The Peace* of Aristophanes or the *Bacchae* of Euripides.

Another awareness which our split society makes it hard for us to keep in the right proportion is that of the popular arts of our technological age. The consequences for all our lives of the mass media of communication become ever more insistent, so that we must either channel them to socially valuable ends or be engulfed by them. The first results of our new discoveries are often as discouraging as when Thoreau scorned the transatlantic cable on the grounds that the initial news that would 'leak through into the broad, flapping American ear' would be that the Princess Adelaide had the whooping cough.

The first results of television would appear to be that it has made conversation impossible in one of its few remaining American strongholds, the barroom, and is debauching the customers with entertainment that is a long throwback to the juvenile days of the penny arcade. But then one recalls how the radio, despite its intolerable deal of soap, has during the past twenty-five years built up a taste for the best symphony music among millions of listeners who would not otherwise have ever heard it. The chief art form of our age, the moving picture, is the compelling reminder of our immense potentialities and continual corruptions. Even now when, in its postwar doldrums, Hollywood seems again to have forgotten that standardization through mass production is more suitable for soup than for art, the great new Italian films are demonstrating the important access of social truth that the art of the film can gain by utilizing some of the solid techniques of the documentary.

I have mentioned these disparate examples of good and bad as a way of enforcing my conviction that we in the universities cannot afford to turn our backs upon them or upon the world from which they come. The proper place for the thinker, as William James conceived it, was at the central point where a battle is being fought. It is impossible for us to take that metaphor with the lightness that he could. Everywhere we turn in these few fateful years since the first atom bomb dropped on Hiroshima we seem menaced by such vast forces that we may well feel that we advance at our peril. But even greater peril would threaten us if those whose prime responsibility as critics is to keep open the life-giving communications between art and society should waver in their obligations to provide ever fresh thought for our own society.

In using metaphors of battle here and now, I am not thinking in an academic void. If we believe that freedom of thought and of speech are the distinguishing features of the culture of a true democracy, we must realize by what a thin margin they now survive in this country. Within the past year there have been the most serious violations of academic freedom, caused, ironically, by officials who are determined to prove that the United States is so much better than any other country that it is above criticism. We must recognize the full gravity of these casualties of the cold war, for they are a product of the very kind of blind suppression that their instigators declare exists only behind what they denounce as 'the iron curtain.'

The most flagrant recent case of national importance has nothing to do with the issue of communism, and thus furnishes a concrete demonstration of how, once official opinion embarks on the course of stamping out dangerous views, every shade of dissent becomes dangerous. Olivet College, as you all here know, was founded in the great pioneering period of our education, when Americans were expanding the frontiers of their thought as well as of their territory. Its recent career, particularly in the period between two world wars, added a notable chapter to our experiments with education by tutorial work and group discussion. When members of its faculty of such national distinction as a Pulitzer prize winner for biography and the candidate for vice-president on the Socialist ticket are dismissed, none of us can stand aloof or feel that we are not implicated.

If what I have just been saying seems an unwarranted digression from the responsibilities of the critic of the arts, I want to correct that impression. The series of awarenesses which I believe the critic must possess lead ineluctably from literature to life, and I do not see how the responsible intellectual in our time can avoid being concerned with politics. It is at this point that my divergence becomes most complete from the formalists who have followed in the wake of Eliot, as well as from Eliot himself, whose reverence for the institutions of monarchy and aristocracy seems virtually meaningless for life in America.

I would like to recall the atmosphere of the early nineteen-thirties, of the first years of the last depression, when the critical pendulum had swung to the opposite pole, from the formalists to the Marxists. I am not a Marxist myself but a Christian, and I have no desire to repeat the absurdities of the moment when literary men, quite oblivious theretofore of economics, were finding sudden salvation in a dogma that became more rigid the less they had assimilated it. But I believe the instinct of that moment was right, as our greatest recent cultural historian, Vernon Parrington's instinct was right, in insisting upon the primacy of economic factors in society. Most artists and students of literature remain amateurs in the field of economics, but that does not prevent them from utilizing some of the basic and elementary truths which economists have made available for our culture.

Emerson held that a principle is an eye to see with, and despite all the excesses and exaggerated claims of the Marxists of the 'thirties, I still believe that the principles of Marxism—so much under fire now—can have an immense value in helping us to see and comprehend our literature. Marx and Engels were revolutionary in many senses of that word. They were pioneers in grasping the fact that the industrial revolution had brought about—and would continue to bring about—revolutionary changes in the whole structure of society. By cutting through political assumptions to economic realities, they revolutionized the way in which thinking men regarded the modern state. By their rigorous insistence upon the economic foundations underlying any cultural superstructure, they drove, and still drive, home the fact that unless the problems rising from the economic inequalities in our own modern industrialized society are better solved, we cannot continue to build democracy. Thus the principles of Marxism remain at the base of much of the best social and cultural thought of our century. No educated American can afford to be ignorant of them, or to be delinquent in realizing that there is much common ground between these principles and any healthily dynamic America.

This is not to say that Marxism gives what I consider an adequate view of the nature of man, or that it or any other economic theory can provide a substitute for the critic's essential painstaking discipline in the interplay between form and content in concrete works of art. But a concern with economics can surely quicken and enlarge the questions that a critic asks about the content of any new work of art with which he is faced, about the fullness to which it measures and reveals the forces that have produced both it and its author. Walt Whitman might have said, in *Democratic Vistas:* 'Man becomes free, not by realizing himself in opposition to society, but by realizing himself through society.' That sentence was actually written by Christopher Caudwell, a young English Marxist who was killed fighting for the Loyalists in Spain. His book *Illusion and Reality,* published in 1937, has recently been reissued, and is having a renewed vogue now with younger writers and students. Their enthusiasm for it, I gather, springs from the fact that Caudwell, despite the sweeping immaturity of many of his judgments, keeps asking the big questions about man in society that the school of close textual analysis has tended to ignore.

I do not mean for a moment to underestimate the value of that school. It has taught us in particular how to read poetry with an alertness and resilience of attention that were in danger of being altogether lost through the habits set up by an age of quick journalism. All I would suggest is that analysis itself can run to seed unless the analyzing mind is also absorbed in a wider context than the text before it.

Mention of Caudwell's name has brought me to the last of the awarenesses that I would urge upon the critic: that of the wide gap which still exists between America and Europe. Henry James discovered long ago his leading theme in the contrast between American innocence and European experience. Although the world that he contemplated has been altered beyond recognition, that theme is still peculiarly urgent when we are faced with the difference between a Europe which has undergone fascism and destructive war at first hand and an America which has come out of the war richer and more powerful than ever before. Stephen Spender has noticed the difference in reading Randall Jarrell's book of poems called *Losses*. For the American, as Spender observes, even when the losses are those of our own fliers, they are something that happens far away on distant continents, they are not yet immediately overhead and inescapable. Allen Tate has described the kind of false superiority that can be engendered by such special isolation:

> The American people fully armed
> With assurance policies, righteous and harmed,
> Battle the world of which they're not at all.

How do Americans become part of that greater world? Not by pretending to be something they are not, nor by being either proud or ashamed of their vast special fortune. It does no good, for example, to adopt the vocabulary of the Paris existentialists in order to emulate the crisis of occupation which we have not passed through. The ironic lines of Tate's 'Sonnet at Christmas' suggest a more mature way of meeting experience. None of us can escape what we are, but by recognizing our limitations, and comprehending them, we can transcend them by the span of that knowledge.

Here is the area where breadth of concern becomes most rewarding for the critic. By perceiving what his country is and is not in comparison with other countries, he can help contribute, in this time of fierce national tensions, to the international understanding without which civilization will not survive. He will also find that he has come to know his own country better.

The art of a country always becomes richer by being open to stimulus from outside, and criticism can find a particularly fertile field in observing the results of that interchange. For one fascinating instance, how much we can learn about both Europe and America from the high estimation that French writers are now giving to the novels of Faulkner. At a period when the French have felt a debilitation in their own tradition, they have turned to the new world for an access of vitality. But what has seemed to them most real in America is not our surface of optimism, but the terrible underlying violence that has possessed the imaginations of nearly all our naturalistic novelists. It may seem a strange paradox that America, spared so far the worst violences of fascism and war, has imagined violence in a way that impresses men who have experienced the savage brutality of both.

But as we look back at America through French eyes, we become more conscious of what the preponderantly genteel reviewers for our organs of mass circulation have done their best to obscure: that Faulkner is not a writer of meaningless sensationalism but one who has seized upon basic forces in our history, particularly upon the tensions resulting from our initial injustice to the Negro. Faulkner may often overwrite and use some of the cheap devices of melodrama, but we should not allow these to deflect us from the truth of his record. If we prefer a more smiling version of ourselves, we are liable to the peculiarly American dilemma of passing from innocence to corruption without ever having grasped maturity. By which I mean the maturity that comes from the knowledge of both good and evil.

In proposing an ever widening range of interests for the ideal critic, I have moved from his central responsibility to the text before him out to an awareness of some of the world-wide struggles of our age. We must come back to where we started, to the critic's primary function. He must judge the work of art as work of art. But knowing form and content to be inseparable, he will recognize his duty to both. Judgment of art is unavoidably both an aesthetic and a social act, and the critic's sense of social responsibility gives him a deeper thirst for meaning.

This is not a narrow question of the wrong right or right left politics. The *locus classicus* on this matter was furnished by Marx's judgment of Balzac, who as a monarchist and Catholic reactionary supported the very forces to which Marx was most opposed. Yet Marx could perceive that, no matter what this novelist's views, his vision of the deep corruption of French society by money made him the most searching historian of his time. Engels proceeded to evolve the principle inherent in this judgment:

> The father of tragedy, Aeschylus, and the father of comedy, Aristophanes, were both very clearly poets with a thesis . . . But I believe that the thesis must inhere in the situation and the action, without being explicitly formulated; and it is not the poet's duty to supply the reader in advance with the future historical solution of the conflict he describes.

A poet describes many other things besides conflict, yet without some sense of conflict there is no drama to engage us. The way in which the artist implies social judgments and entices the critic to meditate upon them may be elucidated by a pair of examples. Wallace Stevens' second book, *Ideas of Order,* appeared in 1935. Until then he had been known by his richly musical *Harmonium,* by what he himself had called 'the essential gaudiness of poetry.' The besetting weakness of criticism, when faced with a new writer, is to define his work too narrowly, and then to keep applying that definition like a label. Stevens had been bracketed as 'a dandy of poetry,' as an epicurean relisher of 'sea surfaces full of clouds,' as one who had found his role in discovering 'thirteen ways of looking at a blackbird,' as identical with his own Crispin in his relish of 'good, fat, guzzly fruit.'

He was, to be sure, all these enchanting things. But no one seemed to have been prepared for the fact that his imagination was so fecund and robust that it would compel him to launch forth, in his mid-fifties, upon the new territory indicated by his explicitly philosophical title. He was also making his own response to the vast disequilibrium that every sensitive mind had to feel at the pit of the depression. He had come to recognize that 'a violent order is disorder.' Or, as Horace Gregory put it more explicitly, Stevens' new poems were demonstrating that he was not merely a connoisseur of nuances, but—not unlike Henry James—a shrewdly trained observer of 'the decadence that follows upon the rapid acquisition of wealth and power.'

Stevens' kind of symbolist poetry never makes the explicit approach. So far as he has any political or social views, they would appear to be conservative. Yet in 'Sad Strains of a Gay Waltz,' the second poem in *Ideas of Order,* he gave to a then young radical like myself a sudden clarification of the clouded time in which we are living. It is this kind of 'momentary stay against confusion,' as Robert Frost has said, that a poem is designed to give, and that becomes one of the measures of its authenticity.

In listening to almost any poem by Stevens, the first thing that strikes you is his past-masterly command of rhetoric, a reminder that, unlike the poets of the imagist movement, he is still rooted in the older tradition that leads from Bridges back to Milton. In this poem his rhetoric is formed into three-lined unrhymed stanzas of a basically iambic pentameter pattern, but with many irregular line lengths which quicken but do not break that pattern. The conflict that constitutes his theme is between an age that is dying and a hazardous potential new birth. He adumbrates this by offsetting a character whom he calls Hoon, a lover of solitude like Thoreau, against the rising masses of men in a still formless society. But his controlling symbols are more oblique, they are 'waltzes' and 'shadows.' Music that has become played out seems to its listeners to be 'empty of shadows,' and by a very effective repetition of the phrase, 'Too many waltzes have ended,' Stevens sets up his counterpoise for a new, more dynamic music that will again be full of shadows:

> The truth is that there comes a time
> When we can mourn no more over music
> That is so much motionless sound.
>
> There comes a time when the waltz
> Is no longer a mode of desire, a mode
> Of revealing desire and is empty of shadows.
>
> Too many waltzes have ended. And then
> There's that mountain-minded Hoon,
> For whom desire was never that of the waltz,
>
> Who found all form and order in solitude,
> For whom the shapes were never the figures of men
> Now, for him, his forms have vanished.
>
> There is order in neither sea nor sun.
> The shapes have lost their glistening.
> There are these sudden mobs of men,
>
> These sudden clouds of faces and arms,
> An immense suppression, freed,
> These voices crying without knowing for what,
>
> Except to be happy, without knowing how,
> Imposing forms they cannot describe,
> Requiring order beyond their speech.
>
> Too many waltzes have ended. Yet the shapes
> For which the voices cry, these, too, may be
> Modes of desire, modes of revealing desire.
>
> Too many waltzes—The epic of disbelief
> Blares oftener and soon, will soon be constant.
> Some harmonious skeptic soon in a skeptical music
>
> Will unite these figures of men and their shapes
> Will glisten again with motion, the music
> Will be motion and full of shadows.

The extension of our sense of living by compelling us to contemplate a broader world is the chief gift that literature holds out to us. This sense is never limited to our own place or time. What makes the art of the past still so full of undiscovered wealth is that each age inevitably turns to the past for what it most wants, and thereby tends to remake the past in its own image. The cardinal example is Shakespeare. What the nineteenth century saw in Hamlet was what Coleridge saw, the figure of a transcendental philosopher absorbed in himself. What we see is a man inextricably involved with his own society, as may be suggested in brief by one of the scenes which nineteenth-century producers usually cut. This is the scene in the fourth act where Hamlet, on his way to England, encounters a Captain from Fortinbras' army. The Captain is bitter at what his orders are compelling him to do:

> Truly to speak, and with no addition,
> We go to gain a little patch of ground
> That hath in it no profit but the name.
> To pay five ducats, five, I would not farm it.

The effect of this speech upon Hamlet is to heighten his awareness of the difference between the Captain's situation and his own, of how he, Hamlet, has every reason for action and yet cannot bring himself to act:

> Examples gross as earth exhort me;
> Witness this army of such mass and charge
> Led by a delicate and tender prince,
> Whose spirit with divine ambition puff'd
> Makes mouths at the invisible event,
> Exposing what is mortal and unsure
> To all that fortune, death, and danger dare,
> Even for an egg-shell. Rightly to be great
> Is not to stir without great argument,
> But greatly to find quarrel in a straw
> When honor's at the stake. How stand I then,
> That have a father kill'd, a mother stain'd,
> Excitements of my reason and my blood,
> And let all sleep, while to my shame I see
> The imminent death of twenty thousand men,

> That for a fantasy and trick of fame
> Go to their graves like beds, fight for a plot
> Whereon the numbers cannot try the cause,
> Which is not tomb enough and continent
> To hide the slain?

As John Gielgud speaks these lines, we feel what Shakespeare meant his audience to feel, the necessity for Hamlet's revenge. But we also bring to the passage our own sense of vast insecurity, our need of being engaged in the public issues of our menaced time, and yet the need of making sure that the seeming issues are the true issues, that we are not betrayed into engagements that are merely 'th'imposthume of much wealth and peace.'

There is a basic distinction between bringing everything in your life to what you read and reading into a play of the past issues that are not there. All I am suggesting is the extent to which our awareness of ourselves as social beings is summoned by the greatest art. That is the root of my reason for believing that the good critic becomes fully equipped for his task by as wide a range of interests as he can master. The great temptation for the young writer at the present moment is to think that because the age is bad, the artist should escape from it and, as a superior being, become a law simply to himself. Some memorable romantic poetry has been written on that assumption, but not the great forms of drama or epic, nor the comparable great forms in prose. However, the critic should freely grant that the artist writes as he must. But for his own work the critic has to be both involved in his age and detached from it. This double quality of experiencing our own time to the full and yet being able to weigh it in relation to other times is what the critic must strive for, if he is to be able to discern and demand the works of art that we need most. The most mature function of the critic lies finally in that demand.

*Michigan Alumnus Quarterly Review,* 1949

# *The Winter Critic*

I GO on the assumption that a review is simply a short piece of criticism, and that it should be as good criticism as its writer can make it. This means a declaration of war on all literary supplements in which you can't tell the reviews from the advertisements, except that the reviewers are a slightly inferior type of publisher's agent. As a reviewer, I think that we ought to pay attention to the kind of letter I received recently from a younger creative writer. 'In books we have dignity enough,' he said, 'but the incalculable force of a Sunday Review is the soft drip that drives a man to the wall.'

Edgar Allan Poe had a similar perception a century ago, and I believe that Poe, who had to support himself by his pen in a very unfavorable market, is still our best model for a reviewer. He protested against what he called 'the cant of generalization,' and excoriated those who used the book nominally under review merely as an excuse for a diffuse essay on what they liked. He was equally astringent against those who went to the other extreme and substituted for the labor of analysis and judgment an easy 'digest or compendium of the work noticed, with copious extracts.'

Challenged by the ghost of Poe, I would submit that what he called 'a critical notice'—preferring himself that term to 'a review'—should at the minimum do three things. It should furnish exposition and description; it should enable you to feel concretely what is being described; and it should give you in the

This piece is printed from an untitled manuscript found among Matthiessen's papers. I have been unable to discover whether it was published. I assume that it was written at about the same time as the chapter on Poe, for the collaborative *Literary History of the United States,* in the mid-'forties.—ED.

process an evaluation. The first of these three functions cannot be satisfactorily discharged by, say, making a digest of the plot of a novel or the chapter headings of a book of history. That will use up all your space and leave you with the compendium without judgment against which Poe so rightly objected. Instead you must interweave your three functions. If the book at hand is a piece of literature, you can best suggest its quality by concentrating your exposition upon a few significant episodes, and by letting your reader feel for himself that quality, not through some illustrative quotations tacked on mechanically at the end, but through the force of a few deftly foreshortened examples woven into your exposition. And if that weaving has been really skillful, you won't be faced with the necessity of a heavy-handed summary for your evaluation. You will have pointed it out lightly, by analytical insights, as you went along.

Beyond that blueprint for the dream review of my future, I should like to dwell on one further responsibility. It is the responsibility of 'placing' the book at hand in relation to what has been previously accomplished in the same field; and our hurried methods of production and changing fashions of the moment make that responsibility the one that we are fulfilling least well. If you are reviewing a novel or a play or a book of poems, you should suggest, however briefly, how that book measures up to the current state of its art, whether it makes a fresh contribution, or whether it is simply more of the same. And if a good new book about Samuel Johnson or Matthew Arnold has appeared, you shouldn't undertake to comment on it unless you are willing to glance back over the already existing work done on the subject, so that you can estimate precisely what has been added.

To anyone concerned with the free play of ideas or with the importance of new works of art, the most depressing feature of our present cultural scene is the continual overpraise of mediocrity. That makes the soft incessant drip which the young artist or thinker feels threatening him with engulfment. Even the destructive 'cutting and slashing' of the old quarterlies was less damaging, for there at least vigorous men were speaking their own minds. Some reviewers may object that Poe's standards are too high for daily use when he insists that the critical practitioner must be concerned with the first principles of art, that, indeed, as he said in his *Marginalia*, 'It is the business of the critic so to soar that he shall see the sun.'

Matthew Arnold would have agreed that the realm of the critic is light, but I will settle for a more homely and a more timely metaphor. Give the winter critic a shovel, and let him get rid of the slush. Demand of him only that he doesn't pretend that what he is dealing with is pure as the driven snow on yonder mountain top. And let him remember that his chief aid is the light of the sun, even if he only feels it on his back.

## II. THE AWAKENING FUNCTION OF ART

*This is the awakening function of art . . . the responsibility of the artist is not to solve in advance the tensions of the society he lives in, but simply—yet this is a task for a lifetime—to give, to the full, existence as he has known it to be. The role of a Hemingway or an Eliot . . . is to keep alive the vital, delicate, and always menaced accuracy of communication, without which there can be no renewed discovery of man by man.*

'FROM THE HEART OF EUROPE'

# Yeats: The Crooked Road

ALL discussion of Yeats should be mindful of the discovery he made, while contemplating the crippled legs and bursting vitality of Henley, that 'antithesis is the foundation of human nature.' Blake had said, 'Without contraries there is no progression.' Yeats' poetry can hardly be described except through such a dialectic, through confronting a series of interwoven paradoxes. Starting out to be a poet, he was so near-sighted and so inattentive of the external world that he was incapable of much visual experience; and what would have seemed to be even more of a liability, he confessed himself tone-deaf. Yet his very bafflement with music may have caused him to listen more alertly to every modulation of the spoken word; and, composing always with great difficulty, he mastered the most resilient and seemingly most effortless rhythms of song. Again, though he would appear to have had no full mystical experience (unless you except the late and special period recorded in his *Vision*), from the start he held poetry to be a mystery cult, a ritual. Yet this theoretical believer in the moment of inspired revelation was in practice the most deliberate and painstaking craftsman. At first distrustful of all rhetoric in the mood of Verlaine, he finally showed himself an inveterate debater and explainer who belonged at journey's end no less with Dryden than with Landor. The most undramatic of dramatists, writing nearly always as though Blake's *Book of Thel* was the criterion and as though he wanted a veil between his actors and his audience, he became in his lyrics our time's outstanding master of the dramatic voice, capable of creating a whole situation by means of a single-line refrain to a ballad and of concentrating a passionate scene into an eight-line poem. Producing poetry over a span of almost sixty

years, he not merely improved to the end, he virtually transformed his talent. He could express what had happened only
through another paradox: that when he was young his Muse had
been old, that as he grew older she had become younger.

These and similar 'contraries' must be the themes in any treatment of his career. Louis MacNeice's book * is, as he says, 'largely
taken up with a discussion of Yeats' subject matter during
various periods of his life.' Writing as a younger Irishman,
MacNeice is in a good position to tell us about Yeats' background, to put into their context the poet's political opinions,
social prejudices, and cultural values. Writing as a conscious
member of a very different school of poetry, MacNeice can also
point out what his generation has learned from Yeats as well as
what it has rejected, and what some of our bearings now are.
MacNeice has written, as always, very deftly; he is knowledge-
able on all the major issues; he has freed his tone of much of the
superciliousness that marred his *Modern Poetry*. The one thing
he does not seem to have brought to his task is the quality of
passion which was Yeats' constant goal both in life and in art.
Consequently, the chief value of his chapters is their neatly
assembled information: we can use this to make the organic
connections that MacNeice hardly attempts, we can bring it to
bear upon the illumination of some of the poems themselves.

One of the themes that must possess a particular absorption
for Americans is what it means to be a national poet. Contribut-
ing in his early twenties a series of articles to a Boston news-
paper 'from your Celt in London,' Yeats formulated the principle
that 'you can no more have the greater poetry without a nation
than religion without symbols.' A dozen years later, in his essay
'What is "Popular Poetry"?' his attention was turned, as was that
of so many other figures in the Irish Renaissance, to the American florescence of the mid-nineteenth century. Longfellow
served him as an excellent example of what he did not want. Such
'popular poetry' 'never came from the people at all.' It was designed for the 'predominant portion of the middle class' who
'have unlearned the unwritten tradition which binds the unlet-

* *The Poetry of W. B. Yeats* by Louis MacNeice. Oxford University Press.

tered, so long as they are masters of themselves . . . and who have not learned the written tradition which has been established upon the unwritten.' On the other hand, Whitman, whom Yeats greatly admired, had made an impossible attempt to break from tradition altogether. For Yeats assumed as a norm that 'the poetry of the coteries' and 'the true poetry of the people' should possess a living bond, since, as Aristotle urged, it is the role of the cultivated poet to think like a wise man but to express himself like the common folk.

In enunciating this norm Yeats was helped by the then recent example of the movements in Scandinavia to restore the folk-life, to revitalize the sense of national history and legend. He wanted a 'unity of culture' in which 'the common man has some share in imaginative art.' He could believe that 'in Ireland today the old world that sang and listened is, it may be for the last time in Europe, face to face with the world that reads and writes.' He could hold that assumption because of the special circumstances of Irish history, because his country had remained largely untouched by the industrial revolution. Therefore, when Yeats thought in terms of classes, he could also hold that 'three types of men have made all beautiful things. Aristocracies have made beautiful manners, because their place in the world puts them above the fear of life, and the countrymen have made beautiful stories and beliefs, because they have nothing to lose and so do not fear, and the artists have made all the rest, because Providence has filled them with recklessness.'

These are the suppositions upon which Yeats proceeded to build all his own work. They wave aside most of existence as it had come to be known in the century of Balzac and Ibsen, the world of the expanding middle class whose activities had encroached overwhelmingly upon both aristocrats and countrymen. MacNeice points out the degree of literary unreality that enters into Yeats' vision of Ireland, the Ireland of the Big House and the peasant. He notes the poet's vague use of 'medieval' as a term of praise, as when he said that Lady Gregory's 'point of view was founded, not on narrow modern habit,' but 'upon her own strange feudal, almost medieval youth.' MacNeice also asserts that the poet's country people generally tend to be myths,

like the Fisherman of the poem of that name, who is not at all
the physical gregarious sportsman but a lonely dreamer, a poet's
projection, 'not to be found on any stream in Ireland.' The
dangers in Yeats' idyllicism came out when he began to general-
ize in social terms. For then, as MacNeice sums it up succinctly:
'The love of tradition merged into support of reaction. Following
his father, who had stressed the *conservativeness* of the Irish
peasantry—"as conservative as the people behind the barriers of
privilege"—he wanted to maintain with the barriers of privilege
around the aristocracy those other barriers (of illiteracy and
penury?) around the peasant.'

At the time when he was in the thick of his work for an Irish
National Theater (1901), he had recognized how little his aspirations could look to the gentry, and had declared that 'all Irish
writers have to choose whether they will write as the upper
classes have done, not to express but to exploit this country; or
join the intellectual movement which has raised the cry that was
heard in Russia in the seventies, the cry, "To the people." ' But
later he came to feel, as he engagingly confessed, that what he
needed was not a social movement but a hostess. And from the
peace of Coole Park, his admiration of vigor led him to a roman-
ticization of oligarchy. He came to think order more important
than justice. He wrote too often as though not merely wealth
and leisure but also human dignity were prerogatives of the land
owners. And since his final explicit statement of his social philosophy—in his pamphlet 'On the Boiler' (1938)—reveals the crucial
danger spot in the thought of our time, it must be added that he
advocated 'the formation of military families' to offset 'democratic plausibility,' that, in brief, his unexamined attraction to
force had brought him close to a sympathy for fascism.

Out of the contradictions of such attitudes he made what he
considered national poetry. In his early dissatisfaction with the
miscellaneous curiosity of Tennyson and Browning, he declared
that 'we must create once more the pure work.' But he did not
mean by this an aesthetic indifference to subject matter. On the
contrary, he insisted that the poet must treat 'those things that
are permanent in the soul of the world, the great passions that
trouble all.' For an Irishman these were to be realized through

the ancient legends, and Yeats aspired to create some new Prometheus through Oisin or Finn, with Ben Bulben or Cro-Patrick
in the stead of Caucasus. Actually nothing could be much farther
from the qualities of Irish saga than *The Wanderings of Oisin.*
As the old Irish poetry appears in the translations by Frank
O'Connor, its world is intensely concrete, hard and often cruel,
with considerably more likeness, as MacNeice says, to Villon
than to Shelley or Blake. Yeats' early narratives and plays smug-
gle into these legends the fruits of his dabbling with theosophy
as well as the vaguest symbolism of Maeterlinck, with the result
that all the tough vigor of the original characters has been lost.
His first 'popular' ballads are equally literary, those of Moll
Magee and Father O'Hart possessing apparently no more roots
in a living folk tradition than do those of the beery England of
Chesterton.

But Yeats' ballads did possess such roots, though no vital
growth was to spring from them until after many years. The
difference from the situation in England is symbolized by Mac-
Neice's remark that 'it is not a mere affectation that a statue of
Cuchulain stands in the Dublin Post Office as a memorial to the
1916 rebels.' Ireland was still a partly primitive country, in which
the saga virtues could stir up associations for the people at large;
she was not separated from her legendary past by the gulf that
separates modern England from the Round Table. The imagination, dwelling long on Cuchulain, could make him a more immediate figure than any of the nineteenth-century re-creations of
Arthur.

What Yeats needed before he could achieve any such vitality
was best expressed by Synge, whose influence upon Yeats' later
work was crucial: 'The strong things of life are needed in poetry
also, to show that what is exalted or tender is not made by feeble
blood. It may almost be said that before verse can be human
again it must learn to be brutal.' In his *Autobiography* Yeats was
to enunciate this aphorism: 'It is so many years before one can
believe enough in what one feels even to know what the feeling
is.' He believed so long in the renewing energy of the legends
that he finally came to the power of possessing his feeling dra-

matically. 'I am of Ireland' has also recaptured the qualities that
Synge stressed:

> 'I am of Ireland,
> And the Holy Land of Ireland,
> And time runs on,' cried she.
> 'Come out of charity,
> Come dance with me in Ireland.'

> One man, one man alone
> In that outlandish gear,
> One solitary man
> Of all that rambled there
> Had turned his stately head.
> 'That is a long way off,
> And time runs on,' he said,
> 'And the night grows rough.'

> 'I am of Ireland,
> And the Holy Land of Ireland,
> And time runs on,' cried she.
> 'Come out of charity
> And dance with me in Ireland.'

> 'The fiddlers are all thumbs,
> Or the fiddle-string accursed,
> The drums and the kettledrums
> And the trumpets all are burst,
> And the trombone,' cried he,
> 'The trumpet and trombone,'
> And cocked a malicious eye,
> 'But time runs on, runs on.'

> 'I am of Ireland,
> And the Holy Land of Ireland,
> And time runs on,' cried she.
> 'Come out of charity
> And dance with me in Ireland.'

This is a very personal version of folk-poetry. Yeats has gotten
rid of everything that cluttered his early work, both the loose
occult symbols and the portrayal of the Irish heroes in the man-

ner of William Morris. We are left with the woman of Holy
Ireland and one heroic man, and once again Synge's influence
can be made explicit, this time in Yeats' own words: 'I did not
see, until Synge began to write, that we must renounce the deliberate creation of a kind of Holy City in the imagination, and
express the individual.' But the content here is not so bare and
forthright as that in the old ballads themselves. The situation
posed in the two stanzas between the refrains is packed with
subtlety. The tension is built up between the man and the be-
seeching woman, but we are not told whether he yields. The
effect is made to depend—through the final repetition of the
refrain—on the fact that whether he goes or whether, cocking his
malicious eye, he refuses, the appeal of Ireland, both physical
and spiritual, is felt in its full fecundity.

That Yeats has made such a richly ambiguous situation into
authentic folk-poetry is attested by the fact that his refrain, as
integral a part of his effect as his stanza, was taken directly from
a fourteenth-century dance song:

> Icham of Irlaunde
> Ant of the holy londe
>     Of Irlaunde.
> Gode sire, pray ich the
> For of saynte charite,
> Come ant daunce wyt me
>     In Irlaunde.

Yeats has introduced one change—'And time runs on'—which is
calculated to increase the tension, but the texture of the stanza
remains unaltered, and yet is indistinguishable from the body of
his poem. Such a poem is no tour de force but the mark of a
living tradition, for he has mastered the old style in his own
terms. And equally in his own terms he has become a national
poet. By eliminating all the descriptive properties he used in *The
Celtic Twilight* he has not become more simple. He has learned
how to command concrete realistic details but he has not abandoned the resources of the symbol. What he has symbolized is
broad and general, but it has become so through the intensification of his particular experience. The voice of Holy Ireland could

be also that of Maud Gonne calling him to participation in the patriots' cause. By being more deeply personal he has finally become universal. But his appeal to his nation is very unlike that of Burns. Yeats had often felt, during the days of his first experiments with popular poetry, that his country's genius 'would in the long run be distinguished and lonely.' Such it has proved to be, at least in the era of Yeats and Joyce.

In his maturity Yeats mastered two styles of poetry, the oblique and the direct. His work in the first lay either in such transformed folk-poems as 'I am of Ireland' and the rest of the Crazy Jane series, or in his equally free re-creations of other symbols, as in the Byzantium poems. His direct style came to fulfillment in the poems in his own person, in his intense dramatic comments, in his tributes to men and women he had admired or loved:

> Speech after long silence; it is right,
> All other lovers being estranged or dead,
> Unfriendly lamplight hid under its shade,
> The curtains drawn upon unfriendly night,
> That we descant and yet again descant
> Upon the supreme theme of Art and Song:
> Bodily decrepitude is wisdom; young
> We loved each other and were ignorant.

This poem is one of many celebrations of a central Yeatsian aphorism, that the arts exist 'to keep our passions alive.' The extraordinary condensation here can best be realized by thinking of the diffuse reveries in the poet's first several volumes. Once again Yeats has traveled by 'the crooked road,' as Blake characterized the road of genius. The 'contraries' involved here are not those in his social attitudes or in his aims as a popular poet. They inhere more completely in his art itself, in his growth into possession of his medium and of his content.

The language in 'After Long Silence' bears his special quality. No other poet of our day has been able to command a diction at once so elaborate and so plain, passing from such words as 'descant' and 'decrepitude' to the statement of the last line. No other poet, not even Eliot, has been better able to release both the precision and the abundance of his words: 'descant' operates here with its double meaning, both as the musical comment on a theme and as the free expatiation of discourse. Yeats' rhetorical skills are just as highly developed: by the antithetical repetition of 'unfriendly' he has shut out the darkness, he has also protected his aging lovers from the scrutiny of light, and he has enclosed for our imaginations an entire stage. The way in which he builds a whole poem out of a single involved sentence and launches its direction with that offhand 'it' near the end of the first line, is testimony of a past master of public speech.

He had come to these excellences from the most unlikely starting-point, since in his first determination to escape from the political rhetoric of the conventional Irish poets and from the scientific humanitarianism of the Victorians, he had cast out all consciously formal skills and any share of intellect, and had thus left himself with an invertebrate style to express a vague sentimentality. As he said in his *Autobiography:* 'I only very gradually began to use generalizations, that have since become the foundation of all I have done, or shall do, in Ireland.' As far as the language in which to clothe these generalizations was concerned, he grew to believe that 'literature is but recorded speech,' and began to seek his model in 'the syntax of impulsive common life.' In an age of journalism and standardized slickness, his distinctive contribution was his enduring resistance to the tyranny of impersonality. He insisted that the idiom of literature must be that 'either of those who have rejected, or of those who have never learned, the base idioms of the newspapers.' How far his goal was from the standards of clipped realism appears when he speaks of 'the delicate movement of living speech' as being 'the chief garment of life.'

He was helped to his goal first of all by the discipline of his decade of working primarily for the stage, whereby he freed himself from the nerveless rhythms of his previous verse by realizing that he must reach an equivalent for 'the interest appealed to by lively conversation or by oratory.' He soon discovered that his early suspicion of rhetoric had missed the point, that the rhetoric of a Macaulay might be crude and mechanical, but that the bolder and more resilient rhetoric of the Elizabethans had empowered their greatest triumphs. Yeats was to develop his own rhetorical resources most characteristically through his formal memorial poems, for which his tribute to Major Robert Gregory set the key. His 'delicate movement,' the hovering variety of his verse, may have been tempered in part by the influence of the Gaelic language, which he did not know. At least Thomas MacDonagh has argued that the musical intonations of Gaelic must have conditioned his ear inescapably. Yeats himself probably defined his debt more accurately when he phrased as the model, which he urged Synge also to follow: 'that English idiom of the Irish-thinking people of the west.'

Such an idiom enabled Yeats to create in prose also a bulwark against the depersonalized style of an era dominated by science. To a delight in Blake's kind of imaginative aphorism he finally brought more resources than may be analyzed here, among them a flair, not to be foretold from his first mystical essays, for the pithy anecdote of the memoir writer. His resultant capacity to range from the most serious to the most witty tone shows what he meant when he laid down the principle that 'we should write out our own thoughts in as nearly as possible the language we thought them in, as though in a letter to an intimate friend. We should not disguise them in any way; for our lives give them force as the lives of people in plays give force to their words.'

That could serve as a precise description also of what he accomplished in a poem like 'After Long Silence.' This poem is saturated with the human wisdom which most critics have found in his later work, although few attempts have yet been made to describe its properties, or to account for why a life which was filled with so many absurdities, from the time when Katharine Tynan remembered the séance where 'Willie Yeats was banging his head on the table,' down to the time when he solemnly asserted to Dorothy Wellesley that George V should have had the ancient gallantry to abdicate in protest when his cousin the Czar was dethroned—why such a life should have been able to yield such a rare attribute. MacNeice furnishes the materials for

defining this wisdom philosophically in what are the most penetrating passages of his book, since the author of 'Plurality' is
well trained in the terms of formal thought.

In the period of 'The Rose of the World' (1893) and 'The
Everlasting Voices' (1899), Yeats wrote as though his Universals
were utterly cut off from human life in some transcendent realm
of their own, and he thereby succeeded only in making their
significance dim and shadowy. After years of meditation he
realized a more dynamic conception of the relation between the
two realms. This relation was voiced for him both by Blake's
'Eternity is in love with the productions of time,' and by the lore
of the Irish peasant, 'God possesses the heavens—but he covets
the earth.' Or, as MacNeice phrases it in connection with the
change in Yeats' own work: 'He had come to recognize the im-
manence of the dream in physical fact while maintaining that it
is the dream which gives the fact its value.' His later poems are
thus more human since he no longer divorced spirit from matter;
indeed, by the end he could incline to the other extreme in
celebrating Tom the Lunatic and Jack the Journeyman, the
simple-minded fool and the natural physical man who, as Mac-
Neice says, 'remain in touch with the truth because their world
remains concrete.' Such men stood in Yeats' imagination along
with the 'passionate fragmentary' men of Homer, and at the
time he wrote his *Vision* (the only period when he read very
much in philosophy), he felt the need of a system that would do
justice to their energies. In his system he wanted most to avoid
Plato's split 'between the worlds of Being and Becoming,' or as
MacNeice continues, 'to vindicate passionate fragmentary men
who do not see beyond their own horizon but are nevertheless
the vehicle of dynamic eternal principles; they need those principles to motivate their actions *but the principles also need them*
as a means to realization.' The later Yeats had inevitably reacted
against Plato's extreme idealism. He had come, as he said, 'to
prefer Socrates to his thought.' It is the poet of Crazy Jane who
says, 'Our bodies are nearer to our coherence because nearer to
the "unconscious" than our thought.' Yet whatever he may have
voiced in certain moods, he was never exclusively a poet of the

particular; his mind was always being caught up into the search
for universals. As the refrain of one of his last poems demands,

'What then?' sang Plato's ghost. 'What then?'

Turning back once more to 'After Long Silence,' its range
would seem to be owing to its balance between the poles of
Yeats' philosophy. The claims both of the spirit and of the body
are given their due, and in their quick juxtaposition consists the
poem's intensity. There is no questioning the magnificence of
such old age of the mind, but the mind's last assertion, 'Bodily
decrepitude is wisdom,' is saved from being empty hyperbole
by the contrasting rhyme-word and the simple final declaration.
Yeats stubbornly refuses to abandon the actual for the ideal, the
living individual for mere abstract reason. The physicality which
Synge first taught him to reckon with remained with him to the
end, and he thereby exemplified the full value of one of his 'Discoveries': 'We should ascend out of common interests, the
thoughts of the newspapers, of the market-place, of men of
science, but only so far as we can carry the normal, passionate,
reasoning self, the personality as a whole.'

Both 'I am of Ireland' and 'After Long Silence' are presentations of Yeats' conception of tragedy; and since the rebirth of the
tragic sense has been the characterizing feature of modern
poetry, the nature of Yeats' conception should be discriminated.
It is important to recall the context of the famous declaration in
his *Autobiography* that 'We begin to live when we have conceived life as tragedy.' That sentence comes as the conclusion to
his reflection that, as life advances, 'we discover that certain
thoughts sustain us in defeat, or give us victory . . . Among
subjective men (in all those, that is, who must spin a web out
of their own bowels), the victory is an intellectual daily recreation of all that exterior fate snatches away, and so that fate's
antithesis.'

Thus Yeats' view of tragedy, like his doctrine of the Mask, is
based on his belief that antithesis is the law of life. But where he
throws his emphasis is not on the disaster that inevitably springs
from the conflict, not on the tragic loss but on the heroic affirma-

tion. When he tries to analyze the tension in personal and psychological terms, he cites Shakespeare's heroes 'who made their
death a ritual of passion,' and he defines passion as 'the straining of man's being against some obstacle that obstructs its unity.'
The triumph in defeat, 'the mingling of contraries,' is what he
finds as the distinguishing mark of all great tragedy. Just as an
individual strives for 'unity of being,' so does a society strive for
'unity of culture,' and Yeats' particular tragic sense came to
maturity as he realized that the one could not be achieved without the other, that the individual must be very incomplete without social coherence to sustain him, and that his own dream for
the cultural wholeness of Ireland, in which his theater could
be a truly national theater as the Elizabethan theater had been,
was not possible of fulfillment. But the double loss, the dangerous isolation of the modern artist and Yeats' sense of the increasing confusion and violence of the world, engendered in him the
passion which alone—as he held—gave life significance.

He describes this passion in terms of joy rather than of suffering. He keeps saying that 'in all the great tragedies, tragedy is a
joy to the man who dies; in Greece the tragic chorus danced.'
This assumption is what caused his distinction between the 'two
kinds of poetry' which 'are commingled in all the greatest works.'
The one kind is produced 'when the tide of life sinks low,' and
the poet, like Keats in the 'Ode to a Grecian Urn' or Virgil at the
plucking of the Golden Bough, makes us 'sorrowful,' since we
share in his 'separation from what he describes.' 'But when
Lucifer stands among his friends, when Villon sings his dead
ladies to so gallant a rhythm, when Timon makes his epitaph,
we feel no sorrow, for life herself has made one of her eternal
gestures, has called up into our hearts her energy that is eternal
delight.' Yeats felt it unnecessary to attribute that final phrase
to Blake; but the contemporary revival of Blake and of Donne,
especially in what modern poets have made of them, has tended
to illustrate Yeats' two kinds. His own poetry is certainly not
'inspired' in the strict sense in which Blake felt his to be, but
Yeats followed him always in celebrating energy, in affirming
that in Ireland, 'where the tide of life is rising,' poets would turn
'to the imagination of personality—to drama, gesture.' On the

other hand, Eliot, repeatedly declaring that the source of poetry is in suffering, has found his kinship in the purgatorial strain in Dante, and in Donne's witty anguish.

Division between the two kinds is not to be made absolute, as Yeats himself indicated, but the great difference in tone between Yeats' poetry and Eliot's may be attributed to the different quality each has stressed at the heart of the tragic experience. Each might well declare of the other that, although he possessed a tragic sense, he had not been able to write full tragedy. Yeats' distaste for 'passive suffering' would doubtless extend to 'Gerontion' as well as to 'The Hollow Men,' and the intermingled doubt and faith of Eliot's later poems would fall far short of the affirmation Yeats demanded—even though Eliot has accomplished Yeats' end of making a fusion between poetry and ritual far more effectively in *Murder in the Cathedral* than Yeats did in any of his plays. Eliot's dissatisfaction with Blake, with the grave limitations that ensue when a poet feels it necessary to create a private mythology, would apply equally to Yeats' Irish mysticism. And it hardly requires Eliot's scrutiny to detect that when Yeats lives up to the demand of his favorite adjectives, when he produces an art that is 'joyful, fantastic, extravagant, whimsical, beautiful, resonant, and altogether reckless,' he is capable sometimes of substituting Irish bravura in place of moral perception. Eliot's excruciated awareness of evil has given him a more unerring psychological grasp: his 'Portrait of a Lady,' as MacNeice suggests, 'throws a cold, cruel light on the sort of woman whom Yeats regarded as a masterpiece of civilization.' It might be argued that this renewal by Eliot of our sense of evil has brought us back into possession of the element without which no tragedy can be created; and that although Yeats is by no means blind to evil, his most characteristic expression is not tragedy, but a special product of the tragic attitude, the 'zest' of the hero, to use another of his favorite words, a zest that could mount in many poems to a final ecstatic frenzy in his exercise of 'an old man's eagle mind.'

MacNeice contends, a little too plausibly, that Auden and his school should be grouped rather with Yeats than with Eliot, on the grounds that theirs also has been a poetry of affirmation. But the evidence of their own first work shows that it was certainly Eliot who, in teaching them to examine the disharmonies of existence, also taught them to be concerned not with the individual but with society. So far as Auden has now receded from that concern, his poetry has become inward in a turgidly romantic vein with little kinship to either Yeats or Eliot. MacNeice, in the 'Eclogues' which still remain his best work, may well have schooled his sensitive versification on Yeats' later music, but his content, the decay of capitalistic society, is exactly what Yeats turned his attention away from.

When Yeats voiced his early conviction that 'personal utterance, which had almost ceased in English literature, could be as fine an escape from rhetoric and abstraction as drama itself,' his father would hear nothing of it and said that 'personal utterance was only egotism.' It became far more than that as the poet matured, even though, as we have seen, the scope of his sympathies was restricted to a few traditional types of men. But as he dwelt upon those he was able to give persuasive viability to his early belief in 'the eternal moods,' to the belief that any moment of deeply realized life shared, through its intensity, in the Universal Mind. Nearly every prose expression he made of this doctrine of the imagination is extremely literary, much closer to Pater than to Blake, as is this surprising echo we find of it in Joyce's apprentice essay on Mangan (1902): 'In that great memory which is greater and more generous than our memory, no life, no moment of exaltation is lost.' The extraordinary thing is that Yeats, by holding to that belief long enough, did come to know what it was his words were feeling for, and thereby to endow his personal lyrics with a wide significance. And Joyce, moving in his realistic period to the opposite pole from his first description of the imagination, returned at the end to project, by means of his enormous resources of dream psychology and folklore, a sense of the mind of the race through the aberrant fantasies of one man.

The religious strain which neither Yeats nor Joyce could escape has caused MacNeice to speak of them both as 'spoilt priests, aiming in their writings at a blend of mysticism and dogma which they could not achieve in their lives.' Yeats, indeed, held always to the position that 'all symbolic art should arise out of a real belief, and that it cannot do so in this age proves that this age is a road and not a resting-place for the imagination.' His own problem, as Michael Robartes phrased it for him, was that he possessed 'intellectual belief,' but was 'entirely without moral faith.' It was not that he did not love order, but that he felt himself continually being confronted with too many philosophical orders to choose from. Maud Gonne, speaking from the political order that she chose, describes how their roads parted, hers leading to jail with Constance de Markievicz. But his, she believes, was the 'more difficult, a road of outer peace and inner confusion, discernible in his later work.' He himself felt acutely that an artist without a more integral bond with society could realize only a small fragment of his essential life. But that fragment placed him among the renewers of literature in English, renewers who have come in the past half century largely from outside of England, Irishmen and Americans, not in poetry alone, but likewise Henry James and Joyce in the novel, and in the drama Shaw and Synge.

*The Southern Review*, 1941

## Primarily Language: John Crowe Ransom

WE have not had enough good minor artists in America. The early nineteenth century, when the traditions of our literature were being established, was the time of expansive aspiration, of gigantic projections; and if it brought us a Whitman and a Melville, it also left us with the inflated ideal of the epic bard and with the dubious dream of the great

American novel. One trouble with that ideal was that it so easily confused size with value. One trouble with that dream was that it set up a sterilizing tension of all or nothing. It invoked a spectral absolute into the realm of the finite and concrete. It did not perceive that one sign of a rich culture is variety rather than singleness, not the striving for one impossible masterpiece but a resilient and far more fertile practice of writing as a craft.

As we look back now to the second phase of the American renaissance, to the period between 1910 and 1930, we can observe, at least so far as poetry is concerned, the pervasive growth of the conception of the poet as craftsman instead of as inspired seer. We can observe also that during that period far more gifted poets emerged than during any other period in our history. The most influential have been Frost and Eliot, although the increasing reputation of Wallace Stevens may now rival theirs. But quite apart from any scale of relative greatness, we can be aware that among our most valuable heritages from that period are the numerous examples of integrity of style, of artistic wholeness within whatever limitations the given poet recognized as his own. In many cases this has meant a spareness of production, as in that of Marianne Moore; or, in that of Cummings, a tendency to keep on producing fresh versions of essentially the same poem. But at the present moment, when so many novelists have lost the sense of social direction in which they were advancing a decade ago, and when both novelists and dramatists have in general failed to dominate the vulgarizations of taste that have flowed back upon them from Hollywood, the usefulness of good minor art should be more and more cogent.

The almost perfect instance of what is implied by the term is the poetry of John Crowe Ransom. The conventional approach to his work is to note that he has not published a book of new poems for twenty years, and so to begin by deploring his lack of capacity for growth or the cultural circumstances of our time that may have crippled him. Such issues are not negligible, but they deflect us from what he has done to what he has not. That kind of critical approach is a phase of the demand for the great American novel. Through its excited attention upon what masterpiece lies next over the horizon, it loses sight of the quality of the work of art at hand.

The limitations of Ransom's production are both natural and self-induced. According to the preface to *Poems About God,* he did not start writing poetry until he was twenty-eight, and in that first book, not one poem of which he has subsequently collected, he showed few traces of his mature style. He did not find his own voice until he was past thirty, and before he was forty he had almost discontinued the writing of verse. But in the interval he had reached such a consistently high level of skill that when he finally came to issue his *Selected Poems* in 1945, it was astonishing that he excluded more than half of both *Chills and Fever* and *Two Gentlemen in Bonds.* From the years after 1927 he added only five poems.

He might well argue that he had provided instances of all his chief themes, and he would be right. His feeling for his region and his particular contrast between the Southern past and present are represented by 'Old Mansion' and 'Antique Harvesters.' His particular contrast between America and older cultures comes out in 'Philomela.' His absorption with the fragility and impermanence of love and his awareness of death form his most recurrent subjects, and give rise to the most notable element in both his style and attitude: the irony that Warren has examined in the best essay devoted to Ransom so far. The theme which— as Warren saw—brings out the fullest resources of this irony is that of the divided personality 'who cannot fathom or perform his nature.' It is phrased most explicitly in 'Man Without Sense of Direction.'

Ransom was probably wise in omitting 'the tale in twenty sonnets,' the title-poem of *Two Gentlemen in Bonds,* since it is a too facile expression of one of his main absorptions, the contrast between the body and the mind—a theme to which he gave his most condensed embodiment in the later 'Painted Head.' He has never shown any great aptitude for the longer poem, and his Biblical narratives, 'Armageddon' and 'Judith of Bethulia,' along with his Harvard Phi Beta Kappa poem, 'Address to the Scholars of New England,' come closest of any of his inclusions to being set pieces. But what one feels for the most part is a regret for

the exclusions. One takes unwillingly the absence of the opening poem of *Chills and Fever,* 'Agitato ma non troppo,' since,
as its title suggests, it establishes this poet's prevailing tone.
And even if no serious themes are omitted, several of the gayest
passages have been sacrificed, perhaps on the ground that they
tended to get out of hand. But a signal loss is involved in 'In
Mr. Minnit's House,' wherein some of the liveliest Skeltonics of
our period also presented the kind of compressed drama over
which Ransom possesses such great command. In fact, as the
reader considers further, he becomes aware that several of the
poems left out could take their stand with the best work in any
representative modern anthology. 'Amphibious Crocodile' may
not have the exact control of 'Philomela,' but it is rich in its social observation of the American abroad. 'Persistent Explorer' is
hardly second to 'Man Without Sense of Direction' in its portrayal of the divided sensibility, and 'Morning' is one of Ransom's sharpest contrasts between free imagination and fixed
reason.

What this last paragraph amounts to is a cumbersome way of
noting that once Ransom established his style, he rarely fell below it. It is also a plea for a collected rather than a selected edition of his two mature books. For what catches the reader's
attention on nearly every page is an extraordinary gift of language, turns of phrase that correspond to perceptions distinct
from anyone else's:

> Tawny are the leaves turned but they still hold,
> And it is harvest; what shall this land produce?
> A meager hill of kernels, a runnel of juice;
> Declension looks from our land, it is old.
> Therefore let us assemble, dry, grey, spare,
> And mild as yellow air.

This opening stanza of 'Antique Harvesters' is among his best-
known instances of what we mean, the full signature of a
matured style. The 'antique' in the title, underscored by the locali-
zation of the scene, in the epigraph, on 'the bank sinister' of both
the Ohio and the Mississippi, sets up the peculiar tone, the kind

of contemplative detachment which may be gained through the deliberately archaic. But the archaisms are not merely literary: in the 'runnel' from the 'meager' hill we hear the old-fashioned country expression, the Elizabethan or seventeenth-century usage that was brought to this country by the first settlers and that has disappeared now except from remote rural and mountain areas, especially in the South. But the particular countryman whom Ransom has devised as the speaking voice or *persona* of this poem is learned to the point of that odd and wryly pedantic use of 'declension.' He can also fall naturally into the elaborate courtly phrases of an older public speech: 'Therefore let us assemble.'

All these means of characterization by language are developed and enriched through the remainder of the poem, but their striking effectiveness is due to Ransom's ability to pack so many of them into a single stanza. He has given us his locale, even to the very look of the Southern autumn with its 'tawny' leaves and 'mild yellow air.' He has given us essential traits of the older cultural South with the thoroughness that only the most accurate and efficient words can command. He has thereby prepared the way to give us also, in three lines, the quintessential expression of his devotion to his region, his distillation of the heroic element in its history:

> We pluck the spindling ears and gather the corn.
> One spot has special yield? 'On this spot stood
> Heroes and drenched it with their only blood.'

How Ransom's sense of proportion has enabled him to avoid sentimentalization of that history—unlike some of the extremists in the Southern agrarian school that followed him—could make an essay in itself. But my concern here remains primarily with his language. That is not to imply that his metrical gifts are negligible, though they are less varied. His usual iambic has considerable variations from the pentameter norm. But his irregularities are seldom casual or haphazard; they are designed to bring out what is essentially a speaking rather than a singing voice. Among the attributes that establish him as an artist secure within his limits is the care with which he has made certain revisions. Perhaps the most interesting case is that of 'Vaunting Oak,' one of his most moving accounts of love's perishability. In reconsidering it, he seems to have felt that it needed tightening up, for he cut out two stanzas. What was far more exacting, he decided to introduce the interlinking rhymes of *terza rima*. The result is very instructive, since such a change—to use some of his own favorite critical terms—inevitably involved the interplay between texture and structure. The middle stanzas are those in which the girl turns to the great oak in the hopeful thought that here at last is a witness to endurance:

### First Version

And she exulted—being given to crying,
'Heart, Heart, love is so firm an entity,
It must not go the way of the hot rose dying'—

For the venerable oak, delivered of his pangs,
Put forth his flames of green with profuse joying
And testified to her with innumerable tongues.

And what but she fetch me up to the steep place
Where the oak vaunted? A meadow of many songs
Had to be traversed; and a quick populace

Of daisies, and yellow kinds; and here she knew,
Who had sorely been instructed of much decease,
Better than brag in this distraught purlieu.

### Revision

And exulted, wrapped in a phantasy of good:
'Be the great oak for its long winterings
Our love's symbol, better than the summer's brood.'

Then the venerable oak, delivered of his pangs,
Put forth profuse his green banners of peace
And testified to her with innumerable tongues.

And what but she fetch me up to the steep place
Where the oak vaunted? A flat where birdsong flew
Had to be traversed; and a quick populace

Of daisies, and yellow kinds; and here she knew,
Who had been instructed of much mortality,
Better than brag in this distraught purlieu.

To make the necessary alterations in the rhyme-words Ransom felt his way back into the meaning of the poem, and strengthened it ponderably. A girl 'given to crying' is a fairly stock figure; she becomes more complexly alive and appealing when her illusion is phrased positively as 'a phantasy of good.' The omission of the usual rose for a more direct apostrophe to the oak is also a shift from a negative to a positive symbol; and 'peace' rather than 'joying' is clearly a more appropriate attribute for the old tree. Though the other two changes here are slighter in their effect, they still bring out some of Ransom's special qualities. 'A flat where birdsong flew' contains his distinctive mixture of colloquial and oblique, as the more conventional earlier phrase did not. The barer statement that results from the omission of 'sorely' may strengthen the drama by not overstating it, and the greater weight of 'mortality' over 'decease' may also contribute to the same effect.

There are several comparable changes in the rest of the poem, and perhaps the only loss in flavor through a new rhyme-word is after the girl's lover has evoked 'a hollow tone' by rapping on the tree's trunk. He originally grieved that 'the old gentleman' is largely 'cadaver,' but that yielded to how he 'holds gallantly' in appearance. The burden of the final stanza is, of course, the falseness of that appearance, how the 'dolorous cry' of the dying tree outsounds even 'the tears of a girl remembering her dread.' The earliest version of that final line—not in *Chills and Fever*, but in the selection issued in England by Robert Graves—said 'discovering.' The deepening of the girl's emotional awareness that is suggested by 'remembering' foreshadows the dominant effect of the later changes.

Thus by examining even such slight details we can perceive the central element in Ransom's conception of poetry, how a poem must be an act of knowing. Each of his poems is designed to afford us a singularly whole experience. His inclusive concern with both feeling and thought has caused him to be referred to as a metaphysical poet, but his style would appear to have developed independent of the revival of interest in the seventeenth century, and, unlike Eliot, he did not borrow any devices directly from Donne. The nearest equivalent to Ransom's irony is from a more immediate background, in Hardy's *Satires of Circumstance*. But Ransom's method is all his own, and can be apprehended only through a whole poem. In the preface to his selections he said that he had arranged them as near to the order of their composition as he could remember, and one surprise to the reader from that arrangement is that 'Dead Boy' comes almost at the beginning. For this poem displays all the aspects of his skill in their full development. By choosing the very kind of theme upon which the nineteenth century spilled out its worst sentimental excesses, it is as though he deliberately set out to demonstrate his complete break with the Southern romantic past:

The little cousin is dead, by foul subtraction,
A green bough from Virginia's aged tree,
And none of the county kin like the transaction,
Nor some of the world of outer dark, like me.

A boy not beautiful, nor good, nor clever,
A black cloud full of storms too hot for keeping,
A sword beneath his mother's heart—yet never
Woman bewept her babe as this is weeping.

A pig with a pasty face, so I had said,
Squealing for cookies, kinned by poor pretense
With a noble house. But the little man quite dead,
I see the forebears' antique lineaments.

The elder men have strode by the box of death
To the wide flag porch, and muttering low send round
The bruit of the day. O friendly waste of breath!
Their hearts are hurt with a deep dynastic wound.

He was pale and little, the foolish neighbors say;
The first-fruits, saith the Preacher, the Lord hath taken;
But this was the old tree's late branch wrenched away,
Grieving the sapless limbs, the shorn and shaken.

The diction works upon us in the ways we have already noted, but here the occasional elaborate-pedantic words are introduced into the very first rhyme for a shock of wit that makes us aware at once through the odd dryness that we are faced with no conventionally moist poem on the death of a little cousin. The unobtrusive thoroughness with which Ransom presents a whole way of life and its milieu can be sampled through the deft off-setting of 'the county kin' against all the rest of the world as 'outer dark.' The usages and values of the Virginia forebears are re-enacted in this dynastic ceremonial, and the saturation of these values in the language of the Bible extends far beyond the words of the Preacher. Phrase after phrase from 'the green bough' through 'outer dark,' the 'cloud full of storms,' the 'sword beneath his mother's heart,' to the 'late branch wrenched away' are either direct or indirect allusions to the rich King James version.

The prevalence of that source in traditional country speech accounts for the mingling in that speech of the simple and the archaic, a mingling which Ransom seems consciously to emulate even in phrases which have no direct connection with the Scriptures. Such mingling gives rise in particular to the quiet compelling eloquence of the fourth stanza where the simple 'box of death' is suddenly more forceful than the expected 'coffin' could be; and where the archaic unfamiliar 'bruit' is by its very unfamiliarity made to release its full store, not only of the 'rumors' of the day, but of the very breath and sound of the old men voicing them. But lest Ransom's combination of the homely and the learned be made to sound too deliberate, we must remember how his diction is always being spiced by the easily colloquial: 'a pig with a pasty face,' 'squealing for cookies.'

These few notes on the contrasting and combining elements in Ransom's language can lead directly into a description of his poetic method, for it also is one of combination through contrast. That is what is meant by speaking of it, as Cleanth Brooks has, as a method of inclusion. In this poem, as we have noted, any expectation of sentiment is undercut in the opening line, and in the first half of both the second and the third stanzas the case is stated against the grief before the grief is described. We are thereby given two views of a situation, the difference, we might say, between what the situation is felt to be and what it really amounts to when seen by the eye of detached common sense. But that latter rational stance, this poem is also saying, is never adequate to the grasp of human values. That is why Ransom is always counterpointing the difference between reason and imagination. Reason alone can merely point to the contrast between a situation experienced from without and from within. And as the poem advances to its end, it is the doubting neighbors, not the involved kinsfolk, who are 'foolish.' Yet the objective view also remains: despite the natural anguish, this boy would not have measured up to much in the world; the older vitality of this heritage is gone.

Ransom's irony became more devastating in some of his poems dealing with the suffering of lovers, for there he was not balancing one view against another to bring out the partial validity of both. He was writing of the tragic limitations of 'desperate men and women.' In one of his latest poems, the haunted 'Prelude to an Evening,' he pushed his expression of frustrated anguish about as far as it could go. That may be why, in his subsequent criticism, he went out of his way to take exception to a poetic method depending too exclusively upon irony and choosing its themes, never from 'human aspirations triumphant,' but always from 'efforts that turned out indecisively, or brought up in the sands.' It is as though he were bidding farewell to his own kind of poetry, and it may be regretted that he has not found another way of expressing other aspects of the concrete 'beauty of the body' which he has always known to be the source of reinvigoration for the too abstract mind. But that regret must not betray us into the error described at the beginning, the error of underestimating the value of the integrated accomplishment. Ransom has not been deluded into the anxious striving to be a poet for the career's sake. He has said what he was compelled to say in a form uniquely his own. He has not attempted to live up to any extraneous expectations, nor watered down his accomplishment by diluted sequels. He has produced some of the best minor poems in our language.

*The Sewanee Review,* 1948

# The Innocent Eye: Mount and Homer

THESE studies of Mount and Homer make valuable contributions to our understanding of two successive generations of our nineteenth-century painting. How careless we have been about Mount, though he was the pioneer of our native genre school, is attested by the painstaking catalogue in this monograph, which still has to state for more than fifty of his works, 'Present Location Unknown.' Only a short biographical essay is needed for all the recoverable facts about this Long Island boy who started out as a sign painter in New York in 1824. But the authors have related his career to the development of American culture, and it is only unfortunate that their stiffly academic writing has not kept pace with the fascination of their subject. The full-length biography of Homer is a different story. Not only was there much more material available, but Lloyd Goodrich has already proved himself, in his comparable book on Eakins, one of our few matured critics in this field. In the ever growing tendency to vulgarize and cheapen our cultural history by reducing it to a series of chatty anecdotes, it is invigorating to hear Goodrich begin by saying that our most important knowledge about Homer is to 'be found in his work, where like every artist he left the most complete record of himself.'

In the light of that record, and of the excellent reproductions in both these volumes, we can see that the critical issue about both Mount and Homer is the same one that raged once about the local-color school, and that rages now about the regionalists

*William Sidney Mount* by Bartlett Cowdrey and Hermann Warner Williams, Jr., with a foreword by Harry B. Wehle. Columbia University Press.

*Winslow Homer* by Lloyd Goodrich. Macmillan.

50

and the various proponents of the American scene, in literature as well as in painting.

Mount first came under the influence of the grandiose manner of Benjamin West, and tried his hand, very clumsily, at 'Christ Raising the Daughter of Jairus.' For those who believe that an American artist can strike vitality only by treating immediate native themes, his shift from such a subject to 'The Rustic Dance' marks a significant victory. As Harry Wehle notes in his foreword: 'It was no mere coincidence that the Jacksonian epoch should have aroused an unprecedented interest in genre painting, a form of art so democratic that it can be enjoyed by anyone who takes pleasure in observing the characteristic behavior of the human animal in his more or less handmade habitat.' Mount, an ardent Democrat, decided to break away from the formal studios and to paint 'by the wayside—in porter saloons, blacksmith shops, shoe shops, wherever character can be found.' He would thus seem to have anticipated by a century John Curry's dictum that 'The artist ought to paint people doing things.' He went back to the country, and, like Whittier, took pride in his reliance upon the common life around him. But he had also responded eagerly to Washington Allston's advice to study such Flemish and Dutch masters as Van Ostade and Steen.

His contemporary reputation was for his 'comic pictures,' such as 'The Truant Gamblers' or 'Raffling for a Goose.' But though these still impress us with the freshness and firmness of vision that mark them off from the easy sentimentality into which most of our subsequent genre painters were to descend, Mount's few best canvases have a somewhat different effect. In 'Eel Spearing at Setauket' and 'Long Island Farmhouses' he is no longer relying upon a humorous or dramatic situation for the main source of his interest. Here he shows what he meant by his resolve to follow nature 'with truth.' Here his broader designs and simple but harmonious tonal patterns show also that he had come to a greater mastery of his medium. These pictures live, not just because they are authentic records of the American scene, but because they project in addition a plastic life of their own.

This same question as to the relative claims of subject matter and technique can be read through the course of Homer's development. Having served as an apprentice to a Boston engraver, he was virtually self-taught as a painter when, almost twenty-seven, he began to work in oils, and gained his first recognition as an illustrator of Civil War scenes. As Goodrich notes, he shunned the heroic, and gave a very full account of how the soldiers looked and acted. It is only when we compare these pictures with Whitman's *Drum Taps* that we realize that Homer's reading of character was relatively superficial. He was an exact contemporary of Howells, and as he proceeded to depict other phases of his milieu, ladies with parasols at the beach, boys playing snap the whip, he expressed something akin to that realist's quiet optimism. His particular distinction, which he had displayed as early as his charming 'Croquet Scene' (1866), was his flair for delicate linear design.

By early middle age he had won his rank as our leading master of genre, several notches above a J. G. Brown or even an Eastman Johnson. Yet the chief interest of his career is how he went on to transcend altogether the narrow limitations of that school, just as Sarah Jewett transcended those of local color in fiction. If we had to judge Homer by his earnest scenes of action like 'The Life Line' or 'The Look Out,' he would fall far below Eakins in the handling of rounded form and in structural massiveness. But, as Goodrich stresses, we must not forget that Homer was also an exact contemporary of the French impressionists, and that, developing quite independently of them, he made his own American reaction to the age's growing interest in the open air. He would never have agreed with Manet's statement that 'The most important person in any picture is the light,' since he always held to a dogged concern with the object in itself. He never reached anything like Renoir's full sensuousness, but particularly after he began to work in water color, at the age of thirty-seven, he advanced rapidly in spontaneity and in a cool luminosity. The biggest single stimulus to his color was his first visit to the Bahamas in 1884. He had previously been a pioneer in painting Negroes, not as an occasion for kindly humor, but as handsome human beings; and his response to their magnificent dark bodies under the brilliant skies of the southern islands brought to his palette a wholly new range.

He was to become our leading water colorist of the nineteenth century, as he continued to add his series in the Adirondacks and on the Canadian streams to those near his final home at Prout's Neck, Maine. When Goodrich remarks that Homer 'saw nature less like a poet than a woodsman,' we realize that he took the same kind of physical delight in his surroundings as a Parkman or a Hemingway. But at a time when we seem determined once again to confuse an artist's surroundings with his performance—or as Sarah Jewett put it, our scaffoldings with our buildings—it is important to note that Homer's essential growth was in more and more flexible control of his medium. His remained the innocent eye. The growth was from within, not from any other painting here or abroad, but it was none the less a painter's growth, not that of a reporter. As Mount had said, 'Originality is not confined to one place or country.' Homer became an original painter, on grounds comparable to those that make Frost an original poet, in contrast to whatever slick or folksy regionalists, be they of Iowa or Maine. Or on grounds that make John Marin our greatest water colorist, in contrast to ditto.

*New Republic,* 1944

## *Essay on Rime*

THIS book may very well be the most remarkable contribution to American art yet to have come out of the war. Its title may suggest to the general reader a bookish piece by a young man growing up in a library and steeped in the period of Boileau and Pope. It happens to have been written by a ser-

*Essay on Rime* by Karl Shapiro. Reynal & Hitchcock.

geant in the Medical Corps who was just completing his third
year of active duty in the Pacific. When Karl Shapiro was
drafted in the spring before Pearl Harbor, his name was probably known only to readers of *New Directions* and the serious
little magazines. He was already in New Guinea before his first
book, *Person, Place and Thing,* was published. He was finishing
this *Essay* in the Netherlands East Indies a year ago, before he
had had any chance to realize that his *V-Letter* had placed him,
among younger readers particularly, at the forefront of the poets
of his decade.

Composed without access to books, this verse *Essay* of over
two thousand lines discusses 'rime' in its widest connotation as
synonymous with 'the art of poetry,' and gives a detailed assessment of that art in our time. It is the kind of production one
would hardly have believed possible in the special circumstances
of soldiering, and yet without the enforced isolation from everything he cared most about and without the equally enforced in-
wardness of his thoughts Shapiro might never have felt the
necessity to take stock of where we now stand 'in the mid-cen-
tury of our art.' What makes the result such exciting reading is
that here we have no formal estimate, with measured dependence upon authority. We have rather the direct statement of
what a poet really knows and believes, what he has absorbed
from thirty years of living and ten of learning his craft.

Shapiro is no eclectic, and makes no attempt to include all the
leading names in modern poetry. In a closing passage he regrets
that he had to leave out certain figures, notably Wallace Stevens
and Frost, since he lacked 'a whole opinion of their work.' Yet
he gives a representative picture of the prevailing influences of
his particular period, of the state of poetry as it has been experienced by someone who began to practice it in the early
nineteen-thirties. He has written thereby a chapter of cultural
and moral history. But he has also written a poem. He has not
availed himself of the technical virtuosity displayed in his previous books. In deliberately roughening his blank verse to the
'flux and reflux of conversation,' he may have produced some
needlessly flat lines. But his language is vivid with the eloquence of conviction, and he enlivens his effect with an occa-

sional tightening rhyme. He does not engage in abstract analysis. He knows the difference between a poet and a semanticist, and, as he says, his wish

> is but to call a rose a rose
> And not a trope.

The poets of his time who have made the most impression upon him are Eliot, Hart Crane, and Auden. Shapiro followed the nineteen-twenties in recognizing Eliot to be the master craftsman of American poetry. In 1933 Hart Crane, who had responded deeply to Eliot's technical innovations but had attempted to refute the disillusion of *The Waste Land* by a new affirmation of Whitman's America, had recently killed himself in despair. Auden, who had also learned much from Eliot, was just starting to express political and social concerns very different from anything articulated in *Ash Wednesday*. With the depression had come a marked break in the sequence of American poets. Between 1910 and 1930 this country had witnessed the emergence of a greater abundance and variety of poetic talents than in any previous period in our history. But during the 'thirties most of our new writers turned to prose, particularly to the novel of social protest. The new signatures in poetry, with an occasional exception like Delmore Schwartz at the end of the period, were predominantly English.

Shapiro does not agree with Yeats' opinion that since 1900 there have been 'more poets of worth' in the English language than in any generation since 1630. He indicates his persistent view by arranging his *Essay* under three headings, 'The Confusion in Prosody,' 'The Confusion in Language,' 'The Confusion in Belief.' He writes with modesty, as one involved with his own age, but also with great firmness. His opening section is the most technical in its references, the most unusual to have been created entirely from memory. Living in the period of the breakdown of formal metric, he takes stock of how and when that came about. He discusses what he has learned of the resources of the past from three monuments of scholarship, Bridges' study of Milton, Lanier's *Science of English Verse*, and Saintsbury's account of prose rhythms.

From his own immersion in the poets Shapiro has found the 'discipline' of Milton's prosody to be the practitioner's 'purest guide' to mastery. Only those aware of the acrid academic debates of recent years will recognize Shapiro's catholicity in being able to admire Milton's supremacy, and yet to assert that 'by far the two great prosodists of our age' are Joyce and Eliot. Academic critics have usually lined up on one edge of that divide, current readers on the other. Shapiro does not argue. He knows as a poet, through the evidence of his ears, that in Eliot 'the triumph of a new form is certain.' He has many fresh things to say about that triumph. He is a judicious appraiser of the artesian interflow that Eliot struck anew between French and English verse; but he values Eliot even more for the way his 'clean conversational voice' cut through 'the late-Victorian lilt.' Measuring his words carefully, Shapiro remarks of the metric of *Ash Wednesday* that

> in a hundred years no poem
> Has sung itself so exquisitely well.

He is even more penetrating in his treatment of Joyce. He reckons with *Ulysses* as 'a thing of rime entirely,' since he believes that it established 'a new rhythmical idiom' through the mating of the possibilities of verse and of prose, such as Lanier and Saintsbury foresaw. But Shapiro is by no means easy in his mind about the influence of Joyce's intricacy. He is aware that the master has fallen into the hands of cultists and has fathered many aberrations. But in summation of the vagaries of our time Shapiro recognizes that it has also been marked by much 'serious invention,' as poets have struggled to find possible verse forms to fit the 'tensile strains' in modern speech.

Confusion in language is of even graver import, since language is the living record of our moral history. Shapiro believes that excessive style is an undeniable sign of disequilibrium, and he is disturbed by the violently diverse phases through which so many of our artists have gone in the age of Picasso and Stravinsky. Auden's is the case history of multiple personality in verse, and Shapiro notes Auden's pursuit through the whole 'lexicon of forms' after 'the lost Eurydice of character.' But he

is by no means forgetful of the immense stimulus to his own
development from Auden's mastery of rhetoric. His passage on
the advent of Auden's group recaptures the excitement of that
moment when

> a set
> Of more or less Oxford radicals unloaded
> Their gear of games and books and politics
> Blazers and alcohol and hockey-sticks
> Into the lap of middle age.

He has high praise for the concrete vocabulary of immediate
things that was thereby inaugurated, but is equally critical of
Auden's subsequent deflection into loose abstraction.

An especially perceptive passage probes farther the effects of
abstract rhetoric induced by our poets' adoption of an international style. Shapiro cites Pound's 'polyglot' *Cantos* as one symp-
tom, and as another the curious influence of such translations as
Spender's Rilke and the various versions of Lorca, which were
then imitated as new idioms. The result was to make much
current verse read like a translation 'where no original exists,'
and the end-product, in a characteristic writer like MacLeish,
has the unreality of 'a linguistic dream.'

The confusion, or rather the failure in belief, is introduced by
an estimate of the poet whose talent, in Shapiro's view, was
greater 'than any, excepting the expatriates,' since Whitman's:

> Crane died for modern rime, a wasted death;
> I make the accusation with the right
> Of one who loved his book; died without cause,
> Leaped from the deck-rail of his disbelief
> To senseless strangulation. When we shall damn
> The artist who interprets all sensation,
> All activity, all experience, all
> Belief through art, then this chief suicide
> May be redeemed.

Crane is the symbol of the most dangerous fallacy in recent art,
the substitution, as traditional faith collapsed, of a frenzied and
catastrophic belief in art itself as 'the supreme criterion of experience.' Other substitute beliefs have been rife in our age,

and Shapiro traces their progression from the Darwinian poet of
progress to the Marxist poet of revolution. He understands why
the political faith of so many of the young radicals of the past
decade collapsed so quickly. They staked everything upon the
immediate fulfillment of their utopian dream, and when that
failed them, their belief failed too. Shapiro reminds us of what
our professional patrioteers would now like us to forget, that
most of our young writers faced the beginning of the war with
little positive conviction. He holds, with quiet discernment, that

> The rime produced by soldiers of our war
> Is the most sterile of the century.

Shapiro is possessed by a very different mood from those prevailing at the close of the last war. He feels neither liberated
nor disillusioned. He is inescapably conscious of the consequences of our trying to live in a 'structural universe' which

> Has neither good nor evil but only true
> And false.

He holds that man is by nature 'a believing being,' and, in a
period of excessive and distracted intellectualism, he also holds
that the writer is responsible for putting his own emotions in
order. He does not indicate his own particular position, but it is
evident here, as it was in *V-Letter*, that Shapiro is increasingly
preoccupied with religious values. The only recent poet who has
impressed him by the integrity of his concern with faith is Eliot.

The recurrent and concluding aim of the *Essay* is to solidify
'the layman's confidence in a plainer art.' Shapiro maintains
that our complex styles, however brilliant, have brought upon
us an unprecedented cleavage between poet and audience. He
thereby raises again the familiar complaint, but he gives to it no
conventional answer. He is fully aware of the difficulties confronting a true popular art in a period so equipped with all the
instruments of vulgarization. His respect for his craft alone would
make him realize that the pseudo-folksy verse carried by the
slick picture magazines, whether called 'Corn' or 'My Country,'
is no poetry at all. Shapiro would also stand with Farrell in

warning against the incalculable corruption already wrought
upon public taste by Hollywood.

But the sure fashion in which he threads his way through
such a maze of horrors is a token of his belief in a continuing
American tradition. His treatment of Whitman is significant, since
he returns to him in all three sections. He declares that the
metric of *Leaves of Grass* is,

> at its best, the strongest
> Link in American prosody,

since it freed us from what was 'fake and effeminate' in our imitation of the forms of Europe. But Shapiro also recognizes how
flaccid Whitman's free verse can be, and thinks that most of his
descendants in our day reflect 'but poorly on the prototype.'
So too with Whitman's language and belief. Vital as it is in its
concrete notations, 'the wide style of the dry Americana' is a very
misleading model when it falls to mere generalizations about
Democracy, Ma Femme. The poet of 'person, place and thing'
had already pronounced 'the word "America"' to be 'the chief
enemy of modern poetry.' He reinforces what he meant by showing how one of Whitman's abstractions, that of the Perfect State,
has become the 'optic illusion of our time.' It has begotten many
swollen epics filled, not with the dramatic tensions of living men
and women, but with the bloodless abstractions of 'the synthetic
myth.' Thus Shapiro affirms his central conviction that a poem is
not the same kind of construction as a philosopher's system or a
political theorist's dialectic:

> Ideas are no more words
> Than phoenixes are birds. The metaphysician
> Deals with ideas as words, the poet with things,
> For in the poet's mind the phoenix sings.

Therefore, despite his response to Whitman's continuing greatness, Shapiro remarks that Poe was

> the last poet
> In the classic signification of the word.

He might have made his meaning less mistakable if he had said Baudelaire, since his concern is to point up the opposition between poetry as craftsmanship and poetry as *Weltanschauung*. Shapiro finds his clearest clue out of the maze by following another substitute belief, that of the Freudian poet, to its dead end. He cites Freud's own final disavowal of psychoanalysis as a *Weltanschauung* and his description of the arts as 'beneficent and harmless forms.' Instead of being dismayed at the reduction of the arts to such a humble status, Shapiro declares:

> This is the sane perspective, one that brings
> The beloved creative function back to scale.

In denying I. A. Richards' claim that 'poetry can save us,' in affirming that all great art must have its tap-root in adequately human moral values, Shapiro would seem to have established a solider 'hope for poetry' than that expressed a decade ago by Day Lewis. The best of Shapiro's own poems so far, ranging with gusto from tenderness to irony to stinging satire, would already augur his important share in bridging the gap between the poet and the democratic audience of the nineteen-fifties.

*The New York Times Book Review*, 1945

## Our First National Style

BY conceiving of his subject in its broadest context, as a manifestation of a major trend in American cultural life during the forty years before the Civil War, Talbot Hamlin has added a valuable chapter to our intellectual history. He is con-

*Greek Revival Architecture in America* by Talbot Hamlin. Oxford University Press.

cerned not merely with technical details, but with what factors in our existence called forth and sustained our first widely national style. He is emphatic in his recognition that the term, 'Greek Revival,' is really a misnomer, since the movement was Greek only in its decorative vocabulary, and it did not seek to revive any past style but to adapt freely and imaginatively for the solution of new structural problems.

Yet elements deeply rooted in our thought and taste determined our eager response to classic forms. Negatively, our hatred of England, stirred up again in 1812, caused a reaction against what Jefferson had denounced as the elaborations of the baroque Georgian. We wanted something simpler and purer, a style more fitted to the aspirations of an early republic. And at that point the positive impulses began to operate, as our first statesmen found their most challenging models for action in the politics of classical antiquity. It soon became widely felt that our own heroic national career should be cast in architectural surroundings of a comparable spaciousness and dignity.

Although the movement was not fully under way until the eighteen-twenties, Hamlin dates its beginnings in 1798, with Latrobe's Bank of Pennsylvania, in Philadelphia. To be sure, Latrobe was an Englishman, but he had brought from England the spirit of growing rebellion against Palladianism. It was his work, therefore, and not Jefferson's which really led the way back to Greek simplicity, since Jefferson's standard remained the grandeur of Rome, which he had discovered for himself in the Maison Carrée at Nîmes. The epoch-making quality of this bank of Latrobe's is that 'it is unlike any bank built before the Revolution, it is unlike any English prototype, and it is certainly unlike any known classic structure.' By such a description Hamlin emphasizes the originality of the movement, and marks off its work from the delicacy and refinement of McIntire, and even of Bulfinch. For that New England school was essentially a continuation of late colonial, and owed much of its impulse to Adam. You might draw a parallel in our literature between such work and the grace and distinction of Washington Irving. And just as Emerson and Melville felt that Irving's talent was too feminine, so our next generation of architects believed that our country

needed a more energetic, a more monumental style. It needed
what Hamlin calls 'a revolutionary classicism.'

He gives justification to that inspiriting phrase by demonstrating that Greek beauty was for these builders a thing to be absorbed but not to be followed slavishly, since archeological correctness was shouldered aside by fresh invention. The basic
reason why their structure and design could be so thoroughly
integrated was that at no other time in our history 'have engi-
neering and architecture been so thoroughly one.' As Hamlin
sums up these general attributes of the style, we are reminded
of how impressed Emerson was by Horatio Greenough's insistence on functionalism, on the fact that we must master Greek
principles for our own life, not copy Greek things. The outstanding instance in our literature of such mastery of the organic
principle, and the closest equivalent to the breadth and firmness
and freedom for which the architects were also striving, are the
quietly classic pages of *Walden*.

But one of the most instructive things about the Greek Revival
was that, unlike the literary renaissance, it did not reach its
summit in the older and more settled parts of the country. In
both Massachusetts and Virginia the more conservative colonial
tradition lingered on, although striking exception must be made
for some of the later developments, such as Alexander Parris'
Quincy Market and Ammi Young's impressive granite Boston
Custom House; and, in Virginia, the college buildings of Washington and Lee, which followed Jefferson's magnificent lead at
Charlottesville in more strictly Greek patterns.

The center of radiation was Philadelphia, and it is notable of
the degree to which a coherent school was responsible for the
wider diffusion that two of the leading practitioners, Robert
Mills (1781–1855) and William Strickland (1787–1854), were
both pupils of Latrobe. Mills claimed that he was the first native-
born American to be regularly trained for the profession. It is
significant that he also believed that an architect should be concerned with all the political and social issues of the day. His
buildings are characterized by a solid massiveness, which can be
noted alike in his Treasury Building at Washington, his New
Bedford Custom House, and his private homes in Richmond and

Philadelphia. Strickland's taste was perhaps surer and certainly less heavy; and his work, extending from the Providence Atheneum to the State Capitol of Tennessee, marks again the range that was exercised by these early masters. A comparable sphere of influence was to be exerted by the New York firm of Town and Davis, which produced state capitols as widely separated as those of North Carolina and Illinois.

But the movement is characterized not by the dominance of a few Easterners, nor of a few big cities, but by the simultaneous flowering in hundreds of local centers. The aims of the movement can be read most clearly in such a pioneering state as Kentucky. There the great name is Gideon Shryock, who, after a year in Strickland's office, returned home to provide his region, in such masterpieces as the Capitol at Frankfort or the new college of Transylvania in Lexington, with buildings commensurate with the dignity of the common man. It is fitting that another of the landmarks of the style should be Andrew Jackson's Hermitage, the product of local builders.

As you follow the movement out through the West, to one of its last great monuments, the San Francisco Mint, it is exciting to observe how rapidly the shacks and cabins of the first settlers gave way to buildings of permanence and to communities planned as a whole. Some of the aspects of this planning, particularly in the older industrial centers, in the workers' houses at Peacedale, Rhode Island, or Manchester, New Hampshire, could be instructive to us now. Hamlin is quite aware that one of the sustaining bases of the style was that agriculture and industrialism were still in balance. He knows that the reasons for its decline were not merely technical, not merely the intrusion of an academic concern with correctness, which gradually robbed the movement of its originality and turned a national style into a national bank style. Hamlin puts the more basic reasons quite simply: 'The emergence of the millionaire was as fatal to the artistic ideals of the Greek Revival as were the speed, the speculation and the exploitation that produced him.'

Some of the difficulties that Hamlin encountered in writing his book are part of our later heritage. He found not only that some of the most beautiful of these buildings are still being destroyed, with no apparent concern on the given city's part for what is thus lost; but, even in the case of those that have escaped destruction, an utter carelessness as to their records, so that he could piece together only tentatively some of the main outlines of his narrative. It is interesting to note how frequently he cites the information provided by the WPA State Guides, which in themselves are a sign of our renewed if belated concern with the cultural community.

*New Republic,* 1944

# Sarah Orne Jewett

B RET Harte, Cable, Craddock, and most of the other local colorists all produced distinctive first volumes and spent the rest of their lives unsuccessfully trying to equal them. Sarah Jewett understood the reasons why: they drew authentic pictures, but they tried to make their material count for everything, and naturally it soon lost its freshness. 'The trouble with most realism,' she observed, 'is that it isn't seen from any point of view at all, and so its shadows fall in every direction, and it fails of being art.' She had grown to perceive the limitations of her own Deephaven sketches; they were accurate transcriptions, but she had stood too directly in the middle of her own experience, and had not been able to see it with any perspective. As her life expanded into wider contacts, and embraced her intimate devotion to Annie Fields, and her friendship with Aldrich and Howells and others of the Boston group, she realized that her books, if they were to be anything, must be the expression of a ripening personality. Amazingly close observation which had been able to echo the very rise and fall of nasal voices had given the sharp tang to her early work, but it was not enough. She had to wait for twenty years, looking back at her treasured scenes from afar, letting her memory dwell on them and recombine them in new shapes, bathing them in the life-giving pools of her imagination, before she could write *The Country of the Pointed Firs.*

The scope of this book is no different from that of *Deephaven*. It simply gives an impression of a summer's life in a fishing village: the subdued hum of daily existence that surrounds Almiry Todd, the famous herb-gatherer, and her old mother Mis' Blackett, alert and gracious for all her eighty-six years; the story of poor Joanna who, having been deserted by her lover, willed to live and die alone on Shell-Heap Island; the idle gossip along the shore; the great expedition up to the head of the bay for the Bowden family reunion. Miss Jewett is not a part of this life; she uses the somewhat pale device of regarding it through the eyes of a visitor to Dunnet Landing, but her visit is really a lifelong pilgrimage constantly to recapture the qualities that lie closest to her heart. She wrote the definition of her own achievement in a letter to her young friend Willa Cather: 'The thing that teases the mind over and over for years and at last gets itself put down rightly on paper—whether little or great it belongs to literature.'

One gets a very exact sense of the way she lingered over her details in the limpid atmosphere that enfolds so many of her later pages:

It was evening again, the frogs were piping in the lower meadows, and in the woods, higher up the great hill, a little owl began to hoot. The sea air, salt and heavy, was blowing in over the country at the end of the hot bright day. A lamp was lighted in the house, the happy children were talking together, and supper was waiting. The father and mother lingered for a moment outside, and looked down over the shadowy fields; then they went in, without speaking. The great day was over, and they shut the door.

This is the final passage in 'The Hiltons' Holiday,' a story which was one of its author's own favorites, and which consists simply in the account of a trip to town made by a farmer and his two small girls. Sarah Jewett's most distinctive quality lies in her ability to enmesh the actual touch of the countryside, a whiff of salt air across the marsh, the flickering shadows over a field of grain. One thinks of the lambent coolness of her sketches in terms of a fresh June day when the lilacs have faded and the peonies are just opening and there is a breeze straight in from the sea; or of the August morning that carries the first hint of autumn when the swamp maple is suddenly a blaze of red.

But there is more to her sketches than atmosphere. She is not merely a poet of nature. She may not tell you many facts about her characters, but they embody a deeply interfused humanity. Her imagination breathes softly through them, and suggests the dimensions of life. You generally think of the stout figure of Almiry Todd as sitting heavily in the stern of a dory, or bent over in a patch of pennyroyal, loquacious, drolly positive, and disconcertingly downright. But in rare moments you also catch a glimpse, behind this daily bustle, of the uncharted depths of a heart that knows the full meaning of love and loss and suffering. Sarah Jewett did not have a sense of tragedy, a limitation which defines her sphere. The daughter of a country doctor was well aware of the stark elements of human nature, but in her temperament these were subordinated to tender pathos and humor. The characters she delineates are not torn by passions, but move on the fringes of life. They have had to give up a good many hopes, but they do not dwell on their hardships. They do not revolt; they do not try to escape. They have long ago settled down to cultivating the pattern of their narrow lives as well as of their rocky squares of garden. They are as much a part of the soil they were born upon as the huckleberries and the pointed firs themselves. The style which Miss Jewett developed to convey their existence has a clarity and precision that suits it exactly to her quiet ends. It is not accidental that her language recalls Wordsworth's in the direct simplicity of its appeal. For her contribution is also one of emotion recollected in tranquillity as she recites her gentle elegies of New England.

*American Writers on American Literature,* 1931

# 'That True and Human World . . .'

ISS Porter's high reputation among nearly all schools of critics may now have reached the point where it is doing her a disservice. She is bracketed as 'a writer's writer,' which she certainly is, so far as that phrase implies that almost any other craftsman can learn important things from her about the handling of both language and structure. But the common reader has too frequently been led to believe that 'style' is something esoteric, and that Miss Porter's relatively slim production must mean that she has not much to say. This misconception has also been nourished unwittingly by her admirers who like her quality so much that they want more and keep urging her to write a novel. But Miss Porter herself, when introducing the work of Eudora Welty, saw that for the master of the short story the novel may simply be the next trap ahead. The assumed superiority of the longer form is a product of our American supposition that bigger must be better, and has blown up many a lyric poet into an abortive epic bard, as well as the content adequate for a decent novel into a limp trilogy.

What we tend to forget is that in such a characteristically French form as the novelette, in the story of twenty to forty thousand words, we have also an American tradition. The kind of intensification that Melville gained in *Benito Cereno* and *Billy Budd*, and that James, working so differently, accomplished in *Pandora, The Coxon Fund, The Bench of Desolation,* and a dozen others, would seem to have much to offer to our period whose syntheses are often so precarious that they may be lost through extension. Miss Porter has set her special signa-

*The Leaning Tower and Other Stories* by Katherine Anne Porter. Harcourt, Brace & Co.

67

ture on this form, as Hemingway has on the contemporary practice of the short story. Not that she hasn't worked brilliantly in
short stories as well, but sometimes hers can seem too fragmentary, as, for instance, do the first half dozen pieces in this
new volume in comparison with the more integrated structure of
*Old Mortality,* which dealt with the same descendants of Kentucky against a Louisiana and Texas background.

Yet these very stories can demonstrate the searching originality of her content. She may seem to be dealing with the stock
material of the local colorists, with older Southern manners and
customs as they persisted down into this century. Yet you quickly
realize, in 'The Old Order' and 'The Last Leaf,' that the human
relationships are being examined with a new depth and honesty,
that the sentimental view of the devoted old slave living on
serenely with her former mistress is punctured once for all by
such a quiet observation as that Nannie thrived on 'a species
of kindness not so indulgent, maybe, as that given to the puppies.'

Such discoveries of the living intricacy in any relationship are
Miss Porter's most recurrent resource. A passage at the end of
'The Grave,' the last of this group, gives a very explicit clue as to
how she comes into possession of her material. This passage records how Miranda, by a chance of seemingly irrelevant association, is suddenly struck with the full violence of an episode long
buried in her childhood, by her first knowledge of the mystery
of birth as it had come to her through seeing a pregnant rabbit
that her brother had shot and was skinning. This passage, too,
long to quote here, reveals Miss Porter's understanding of how
much enters into any mature experience, of how deeply bathed
in imaginative richness any event must be if it is to become a
fluid and viable symbol.

The frequence with which violence lies at the heart of her
discoveries helps to explain a main source of strength in her
delicate prose. 'The Circus,' the best short story here, conveys
the naked agony with which Miranda, too young to grasp the
conventions, reacts to the dangers and brutalities of the show.
What the others can take in the comic spirit presses upon her a
first initiation into the pity and terror of life. Violence in modern
fiction has been so often a substitute for understanding that Miss

Porter's ability to use it to reveal ethical values is another of her particular distinctions, as she showed especially in *Noon Wine*. In 'The Downward Path to Wisdom,' one of the three longer stories in this collection, her control seems far less sure, since the brutalities which are poured down upon the helpless child by his elders are not sufficiently motivated to make a coherent pattern. Violence seems to have been manipulated almost for its own sake.

Still another of Miss Porter's distinctions has been her refutation of the local colorists and other narrow regionalists by her extraordinary ability to portray a whole series of different environments. It may only be our anticipation of so much variety from her that causes a story like 'A Day's Work' to seem for the first time a repetition of material handled more freshly in 'The Cracked Looking-Glass.' In comparison with that earlier story, which was a sustained miracle of Irish feeling and rhythm, both the situation and characters here may seem slightly expected. But when we turn to the longest story, to the novelette which gives title to the volume, we have again the rare combination of virtuosity with moral penetration.

Here Miss Porter uses a controlling symbol in the way that James often did, since the leaning tower not only is a souvenir of the Berlin landlady's long past happiness in Italy, but also becomes a compelling image for the tottering balance of the German world in the year before Hitler's rise to power. Many best-selling accounts have now been written of that time, and yet it seems doubtful whether any of them will preserve its form and pressure longer than Miss Porter's presentation of it through the consciousness of a young American painter. The reason for her success may be suggested by a comment James once made when noting that Turgenieff's *Memoirs of a Sportsman*, dealing with the question of serfdom, had appeared in the very same year as *Uncle Tom's Cabin*: 'No single episode pleads conclusively against the "peculiar institution" of Russia; the lesson is the cumulative testimony of a multitude of fine touches—in an after-sense of sadness that sets wise readers thinking . . . It offers a capital example of moral meaning giving a sense to form and form giving relief to moral meaning.'

Some of Miss Porter's 'fine touches' consist in her recurrent stress on the city's poverty, through Charles Upton's gradual realization of the difference from the depression he had left behind at home, where everybody took it for granted that things would improve, whereas in Berlin 'the sufferers seemed to know that they had no cause for hope.' No journalist or social historian analyzing the collapse of the republic has come closer to the central cause. And concerning the interpenetration of form and moral meaning, a comparison with Christopher Isherwood's *Good-Bye to Berlin* is instructive. Isherwood looked back to the same kind of student and boardinghouse life, and he dealt more explicitly with some of the manifestations of social decay. But his characters seem self-consciously worked up from a Freudian handbook, or they exist to shock like the figures in a cinema thriller. They have none of the deep authenticity that springs from Miss Porter's humility and tenderness before life. She has been able to apprehend many kinds of Germans, ranging from the lumpish solemn mathematician who 'loves study and quiet' to the young aristocrat whose new cheek-wound brings out in his expression a mixture of 'amazing arrogance, pleasure, inexpressible vanity and self-satisfaction.' Miss Porter does not slight the bestial brutalities in this hard city. No more, however, does she indulge in easy propaganda. When Charles Upton remarks lightly that Americans are sentimental and 'like just everybody,' the young mathematician stares at him earnestly and says: 'I do not think you really like anybody, you Americans. You are indifferent to everybody, and so it is easy for you to be gay, to be careless, to seem friendly. You are really cold-hearted indifferent people.'

As a result of weaving back and forth through contradictions and incongruities, from one flickering center of human conviction to another, Miss Porter has done again what she did in *Pale Horse, Pale Rider*. She has created the atmosphere of a haunting moment of crisis. In that earlier novelette she gave us the end of the last war as it was felt in America through the crazy fever of the flu epidemic. Here, as she brings her group of students close together for a moment of New Year's Eve conviviality, what reverberates through their every speech and gesture is a premonition of disaster. In writing of Miss Welty, Miss Porter warned the artist against political beliefs, but here we can see that her remark was not the reactionary one that such a remark generally is. For she has penetrated into the economic and social sickness that brought on fascism, but she has also held to her knowledge that the realm of the creator of fiction must be broader and more resilient than theories or opinions, that it can be nothing less than 'that true and human world of which the artist is a living part.'

*Accent,* 1945

## Late-Summer Wine: Wallace Stevens

WALLACE Stevens continues to exhibit the fecundity which has made the last decade more prolific for him than all the rest of his previous career. Until 1936 all his published poems were included in *Harmonium,* but since then he has added *Ideas of Order, The Man With the Blue Guitar, Parts of the World,* and now this present book. At sixty-seven his subject, like that of the later Yeats, is increasingly the imagination itself. Indeed, some of the titles here—'The Motive for Metaphor,' 'The Creations of Sound,' 'The Pure Good of Theory' —might suggest that he has veered over the line into being more critical aesthetician than poet. But the full-bodied connotations set by the book's title are reinforced by the excitingly physical expectations of 'The Dove in the Belly' or 'Mountains Covered With Cats.'

*Transport to Summer* by Wallace Stevens. Alfred A. Knopf, Inc.

Stevens' thoughts are generally drenched with the life of his senses. This vibrant fact forms the core of his exploration of the interplay between the mind and reality. He approaches that interplay from a variety of angles and stances. Sometimes, in the poems that are most analogous to a painter's still life, he says: 'Let's see the very thing and nothing else.' Sometimes he is absorbed with the differences between the observed thing and what the imagination can make of it, a contrast which calls out his recurrent symbol of the differences between sunlight and moonlight, between the stark actual and the release given by soft shadows and oblique half-tones. (Nathaniel Hawthorne, whose many days in a customs house are comparable to those spent by Stevens in his insurance office, often used the same symbols for the same purpose.)

Most frequently and most characteristically this poet of nuances is given over to speculations upon what the imagination can be said to add to reality. He knows, as the true artist must, that

> Description is revelation. It is not
> The thing described, nor false facsimile.

Rather, it produces a heightened reality, 'intenser than any actual life could be.' In such speculations Stevens often seems closely akin to Santayana's conception of 'essences.'

'Notes Toward a Supreme Fiction,' running above six hundred lines, is the longest and most ambitious poem in this collection, and provides the most numerous variations upon Stevens' central theme. Its division into three parts of exactly equal length, entitled 'It must be abstract,' 'It must change,' 'It must give pleasure,' suggests again the dangers risked by Stevens' latest manner. The development of these propositions in unrhymed three-line stanzas of Stevens' formal pentameter can become such a set piece as the more varied liveliness of 'The Man With the Blue Guitar' fully escaped being.

Stevens is often more completely successful in his shorter poems, as in the happily named 'Holiday in Reality.' For there, to express his conviction that the artist must always make a fresh and personal discovery, he brings into play his lightness and ebullience:

> After all, they knew that to be real each had
> To find for himself his earth, his sky, his sea.
> And the words for them and the colors that they possessed.
> It was impossible to breathe at Durand-Ruel's.

The sense of unexpected deadness that can overtake you in a gallery, that can make a museum and a mausoleum akin, is what Stevens develops in the second of the three propositions for his 'supreme fiction.' He is at his best in those poems which embody his conviction that a work of art is a moment of stasis out of movement, an equilibrium as difficult as it is delicate. The heaviness of spirit that can descend from the period pieces in Durand-Ruel's is because 'nothing had happened because nothing had changed.'

Stevens knows that a poem is not a proposition, or, as he puts it in 'Man Carrying Thing': 'The poem must resist the intelligence / Almost successfully.' He conveys the value of change most compellingly, not by direct statement, but by such devices as his wonderfully effective recurrent symbol of the endlessly fascinating movement of clouds. His greatest resource has always been in the gaiety of his language, in the way he employs also the nonsensical and the grotesque to break through the restrictions of the fixed and dry rational into what he calls 'the lingua franca et jocundissima.'

All of Stevens' later work has been written against the realization that we live in a time of violent disorder. The most profound challenge in his poems is his confidence that even in such a time, even on the verge of ruin, a man can re-create afresh his world out of the unfailing utilization of his inner resources. The value of the creative imagination, of 'supreme fictions' in their fullest abundance, lies in the extension, even to the point of grandeur, that they add to our common lives. I suppose that Wallace Stevens, in expressing such truths with the mellowness and tang of a late-summer wine, has about one reader to every hundred of the latest best-seller. Yet Stevens, who did not publish a poem until he was thirty-five, will increasingly be recognized to belong in the company of Henry Adams and Henry James, with that small body of important American artists who have ripened as they matured, and who have been far more productive beyond their middle years than during their green twenties and thirties.

*The New York Times Book Review,* 1947

III. THE ARTIST AT WORK

# Melville as Poet

T HROUGHOUT the last half of his life, over a span of
thirty-five years, Melville, who, in *Moby Dick,* had reached
levels of imaginative writing unsurpassed by any other American, wrote little more prose. When he had finished *The Confidence Man* in 1856, he had produced ten books in less than a
dozen years and had had his bellyful of trying unsuccessfully to
gain a comprehending audience and to support himself by his
pen. But he had not lost his interest in self-expression, and,
turning to verse, he had, by the spring of 1860, a volume ready
for publication. This was to find no publisher, and not until the
year after the end of the Civil War did he at last make his appearance as a poet. The book then issued was *Battle-Pieces,* a
series of seventy poems that form a running commentary on the
course of the war, though most of them were inspired, retrospec-
tively, by the fall of Richmond. The book had slight critical
success, and from that time forward Melville, who had failed in
various applications for a consular appointment, was employed
for twenty years as a customs inspector in New York, and possessed only intermittent time for writing. But he managed to
bring to completion *Clarel,* a narrative poem of several thousand
lines, which grew out of the meditative pilgrimage he had made
to the Holy Land during the year after the career as a writer of
fiction had seemed to him finally unreal. *Clarel,* as Melville himself noted, was 'immensely adapted for unpopularity,' and could
be printed in 1876 only as the result of a gift from a Gansevoort
uncle. After his release from the customhouse at the end of 1885,
Melville felt a resurgence of his creative energies, and made one
major return to fiction in *Billy Budd.* But this story was still in
The Introduction to a selection of Melville's poems.—Ed.

77

manuscript at his death, and his final efforts to publish were two small volumes of verse, each privately printed in twenty-five copies, *John Marr and Other Sailors*, 1888, and *Timoleon*, 1891. One section of the latter, 'Fruits of Travel Long Ago,' would seem to be at least part of what he had designed as his first book of verse three decades before. Left among his papers at his death were more than seventy further poems, in addition to fragments of varying length.

All the above poetry, with the exception of a few of the manuscripts, comprises three volumes of Melville's collected works. But since that edition appeared in England twenty years ago, was limited to 750 copies, and is long since out of print, the range of Melville's verse is virtually unavailable for the common reader. The selection here presented tries to take advantage of all the various interests attaching to any part of Melville's work. Some poems have been chosen because they embody the same recurrent symbols that give an absorbing unity to his prose. These symbols appear most often in his reminiscences of the sea: 'To Ned' shows that he kept through life the image of Typee, of primitive existence unspoiled by civilization; 'The Berg' presents a variant of the terrifying white death of Moby Dick; the 'maldive shark' glides also through the lines 'Commemorative of a Naval Victory.' Other poems serve to light up facets of Melville's mind as it developed in the years after his great creative period: 'Greek Architecture' indicates his understanding of a balanced form far different from any he had struggled to master; 'Art'— whose lines are scratched out and rewritten with many changes in the manuscript—tells how painfully he understood the tensions of the struggle for the union of opposites.

Few of his poems reveal anything like the mastery of organic rhythm to be found in his best prose. He had become an apprentice too late to a new craft. Although he tried his hand at a variety of metrical forms, he seldom progressed beyond an acquired skill. He was capable of such lyric patterns as 'Shiloh' or 'Monody,' but he could often be stiff and clumsy. Yet what he had to convey is very impressive. I have included enough of *Battle-Pieces* to show the depth of his concern with the problems of war. Wholehearted in his devotion to the Union's cause, what

he urged at the close was forbearance and charity on the part
of the North as the chief guide to reconstruction; and he prayed
'that the terrible historic tragedy of our time may not have been
enacted without instructing our whole beloved country through
terror and pity . . .'

*Clarel* took his thought into some of the problems of his society's future and of our present. It falls into the tradition of
those poetic debates of the mind which formed so much of the
substance of Clough and Arnold and Tennyson. Since its characters voice a bewildering variety of creeds, and since Clarel, the
disillusioned young divinity student, is about the most shadowy
in the group, it is impossible to determine from the poem exactly
what Melville believed. The passages selected are among those
where he persevered farthest from the beaten tracks of his day,
where he doubted the value for the world of the dominance of
Anglo-Saxon industrialists, where he foresaw class wars, and
where, with the decay of Protestantism, he also foresaw a grim
duel between 'Rome and the Atheist.' To put the gloom of some
of these conjectures into its proper context, we should remember
his reaction to Thomson's *City of Dreadful Night:* 'As to the
pessimism, although neither pessimist nor optimist myself, nevertheless I relish it in the verse, if for nothing else than as a
counterpoise to the exorbitant hopefulness, juvenile and shallow,
that makes such a bluster in these days.' We should also remember that the 'Epilogue' to *Clarel* dwells upon Christian hope, and
that 'The Lake,' the most sustained poem left by Melville in
manuscript, celebrates the theme of seasonal death and rebirth.
And to counteract his forebodings of the possible degradation
of democracy, we should recall his celebration of the heroic
possibilities of the common man—one of the most recurrent
themes of his fiction, from Jack Chase to Billy Budd.

A reward that awaits the reader who follows these selections
on to Melville's collected works is the frequency with which his
mediocre poems are illuminated by passages where the poet is in
supreme control. That being the case I have not scrupled in
three instances beyond *Clarel* ('Sheridan at Cedar Creek,' 'On
the Slain Collegians,' 'Commemorative of a Naval Victory') to
release such passages from their hampering surroundings. One

further such passage, the concluding quatrain to 'The Coming Storm,' an otherwise undistinguished reaction to a painting by Sandford Gifford, is perhaps the best poetry Melville wrote. Indeed, as I have said elsewhere, these lines constitute one of the most profound recognitions of the value of tragedy ever to have been made:

> No utter surprise can come to him
>   Who reaches Shakespeare's core;
> That which we seek and shun is there—
>   Man's final lore.

Such lines suggest Melville's master preoccupation, in verse no less than in prose. If it would not have risked confusion, I should have called this selection by the subtitle of *Battle-Pieces*—'Aspects of the War.' That would have suggested Melville's continuing concern with the unending struggle, with the tensions between good and evil: within the mind and in the state, political, social, and religious.

*Herman Melville: Selected Poems,* 1944

## The Private Poet: Emily Dickinson

ACCORDING to the advance agents, a historic event occurred this spring in the annals of American literature, and we are the richer by over six hundred more poems by 'Emily.' Nearly everyone who writes about her plunges at once

*Bolts of Melody: New Poems of Emily Dickinson,* edited by Mabel Loomis Todd and Millicent Todd Bingham. Harper & Bros.

*Ancestors' Brocades: The Literary Debut of Emily Dickinson* by Millicent Todd Bingham. Harper & Bros.

to cozy first-name calling with this poet who did not enjoy such liberties when she was alive and could prevent them. Millicent Todd Bingham, the editor of this new collection and the author of a volume explaining why it was not published fifty years ago, is no exception. She also goes on the once fashionable assumption that Miss Dickinson 'has always been shrouded in mystery,' just as though George Whicher had not published seven years ago the biography which places her career so lucidly against its local and intellectual backgrounds. To be sure, Mrs. Bingham no longer engages in that favorite guessing-game of the 'twenties, 'Who was Emily Dickinson's lover?' But the ground of extraneous interest has now shifted to the poet's brother and sister and sister-in-law, and the breathless drama builds around a lawsuit brought by Lavinia Dickinson against Mrs. Bingham's mother a decade after the poet's death. This suit involved a strip of land willed by Austin Dickinson to Mrs. Todd, and its one importance to literary history is that it broke off all plans which that first editor of Miss Dickinson's poems had had for carrying that work further.

But Mrs. Bingham could not leave it at that. She apparently had to avenge her mother's memory with a detailed account of Vinnie's virulence (her 'mouth was perfectly hideous and full of false teeth'), and of the violent tensions that existed between this old maid and the Dickinsons in 'the other house.' Mrs. Bingham's narrative has been so successful as to inflame Bernard DeVoto's imagination with the notion that this is 'incomparably the best book ever written about Emily.' And he has pushed the present flurry to its limit by declaiming that 'they were all burning . . . they were all damned . . . Emily Dickinson was the supreme poet of hate.' That climactic statement can, of course, be corrected by comparing it with nearly every line and implication of Miss Dickinson's verse, but not all readers of 'The Easy Chair' will go that far.

Amy Lowell once projected a biography of Emily Dickinson in which the effect upon her of each member of her family would be analyzed. Such a book, doing its best to reconstruct the young and formative period of her life, and probing her strong fixation upon her father, might have been valuable. But Mrs. Bingham has not even attempted to write it, since her story begins only with the arrival of Professor and Mrs. Todd in Amherst, less than five years before Miss Dickinson died. The jealousy-ridden Lavinia whom Mrs. Bingham portrays is not the devoted younger sister whom Emily knew. This biographer's material is the unhealthily closed circle of a New England family at the time of its decline, but, though she insists on modern 'frankness,' her story does not read very convincingly. Why, after some years of collaboration, did Lavinia turn so fiercely upon Mrs. Todd? Why, to Mrs. Todd's consternation, did the lawsuit go against her and for Lavinia? Mrs. Bingham hints at some 'sadness' in her mother's life, and just mentions the Amherst gossip of an attachment between Austin Dickinson and Mrs. Todd. If you set out to withhold no 'pertinent' facts in such a drama, you can't give only a highly colored version of one side, especially if you are bent on proving that 'truth, like ancestors' brocades, can stand alone.'

Mrs. Bingham would much better have confined herself to the circumstances of the first publication of Emily Dickinson's poems, though that was hardly the subject for a whole book. As it is, she has printed every scrap of a note that passed between Mrs. Todd and Higginson and the printers of both the poems and letters, without any perspective or principle of selection. The only portions indispensable to our knowledge of the poet are those chapters which extend the already grim picture of the state of the printed text of her poems. No one now needs further persuading of the hopeless inaccuracy in every function of an editor of Austin and Sue Dickinson's daughter, Martha Dickinson Bianchi; but Mrs. Bingham helps clear up a great number of misreadings. She demonstrates how frequently lines were confused, stanzas omitted, and even two poems run together as one. Her most spectacular though by no means most important correction is that involving the final stanza of one of the *Further Poems* of 1929. Instead of the almost meaningless ending,

> Mine be the ministry
> When thy thirst comes,
> Dews of thyself to fetch
> And holy balms,

Emily Dickinson characteristically wrote,

> Dews of Thessaly to fetch
> And Hybla balms.

Unlike Madame Bianchi, Mrs. Todd was a painstaking and accurate transcriber, and her daughter takes after her in this valuable respect. But the paradoxical result is to destroy the one remaining plank of confidence regarding the text as we have it. Hitherto it has been generally assumed that the Higginson-Todd editions gave their poems as Emily Dickinson wrote them, but it now appears that the case was more complicated. In her chapter called 'Creative Editing,' Mrs. Bingham recounts the dilemma with which the original editors felt themselves confronted. They wanted to present their poet to the world, but they did not want the world of the 'nineties to find her too queer, and there was the problem of her eccentric syntax and grammar, to say nothing of her rhymes. Sometimes the issue was that of conventionally correct versus actually spoken usage, for Emily Dickinson, as the new poems show, was quite capable of writing 'It don't sound so terrible, quite, as it did,' or of revealing our native fondness for 'r' by rhyming 'India' with 'too near.' Mrs. Todd seems to have acted as a brake on Higginson in the matter of changes, for though she accepted his arrangement under the general (if not too illuminating) categories of Life, Nature, Love, Time, and Eternity, she doubted the validity of the titles he bestowed upon individual poems, and was quite staunch in the kind of resistance that prevented the dog's feet 'like intermittent plush' from being altered to 'in intermittent plash.'

But there were many stanzas that seemed to go flat for want of a rhyme—for instance,

> or later,
> Parting with a world
> We have understood for better
> Still to be explained.

The now familiar final line, 'Still it be unfurled,' is an example, as Mrs. Bingham says, 'of the kind of thing they felt called upon to do.' Despite conscious resistance to temptation on Higginson's

part also, compromises were yielded to, and, in the end, 'a good
many changes were made.' Sometimes these involved the editors
fairly deeply in the texture of the verse, to the point of four
changes in the first two stanzas of one of her best-known poems:

> I heard a fly buzz when I died;
> The stillness in the room
> Was like the stillness in the air
> Between the heaves of storm.
>
> The eyes around had wrung them dry,
> And breaths were gathering firm
> For that last onset, when the king
> Be witnessed in the room.

In order to provide a rhyme, that first 'in the room' became
'round my form.' That led, to avoid repetition, to 'around,' in
the opening line of the second stanza, being changed to 'beside.'
Then 'firm' became 'sure,' and was made to rhyme by substituting for the second 'in the room,' the wholly new phrase 'in
his power.' As a result the rhymes click—or almost—but what
has been lost is the peculiar desolate effect provided by the echoing 'in the room,' which does not lift the sufferer to God's power,
but reverberates with the loneliness of dying.

Sometimes the creative editors omitted a whole stanza that
seemed too odd, and in the view of Mrs. Bingham, though such
an omission 'might sometimes improve a poem, it was more often
a mistake.' Both editors possessed some literary tact, and some of
their interpolated rhymes may very well have served to quicken
the energy of a verse; but if what is wanted are the poems of
Emily Dickinson, every kind of alteration was a mistake.

In her own editing Mrs. Bingham really proceeds on that latter
assumption; but in presenting the further poems and fragments
that remained in Mrs. Todd's hands at the time of the rupture—
the very large number of which Lavinia seems not to have been
aware—Mrs. Bingham hardly lives up to her opportunities as an
editor. She realizes that the poems 'should eventually be arranged in the order of composition,' but though she has at her
command some of the evidence for dating, particularly that furnished by the three markedly different periods of Miss Dickin-

son's handwriting, she has put the reader in effectual possession of none of it. She contents herself with such tantalizing withholdings as that 'many of these poems were written comparatively early in life,' or that some of the love poems had 'a very special person in mind.' She recognizes the value that could accrue through seeing the chronological progression of Miss Dickinson's poems dealing with specific themes—for instance, with fame, to which she is popularly supposed to have been indifferent, but to varied meditations about which she kept returning to the end. But having noted such a point, Mrs. Bingham then seems to forget her mother's objections to Higginson's titles, and arranges her volume under a series of allusive headings. These are all borrowed from phrases in the poems, to be sure, but out of its context 'Italic Faces' may seem mannered and obscure for a title covering twenty poems, and 'My Pageantry' and 'Our Little Kinsmen' verge on the sentimental.

The poems themselves possess nearly all the qualities to have been found in Miss Dickinson's work before. There is the same exciting verbal action; the familiar liking for plush and satin and purple; the alternation of themes between tension and escape, with her fondness for battle imagery to express the one and her equal fondness for words of romantic distance—Cordillera, Himmaleh, Venetian—to enhance the other. And to counterpoise her recurrence to isolation and death is the quality that so often forms her special signature, her expectant intimacy with nature, and particularly with its smaller denizens, frog, robin, squirrel, spider, and bee. One revelatory new phrase—under which Mrs. Bingham groups some of the most effective of these poems—is 'an ablative estate.' What Miss Dickinson meant by it she indicated thus:

> I'd rather recollect a setting
> Than a rising sun.

And she gave this reason for her choice:

> Because in going is a drama
> Staying cannot confer.

Whether or not she was consciously balancing her ablative case against Emerson's emphasis upon 'the optative mood,' the difference between wishing for a more radiant future and accepting the finality of removal is the difference between these two poets, marking the distance traversed between the beginning and the end of the New England renaissance. It marks also why Miss Dickinson possessed the dramatic, indeed, the tragic sense so lacking from Emerson's radiant eloquence. In celebrating the dawn of a new era, he threw to the winds not merely Calvinism but all traditional belief in the inescapable tension between good and evil. She noted, in the final poem in Mrs. Bingham's collection, some of the unforeseen consequences of his emancipation:

> Those, dying then, knew where they went,
> They went to God's right hand;
> That hand is amputated now
> And God cannot be found.
>
> The abdication of belief
> Makes the behavior small—
> Better an *ignis fatuus*
> Than no illume at all.

This poem is one of the most impressive of those now added, and if we reckon with whole poems rather than with flashes of quality, comparatively few here rise very near her first rank. Of course, any judgment of such short lyrics as most of hers is extremely subjective, as Higginson remarked in noting that nearly every reviewer of the first collection picked a different favorite. But to specify some of the types of her greatest successes, I doubt whether there could be found here any quatrain with the epigrammatic terseness of 'Presentiment is that long shadow on the lawn'; any longer poem with the dramatic intensity and wholeness of 'I cannot live with you' or 'The last night that she lived'; or any poem with the kind of union between metrical delicacy and philosophical discovery that makes 'Safe in their alabaster chambers'—to this reviewer's taste—her rarest contribution of all. Nor at her polar moods of loneliness and exuberance is there anything quite to match either the starkness of 'My Wheel is in the dark' or her way of outdistancing the release of Emerson's

'Bacchus' by proclaiming herself 'the little tippler / Leaning against the sun.' And though there are a few affecting additions to her never numerous poems of somber compulsion—particularly a poem of suicide beginning 'He scanned it, staggered, dropped the loop' and another, 'The waters chased him as he fled,' which conveys the terrified sensation of being pursued—these again do not approach the sustained horror of the poem which seems to have risen most obsessively from her subconscious, that drama of agonized repression and flight: 'In winter in my room / I came upon a worm.'

Altogether these new poems, though they increase the body of her previously published work by more than a third, will hardly serve to increase the bounds of her reputation. The final critical estimate of such a poet will always depend upon a winnowing, whereby her inevitably few accomplished poems can be shaken free from many pieces which are hardly more than abandoned beginnings of themes that she managed to develop on another occasion. Her work—and its editing—present all the peculiar problems of the private poet.

She was a private poet in a different sense, say, from Hopkins. In reaction against the current modes of Tennyson and Swinburne, he set himself, in his isolation, deliberately to shape a new style in poems that could not have been more highly wrought. Her process was almost wholly instinctive. No matter what shades of difference between her religious values and Emerson's, her way of writing continued to illustrate his conception of the Poet. That she believed no less than he that poetry could be written only in all-sufficient moments of inspiration is apparent from the state of her manuscripts. She wrote on every conceivable scrap of paper, brown grocery bags and the backs of drug store advertisements, with a partiality for the insides of used envelopes. Her verses were set down to satisfy an immediate need, and variant words were added as fast as they occurred to her. Several such manuscripts are given in facsimile by Mrs. Bingham, and it should be obvious that they simply are not subject to customary editing. The present editor states her principle of choice: 'in most cases I used the word she wrote first'; but

82888888888

even if that word was more surely establishable than the fac-
similes indicate, Miss Dickinson would presumably have favored
more often the last alternative that struck her. How confusing
this question can become may be noted from a single poem, 'A
sparrow took a slice of twig,' which Mrs. Bingham prints without variants, even though the facsimile yields readings as far
from those chosen as 'epicure of vehicles' is from 'a familiar
saddle,' and at least a dozen choices for its final line.

It must be recognized henceforth that such poems were not
finished, that they existed for Emily Dickinson's eyes alone, and
that we cannot tell what she finally intended or whether she had
made up her mind. She seems to have tossed many of these
fragments aside as soon as her initial impulse was spent; and if
they are printed, they can be given accurately only as work-
sheets, with all the variants included. Lest the reader fear that
such publication would swamp his interest, it should be added
that a leading value of such fragments is to give us an insight
into the poet's process of creation, and that our sense of her
verbal resources is heightened by watching her alternate from
'the blissful oriole' to 'the reeling oriole,' and remain undecided
as to whether to call him also 'confiding prodigal' or 'minute
Domingo.'

And fortunately, a great number of Miss Dickinson's poems
do not deliquesce in this fashion, for those eight or nine hundred
which she had copied out and sewed together in fascicles, and
which formed the basis for the Higginson-Todd editions, contained a far higher proportion of her final choices. Yet even several of the best known must be printed ultimately as private
poems still, with the variants noted not too distractingly in small
type at the foot of the page. For example, in the final line of 'He
preached upon "breadth" till it argued him narrow,' she thought
of calling this individual, with varying shades of irony, 'so religious (enabled, accomplished, discerning, accoutred, established, conclusive) a man!' We cannot rely on any creative editing, for even though the Higginson-Todd choice of 'enabled'
was a sensitive one, still Miss Dickinson underlined 'religious,'
apparently to indicate her choice. If we are to enter into the full

nature of what it meant to be a poet in her circumstances, we must print each manuscript *in toto* as the special case it is.

Otherwise—and that is the reason for bringing up all these editorial issues here—we will almost certainly misconceive her. Indeed, ever since her rediscovery in the 'twenties, she has been variously misunderstood by those who have failed to reckon with enough of her actual background. Since her revival coincided with our renewed taste for the seventeenth-century metaphysicals, some critics wrote as though she was a conscious follower of Donne. But she had none of his sustained control over rhetoric, though she shared with Emerson and Thoreau their great liking for Browne and Herbert. She copied out, late in life, the second and third stanzas of Herbert's 'Matins,' beginning 'My God, what is a heart?' as though to indicate her kinship with some of his spiritual values and with his way of conveying them through the homeliest words. It was a natural mistake for Mrs. Bingham to regard these stanzas as Miss Dickinson's own, and to print them as the climactic poem of one of her sections.

Yet whatever Emily Dickinson's debts to the seventeenth century, it should never be forgotten that Emerson was the great figure in her foreground, and that her conception of poetic language, of how 'the word becomes one with the thing' in the moment of inspired vision, was basically his. She expresses that conception explicitly in one of these new poems, emphasizing the *inwelling* of a mysterious force beyond conscious control:

'Shall I take thee?' the poet said
To the propounded word.
'Be stationed with the candidates
Till I have further tried.'

The poet probed philology
And when about to ring
For the suspended candidate,
There came unsummoned in

That portion of the vision
The word applied to fill.
Not unto nomination
The cherubim reveal.

In another poem, where the subject is also language—'Your thoughts don't have words every day'—she dwells, as Emerson also had, upon the inevitable intermittence of inspiration. This poem should serve as her own warning to those who are bound to find superlative adjectives for every scrap of verse she left behind her. Criticism in this country still tends to make up for former neglect by erecting exaggerated monuments. It seems doubtful whether we are enabled better to perceive Emily Dickinson's rare distinctions when she is loaded with such a formidable weight as Mark Van Doren's foreword description of her as 'one of the great poets of the world.' Calling her such a thing as that plays directly into the hands of those who are determined to justify her every syllable, even some which, it now appears, she did not write.

Take, as a symptomatic case, the vexed question of her rhymes. Because Aldrich, the most genteel of our Victorians, wrote an essay about her called 'Un Poète Manqué' and had the further fatuity to provide his own better-rhymed version of 'I taste a liquor never brewed,' her anti-Victorian defenders have rushed to declare that her every imperfect or off-rhyme was not merely intentional, but a subtle refinement. Without gainsaying her fondness both for assonance and for the suspended rhyme (in which words ending in different vowel sounds followed by the same consonant are made to serve), it should be palpable now that in many cases she missed, in her constrained haste, finding even approximately the right word. Her great gift was for poetic thought—a very different thing from the customary nineteenth-century reflecting in verse—since it involved a fusion between her thought and the image which embodied it. But these further poems make even clearer than it was before that she possessed no comparable gift for versification. Her almost standard measure was the familiar ballad stanza, which was also the 'common meter' of the hymn books of her heritage. She seems hardly to have been concerned with the possibilities of metrical experiment, and many of her best poems are those wherein the vividness of what she had to say stirred her small stanzas with fresh irregularity. In any such long sequence of her less successful work as is provided by much of this new collection, the cumulative impression cannot escape monotony.

Discrimination, therefore, is imperative if the Emily Dickinson boom is not finally to collapse in deflation. As a check to the widespread notion that the 'twenties were entirely responsible for her discovery, it should be recalled that a not undiscerning popularity greeted the three series of poems as they were issued between 1890 and 1896. The review by Howells (Mr. DeVoto's remotely distant predecessor in 'The Easy Chair') penetrated at once to her originality. And although Howells was taken to task by Andrew Lang and other British reviewers for praising 'this farrago of illiterate and uneducated sentiment,' Alice James, writing near the end of her life in an English sanitarium, may be allowed the last word on this matter: 'It is reassuring to hear the English pronouncement that Emily Dickinson is fifth-rate—they have such a capacity for missing quality; the robust evades them equally with the subtle. Her being sicklied o'er with T. W. Higginson makes one quake lest there be a latent flaw in one's vision . . .'

But whatever Higginson's limitations, he and his friends—whom Mrs. Bingham cites—were at least able to place Emily Dickinson against her background. As William Roscoe Thayer wrote: 'Surely our New England Calvinism never brought forth any other flower so sweet and un-Calvinistic.' Several of her most sensitive first readers kept probing the question of her form, as they responded to her compressed intensity. Noting too her particular flavor of New England isolation, Samuel G. Ward called her 'the articulate inarticulate.' Maurice Thompson tried to express the sensation that many others have felt in her straining effort to give order to her material: her 'verse suggests to me a superb brain that has suffered some obscure lesion which now and then prevents the filling out of a thought—as if a cog slipped in some fine wheel just at the point of consummation.' That may overstate the element of strain, but one often feels an almost desperately maintained poise in her letters as well, and she herself summed up for Higginson her frequently defeated struggles for form: 'When I try to organize, my little force explodes and leaves me bare and charred.'

Detailed criticism of her poems, notwithstanding the work of Genevieve Taggard, Tate, Blackmur, Winters, still has much to do. A systematic study of her diction would bring to light many facets of her mind and sensibility—for instance, no one yet has quite given due attention to the pervasive presence of such terms as 'decree,' 'degree,' 'election,' 'capacity,' 'covenant,' 'confirmed,' 'condemned,' 'espoused.' Miss Taggard believes many of these to be owing chiefly to the legal vocabulary of Emily Dickinson's father, but they are more likely to have risen from the theological residue which must always be considered in reaching the nuances of her thought. A valuable essay also remains to be written about her recurrent symbols. The exacting task of arranging her poems around their leading themes cannot be fully undertaken until the manuscripts are available. So far as these are still in the hands of Madame Bianchi's executor, they do not seem likely to come into the public domain where they belong. But Mrs. Bingham has enough material upon which an important beginning could be made, and her unpossessive tone would augur for her willingness to share it. Only when some approximation of chronological order has been established, will we be able to perceive accurately for the first time how often Emily Dickinson kept writing essentially the same poems again and again. We will then be able to follow her, through tentative beginnings and rejected fragments, to her few delicate yet full-blooded marriages between spirit and form.

*Kenyon Review*, 1945

# William Vaughn Moody

WILLIAM Vaughn Moody has been unusually fortunate in the tributes paid him by his friends. John M. Manly was the editor of his collected works; Daniel Gregory Mason brought out his letters; and now, after twenty years have elapsed since the poet's death, Robert Morss Lovett, a contemporary of Moody's both at Harvard and later on the teaching staff at Chicago, has added his long essay of reminiscence. Moody's personality made a strong impact on all of them. They unite in praising his vigor, his grace, his humor, his courage, his austere reserve as well as his abundance, the sweetness and sanity of his mind as much as its bold constructiveness, and, above all else, his broad humanity, the hearty acceptance of life as a whole which stood out as his most significant trait.

Mr. Lovett reiterates the scope of his importance. He reminds us that Moody was not only a lyric poet, but that he also had an impressive share in the revival of poetic drama, and that his prose plays, *The Great Divide* and *The Faith Healer,* were the one serious effort of his period to bring the American stage to the movement started by Ibsen, and make it a vehicle for actual criticism of life. But he values Moody most of all for having worked in the great tradition of the poetry of the world, and gets from his best lyrics the sense of exhilaration that only great poetry can give. This evaluation is very like that made by one of the most sensitive judges of poetry in Moody's time, the late Charlton Lewis of Yale. Writing in the *Yale Review,* in 1913, Professor Lewis took deep satisfaction in the mingled fineness and robustness of Moody's work, and particularly in its final effect of masculine directness, a quality that made him feel that

*Selected Poems of William Vaughn Moody,* edited, with an introduction, by Robert Morss Lovett. Houghton Mifflin Co.

it spoke to him of his own thoughts and aspirations in a way that
the great Victorian poets of his youth were unable to do.

Such an evaluation is very difficult for a contemporary reader
to respond to. The element that all Moody's critics agree in
praising most highly, his rich gift of expression, is the very element that makes his poetry seem artificial. Affected partly by the
symbolists, working partly in a vein similar to that of Meredith,
metaphor was his natural vehicle; he wanted his image to be the
complete embodiment of his thought. But whether in the somewhat florid exuberance of his talk and letters, or in the even
more studied figures of his poems, one feels that he has so
strained and squeezed his image to make it yield every subtle
implication that, as in the case of 'the gallant, gallant ship' of
'Gloucester Moors,' instead of giving the reader a more vivid
realization of the idea, the image itself simply catches him in its
meshes. Probably the chief reason why one feels this quality of
overabundance is that the diction, as well as the figures, seems
too strenuously sought after. Moody thought himself as enthusiastic a pioneer in language as the Elizabethans. 'You are
not tolerant enough,' he wrote to Mason, 'of the instinct of con-
quest in language, the attempt to push out its boundaries, to win
for it continually some new swiftness, some rare compression, to
distill from it a more opaline drop.' But that very passage, particularly its closing phrase, reveals the limitations of Moody's
pioneering. Sometimes he brought a fresh word from the ver-
nacular, as in the effective humorous line in 'The Menagerie': 'a
little man in trousers slightly jagged'; but more often he studded
his language with the archaic and literary, 'energic,' 'margent,'
or 'blooth.'

Both his manner of expression and his language would indicate Moody as an eclectic poet. He was seldom imitative in the
narrower sense of being completely under the sway of any one
writer, but the range of his debts was very wide: Browning,
Keats, Shelley, Swinburne, and later Milton and the Greek
drama, especially Euripides' *Bacchae*, Francis Thompson, and
Verlaine all contributed to his broad and diverse culture. The
richness of that culture is known to every one who is familiar
with his brilliant edition of Milton, a very mellow achievement;

but for a poet such a large number of masters might seem to
argue a lack of inner fiber of his own, an aloofness from life, an
academic want of passion. Such a conclusion in the case of
Moody, however, would be wholly false. Writing of his *Masque
of Judgment*, he speaks of its most important theme being 'the
plea for passion as a means of salvation,' and again and again his
voice reverberates with the statement:

> Who loves not life
> Receiveth not life's gifts at any hand.

The fact is that the deeper one penetrates into Moody's work,
the more one becomes interested in his ideas, and impressed by
their solid quality and by the range and energy of his conception of life. He was indebted to America as well as to literature.
His father was a steamboat captain on the rivers between Pitts-
burgh and New Orleans; his mother was a daughter of one of
the earliest families to settle in southern Indiana; and through
these parents Moody shared strongly in the pioneer heritage of
devotion and patriotism. In his formative years he also came
under the spell of Henry George and Hamlin Garland; so it was
natural that his poems should cope directly with the issues of his
day. Nowhere in our poetry is there a more fearless denunciation of blind and greedy imperialism than that in 'An Ode in
Time of Hesitation' or 'The Quarry,' nor a nobler scorn of a base
cause than that expressed in the lines 'On a Soldier Fallen in the
Philippines.' In such poems as 'Road Hymn for the Start' and 'I
Am the Woman,' Moody is also strongly in the main tradition
from Whitman, for, despite his antipathy to the form of *Leaves
of Grass*, his vision of the potentialities of modern life, and,
even more deeply, his mingled quality of being both pagan and
mystic, have much in common, though given a more educated
expression, with the nature of the elder poet.

The poems which Moody regarded most seriously, over which
he brooded longest, and which contain the large bulk of his
speculations on the meaning of life, are his poetic dramas, *The
Fire Bringer, The Masque of Judgment*, and the unfinished
*Death of Eve*. Their scope and intention owe much to Milton;
they are designed to do no less than to effect a reconciliation

beyond that conceived of in the seventeenth century, to justify the ways of man to God. The first member of the trilogy is perhaps the least original in its treatment of the reaction on the human race of the effort of Prometheus to make man independent of God; *The Masque of Judgment* is much bolder imaginatively in the way it reveals how, through His destruction of mankind at the Judgment Day, God is Himself destroyed; *The Death of Eve* was intended to show the impossibility of separation between the Creator and His creation, the essential unity between them. These plays are philosophical poetry, and not an ordered scheme of philosophy, and are therefore inevitably more interesting in parts than as a whole. Moody never had a more generous conception of character than that of the broad humanism of Raphael in *The Masque of Judgment;* or a more thrilling poetic idea than that of portraying Eve in her old age, who, finding herself failed by every one else, seeks out Cain, her child of passion, and returns with him to the Garden to lay her life before God, not in fear or humiliation, but in the sense of having fulfilled through long years the deepest laws of the nature of woman.

Through exploring Moody's ideas one comes to have a high respect for him, and it is largely this approach which has produced the recent very favorable judgments of his work by the French and German critics, Régis Michaud and O. E. Lessing. Any final estimate of him must bear in mind that he was an exact contemporary of Edwin Arlington Robinson's, born in the same year, and that the two of them together were responsible for the rebirth of American poetry, which had sunk into decay after the death of Whitman. No one can examine Moody's work without feeling his excellent qualities: he is never trivial or sentimental; above all else he is calm, self-possessed, and of great dignity, but saved from pompousness by a salty humor. Yet even in the lines where one comes closest to his spirit, in the poignant tribute to his mother in 'The Daguerreotype,' in 'Jetsam' where he tells how after long struggle he feels 'strong now at last to give myself to beauty and be saved,' in Pandora's stirring song of victory achieved through defeat, a great deal of the implied emotion is drowned in rhetorical virtuosity. He could not seem to escape the overstuffed opulence of the late Victorian age, the defect of Pater, even of Meredith. But by far his worst limitation is his too elaborate assumption of the singing robes. As he grew older he became less studiously poetic in his expression, and, had he lived, he might have advanced even farther along this road, but just how far is doubtful in view of his early too complete insulation in literature. No one could have been more earnest in his desire to be a poet, no prayer could be more heartfelt than the lines in which he says:

> All my spirit hungers to repay
> The beauty that has drenched my soul with peace.

But he never quite found an authentic voice of his own. He was so striving in his effort to create that it left a pale cast of heavy deliberateness over nearly all of his lines, so self-conscious in his determination to be a poet that it almost incapacitated him for writing poetry. In fact, his kind of eclectic reliance upon the past and absorption in its ways of expression became finally so oppressive that it was the very thing which caused the violent break of our contemporary poetry away from nineteenth-century literary tradition.

*The New England Quarterly,* 1931

# A Monument to Howells

HOWELLS is one of the most disconcerting figures in our past. He came so near to being the great American novelist. He seemed to possess everything: the widest variety of experience afforded by his frontier Ohio boyhood, his journalistic

*Life and Letters of William Dean Howells,* edited by Mildred Howells. Doubleday Doran.

training, his appointment at the age of twenty-four to be consul in Venice during the last years of the Austrian occupation, his pilgrimage to Cambridge and the subsequent editorship of *The Atlantic Monthly,* which brought him a constantly expanding horizon and an intimate knowledge of Boston, and, later, his equally wide contacts with life in New York. Add to this, critical penetration which understood the superiority of Balzac, Flaubert, and Tolstoy to Thackeray and Dickens, and made him the vigorous champion of realism; and, above all, the perfection of a style as deliberately clear as it was unaffected. When you set down all these qualities, you wonder why it is that even the names of most of his books are now forgotten. Then you recall that, in spite of the acute power of many passages, the account of the street-car strike in *A Hazard of New Fortunes,* the dinner party in *The Rise of Silas Lapham,* where the pathos of the self-made man trying to cope with the inbred Boston taboos is revealed with extreme poignancy, in spite of an abundance of accurate description and lambent irony, not one book seems to realize itself as a whole. There is always a strange dying away of the creative energy, an impalpable thinness which Howells himself came close to defining when he wrote to Charles Eliot Norton in 1905 with regard to certain critical remarks that had been made about him by Henry James:

> In a way I think their criticism very just; I have often thought my intellectual raiment was more than my intellectual body, and that I might finally be convicted, not of having nothing *on,* but of the worse nakedness of having nothing *in.* He speaks of me with my style, and such mean application as I was making of it, as seeming to him like a poor man with a diamond which he does not know what to do with; and mostly I suppose I *have* cut rather inferior window glass with it. But I am not sorry for having wrought in common, crude material so much. That is the right American stuff . . . I was always as I still am, trying to fashion a piece of literature out of the life next at hand.

His aim was so right that it is hard to see just what caused the arrow to waver on its way to the mark. Certainly his curiosity and interest in his country were unflagging. Nothing in these letters stands out with greater sharpness than his growing perception of our national tendencies. In 1862 he is writing from Venice about 'the strife and combat, which make America so glorious a land for individuals,' and reminding his sister Victoria that as a people we are 'so much purer and nobler and truer than any other.' By 1887 he has undertaken the defense of the Chicago anarchists with an outspokenness equal to that of present-day writers in the cause of Sacco and Vanzetti, and with the same helpless frustration. He has now progressed to the point of despair about the ruthless competition that had formerly seemed so splendid, and declares that 'after fifty years of optimistic content with "civilization" and its ability to come out all right in the end, I now abhor it, and feel that it is coming out all wrong in the end, unless it bases itself anew on a real equality.' Similar strictures appear frequently in his later books, and yet somehow, in spite of all his observation and all his honesty, there is in him a kind of nice restraint which amounts almost to complacency. He is always perfectly controlled: his words flow in a quiet stream, they never boil or snarl through any rapids. He once wrote to Henry James about the fascination of New England, 'a sort of strange, feminine fascination. It is like a girl, sometimes a young girl, and sometimes an old girl, but wild and shy and womanly sweet, always, with a sort of unitarian optimism in its air.' This spirit is Howells' passionless muse.

It is ungracious to convict a man from his own frank words. Howells had no illusions about his achievement: he wrote enthusiastically to James about 'the fullness, the closeness, the density of your work'; he felt that his own was meager beside it. He was forever saying how Mark Twain would 'bask in the same light with Cervantes and Shakespeare' when his name would be forgotten. So it is better to remember that both Stephen Crane and Frank Norris felt everlastingly indebted to him, and that Howard Pyle wrote to tell him that he had 'done more than any other living man in his country to teach a younger generation what is true art as distinct from what is false.' Perhaps the next generation will see more than we do in his cool, classic pages. At least social historians will discover nowhere else such a complete picture of everyday American existence in the last

Indiana University
Gary Center Library

half of the nineteenth century. But for the time being these two
volumes of Howells' letters stand as a monument to what
Stephen Crane called his 'kind, benevolent life,' unhappily with
no more meaning for us than most monuments have.

*New Republic,* 1929


# Edwin Arlington Robinson


I N preparing the first full-length biography of Robinson, Hermann Hagedorn possessed the advantage of twenty-five years
of close acquaintance with the poet. He was also in touch with
the whole small circle of Robinson's other friends, and devot-
edly gathered their letters, reminiscences, and anecdotes. He
has thus preserved much that would otherwise have been lost,
and his book must be the source for any further study. His dis-
advantages are that he was too close to his material always to see
it in proportion: many of his anecdotes are strung out quite beyond their significance, and others are handled so elliptically
that they hardly convey a direct meaning. For instance, the
chatty description of Isadora Duncan's rapid fascination with the
unresponsive poet only serves to make the whole incident sound
unreal. Nor is the firmness of Hagedorn's narrative increased by
his fondness for such evocative phrases as 'the gifted sylvan
being,' or 'a lovely colorful butterfly,' when describing the wives
of two of Robinson's friends.

This biography makes no effort at criticism, yet from it we
can gather the materials that are essential to an understanding
of Robinson's poetic career. In this review I want simply to
note a few of the problems and triumphs of that career which
*Edwin Arlington Robinson* by Hermann Hagedorn. Macmillan.

Hagedorn has thrown into sharper light. In the first place, he gives us intimate, if fleeting, glimpses of the cultural life of Gardiner, Maine, in the eighteen-seventies and 'eighties: a provincial town where several lonely New Englanders were still aspiring to culture, and where Robinson as a high-school boy met weekly with a group composed of one of the early graduates of Radcliffe, a local doctor, and a local judge, all of whom wrote verse and alternated the reading aloud of their own latest things with Villon or Verlaine. The boy brought to that group a fondness for exploring the meanings of words that he seems to have had from the age of ten. The youngest son of a prosperous storekeeper and of a mother with a tenuous gift for literary composition, Robinson was neither the student nor the man of action that his two considerably older brothers had respectively shown themselves to be. From his schooldays he regarded himself as a misfit, with a fatal lack of energy and with an apathy toward everything that practical New England valued as success.

The succession of tragic events against which he grew to maturity can hardly be exaggerated. His family's fortunes had declined before the death of his father; his two promising brothers both came to disaster and died as alcoholics; his mother met a horrible death from black diphtheria. These events, spaced over several years, conditioned the world in which Robinson had to find his way. An early injury to his eardrum, neglected while a child until the bones had become diseased, made him dread for long periods that his brain might be threatened. He had already learned, by the time he was a special student at Harvard, that 'life is a terrible thing,' but his response to it was far less somber than has often been supposed. His first strong tastes had been for Dickens and Kipling, and he continued to possess the interest in character of the one, and the fresh delight in common speech which had been stimulated in him by the other. At Harvard he came into his own heritage: he distinguished the wide separation between Emerson's value and Longfellow's, and when a friend read to him 'When lilacs last in the dooryard bloomed,' he said, 'If that's not poetry, it is something greater than poetry.' Santayana's verse struck him as though it had been written 'by a highly sophisticated corpse'; and he judged that Moody had

'many things to unlearn.' Robinson often felt himself drifting
without purpose, and years later he was still uncertain whether
he really knew how to write, but his keenness to speech rhythms,
quickened by a special fondness for Crabbe, had brought him
by his mid-twenties to his formed style.

What he most wanted to say in those early years is contained
in his first long poem, *Captain Craig*, finished in 1899. The gar-
rulous old man who is its hero is impoverished, a failure by all
worldly standards, and yet insists that

> There is no servitude so fraudulent
> As of a sun-shut mind.

He provided Robinson with the opportunity to test his theory—
laconically phrased to Laura Richards—that 'it is possible to
apply good natured common sense even to the so-called serious
events in life.' Through the figure of the Captain the poet developed his fondness for what he termed 'semi-intellectual humor,'
which to him was 'the only real kind—that is, the only kind that
has to do with the realities.' Failure to perceive the subtle play
of ironic comedy even in Robinson's most somber passages has
often caused him to be misunderstood. It is Hagedorn's contention that the poet's difficulty in finding a publisher for *Captain
Craig*—it kept going from office to office for three years—
robbed him of an initial buoyancy which he never recovered.
Certainly those were the years when he was existing most precariously in New York, and when he began to drift into seeming aimlessness and hypochondria. He often said, 'We are living
in hell,' but he grew able to accept and endure that fact, and
his endurance finally allowed him to write a poem like 'The
Man Against the Sky.' He had early confessed his weakness in
abstract thought; he had said that he lacked 'the stamina to be
a Christian,' yet his concern with the 'light,' his dogged conviction that there was something beyond materialism, composed
the substance of all his meditations. In a letter written in 1931
he was still insisting that he should not be called a pessimist,
that the acceptance of life's actual horror could give one at last
the release that belongs to tragedy.

As a child Robinson had dreaded that he was never going to be able to elbow his way to 'the trough of life.' As a young man he was sure he would die young. Yet his strangely resistant passiveness, the quality which enabled him to say, when his prospects were bleakest, that he could 'keep on waiting for some time longer in the dark,' carried him through to old age. From the time when he first went to the MacDowell colony (1911), his external routine finally began to be regularized. That kind of induced stability saved him from his worst loneliness and checked his drinking. He became far more prolific, but it is questionable whether that in the end was a good thing. The long series of narratives which occupied most of his last twenty years lack the intensity of his character studies. Into his short portraits he had distilled his suffering and tenderness over the disorder of men's lives, and had expressed the heart's strength in meeting failure.

*American Literature,* 1941

## An Absolute Music: Hart Crane

I N giving his biography the subtitle, 'The Life of an American Poet,' Philip Horton has found in Crane's career a symbol of our recent culture in much the same degree as Edgar Lee Masters found one when writing about Vachel Lindsay. Coming from Ohio to New York in 1916, Crane began immediately to participate to the full in the poetic renaissance. With a poem accepted in Margaret Anderson's *Little Review* when he was seventeen, he had already stated that Pound was second only to

*Hart Crane: The Life of an American Poet* by Philip Horton. W. W. Norton & Co.

Yeats among poets then writing in English. But it was Eliot's
early work that left a far more lasting mark on Crane's own
style. However, from the moment of his first absorbed admiration of *The Waste Land,* he declared that he wanted an almost
complete reversal of Eliot's direction; he felt that he could profit
enormously from Eliot's technical discoveries, but he would bend
them 'towards a more positive, or (if I must put it so in a skeptical age) ecstatic goal.' He felt the closest kinship with Whitman's affirmation of American possibilities.

His dilemma has already been suggested. In his intense desire
to embody an idealistic vision, to assert the present as a splendid bridge to the future, and then, as he tried to center on his
creation, in his growing confusion as to the contours of his
vision, in his uncertainty as to the foundations of his bridge, he
illustrated both the buoyant aspirations and the sudden bewildered despair that fought in the American temperament in
the postwar decade. The strength with which Mr. Horton makes
his reader share in such conclusions is owing to his remarkable
avoidance of loose generalization. By assembling with rare
patience and tact the details of Crane's extremely complicated
existence (a task in which he had the generous co-operation of
the poet's mother), and by weaving them into the intellectual
and social patterns of postwar life, he has revealed that Crane's
tortured violence cannot be regarded as an anomaly but as a
heightened response to some of the tensions of these years. And
owing to the even more notable maturity and detachment with
which he has avoided the temptation to indulge in amateur psychoanalysis in accounting for Crane's suicide, Mr. Horton has
shown that event as an organic result of forces straining at the
poet's being from the time of his high-strung boyhood. An
only child of well-to-do parents, he suffered the full shock of
their uncontrolled incompatibility. Torn by their quarrels, his
confidence in human emotions was so fully destroyed that he
never mastered any equilibrium, but veered in later life from
impossible demands on affection to a recoil into savage egoism.
His parents' self-indulgence also launched him with sketchy education and no knowledge of discipline, thus rendering his impulsive eagerness for experience and his warm belief that the

artist should identify himself with all of life an easy prey for the rootlessness of the megalopolis.

Mr. Horton's work has been biography rather than strict criticism. He asserts Crane's value as a poet, but does not demonstrate it through close analysis. It is clear, however, that he considers Crane a major figure in contemporary poetry, an opinion shared by others of his generation, by the generation now about twenty-five, who might have been undergraduates when *The Bridge* was published. These readers do not seem to be bothered by such objections as those raised by Allen Tate—in the most thoughtful evaluation yet made of Crane—that *The Bridge* is in the last analysis a failure owing to the fatal cleavage between what Crane was determined to announce about the glowing promise of contemporary life and the chaotic actuality that he was beginning more and more to realize. But even if Crane did not succeed in building a philosophical structure that would give form to the course of America's development and satisfy his desire for a symbol of 'the continuous and living evidence of the past in the inmost vital substance of the present,' he did envisage and create separate sections of the poem, as for instance 'The River' or 'The Harbor Dawn,' with magnificent wholeness. When he spoke, during the weeks of his most heightened concentration on his work, of sensing 'an absolute music in the air,' he was not engaging in hyperbole. For he was more greatly endowed than any other poet born in America since Eliot with the essential talent of being able to conceive of his poems not as 'ideas,' nor as expressive lines and passages, but as complete rhythmical entities. The obscurity for which he has been much attacked was never deliberate; it resulted from his fumbling need to find words that could articulate a musical ecstasy that he knew to be as real as that of Rimbaud. He may have been betrayed at times by a dangerous analogy between poetry and painting into trying to use words plastically, to manipulate their colors and shapes, but he never lost sight of his fundamental conception of a work of art as 'simply a communication between man and man, a bond of understanding and human enlightenment.'

*Yale Review*, 1938

# Louis MacNeice

LOUIS MacNeice is an exact contemporary of Auden's, but at thirty has been far less prolific. He offers now a collection which retains only four poems from his first volume, *Blind Fireworks*, 1929, and adds to his volume of 1935 about fifteen poems more. He showed his Irish sense of humor in choosing the title for his early poems 'because they are artificial and yet random; because they go quickly through their antics against an important background, and fall and go out quickly.' The short musical exercises that he has decided to keep from these pieces possess what Eliot, in talking about Blake, recognized as the more likely kind of promise; instead of crude efforts to encompass something grandiose they are 'quite mature and successful attempts to do something small.' The distance he traveled between the less distinct remainder of that volume and the *Poems* of 1935 is considerable. In the two years preceding his second book he developed a distinguishing style, a rhythm unmistakably his own. He seems to have profited most from Hopkins in learning how to give to the conventional line a more resilient conversational tone. But his feeling that Hopkins was wrong to bind his sprung rhythm to the arbitrary frame of an equal number of accented syllables for every line has enabled Mac-Neice to gain a greater fluency, and a very deft approximation to an actual speaking voice.

Although he was at Oxford at the same time as the group of young English poets who have hitherto been more widely discussed, MacNeice's course has been fairly independent of theirs. His is not 'fighting' poetry. His impulse has not been contentious and hortatory like Auden's; he has not joined Spender in

*Poems* by Louis MacNeice. Random House.

romantic proclamations of faith. He has recently remarked: 'Poets are not legislators (what is an "unacknowledged legislator" anyway?), but they put facts and feelings in italics, which make people think about them and such thinking may in the end have an outcome in action.' Such an attitude may seem too passive for much contemporary taste; and it has not brought into poetry the wide subject matter of economics and science which Auden's unflagging curiosity has explored, nor the more mechanically manipulated culverts and pistons and other modern properties of Day Lewis. In 'Turf-Stacks,' written in 1932, Mac-Neice formulated his lack of political position:

> For we are obsolete who like the lesser things
> Who play in corners with looking-glasses and beads;
> It is better we should go quickly, go into Asia
> Or any other tunnel where the world recedes,
> Or turn blind wantons like the gulls who scream
> And rip the edge off any ideal or dream.

But he has not embraced either of the alternatives offered in that stanza, though ironically bitter contemplation of his own country has brought him closer to the last one. He has never made of poetry an easy vehicle for evasion, for although he has a warm feeling for landscape, he knows that he always carries a city-bred mind with him. He has, however, set himself fairly deliberately to writing descriptive poetry, as when he states in 'Train to Dublin':

> I give you the incidental things which pass
> Outwards through space exactly as each was.

He knows that this demands an exacting discipline. Unlike most other poets who have been influenced by Eliot he has learned and declared that 'You must walk before you can dance; you can't be a master of suggestion unless you are a master of description.' He has consequently evolved the neat craft of making the inner coherence of a poem depend on the subtle and precise interrelationships of a series of things observed. But success in this kind requires tightrope technique, for if any image asserts

itself too vividly, the balance is quickly upset, and the whole
effect falls into obtrusive fragments.

Nor is it conceivable that a poet could describe anything
exactly as it was without betraying some point of view towards
his material. MacNeice's frequent fascination with catching the
effects of sunlight and smoke suggests that he has the eyes of a
painter, but his interest is never confined merely to recording
surface textures. In some passages he may reveal that

> . . . there is beauty narcotic and deciduous

in the very midst of the sinister chaos of a modern city. But though
his subject matter is seldom political, he is increasingly aware of
the social implications of what he sees. He quoted last fall: ' "Other
philosophies have described the world; our business is to change
it." Add that if we are not interested in changing it, there is really
very little to describe.' And the close of 'Eclogue from Iceland,'
1936, to which he traveled with Auden, finds him in a much
more positive mood than that of the young Irish intellectual who,
in 'Valediction,' had two years previously turned away from
his own country in the manner traditional to the *Portrait of the
Artist as a Young Man*. For in the 'Eclogue' the ghost of Grettir
tells the two summer visitors that they had better go back to
where they had come from, and that in spite of the enormous odds
against their being able to make anything prevail:

> Minute your gesture but it must be made—
> Your hazard, your act of defiance and hymn of hate,
> Hatred of hatred, assertion of human values,
> Which is now your only duty . . .
> Yes, my friends, it is your only duty.
> And, it may be added, it is your only chance.

Notwithstanding the dramatic tension here, MacNeice's talent
so far seems fundamentally lyrical. In saying that I bear in mind
that he has already published a translation of the *Agamemnon*
and a two-act play of his own, *Out of the Picture*. But whereas
the translation displays a firm controlled simplicity that re-
creates much of the original passion, his own play is the one
occasion where MacNeice seems to have collapsed into being

affected by the least valuable elements in Auden, and has produced a loosely blurred mixture where it is hard to say whether
the intention is satire or farce, since nothing comes through
clear. Moreover, in his poems, MacNeice's continual subject is
Time, conceived wholly in the lyric mode of dwelling on the
moment's evanescence, as when he advises a Communist that
before he proclaims the millennium, he had better regard the
barometer—

> This poise is perfect but maintained
> For one day only.

Both his mind and imagery are so possessed with this theme that
he finally tries to shake off his preoccupation by affirming that
he does not want always to be stressing either flux or permanence, that he does not want to be either 'a tragic or a philosophic chorus,' but to keep his eye 'only on the nearer future.'
From the stuff of that 'nearer future' he makes his most balanced
and proportioned poems.

In an ode for his son, which owes something to Yeats' 'A
Prayer for My Daughter,' he would ward off from him the desire
for any absolute 'which is too greedy and too obvious.' Mac-
Neice cannot accept the 'easy bravery' of being 'drugged with a
slogan,' and can hand on to his son neither decalogue nor formula but only symbols, and those only so far as he can feel them
emerge from close and concrete samples of experience. Most of
all he would pray:

> let him not falsify the world
> By taking it to pieces;
> The marriage of Cause and Effect, Form and Content,
> Let him not part asunder.

The desire for such fusion has found fulfillment in the architectural structure of many of his longer poems, and it is the chief
evidence for MacNeice's skill as an artist that his clearest successes are in their complex harmonies rather than in his simpler
short pieces. In 'Homage to Clichés,' for instance, he has devised
and developed a series of repeated images to celebrate his delight in the familiar: the expected response of his companion is

elicited as though by stroking a cat, or is angled from the stream
of their conversation as the fish swim into the net and the
drinks swim over the bar. Here his observations intermesh so
intricately that even though you can take surprised delight in
a single example:

> . . . an old man momentously sharpens a pencil as though
> He were not merely licking his fur like a cat,

it becomes the best tribute to the unity which the poet has
created that no adequate illustration is possible short of the entire poem. For here his attitude is less bald than in the somewhat stagy declaration in his 'Epilogue' that he drinks Auden's
health before 'the gun-butt raps upon the door.' For, in 'Homage
to Clichés,' the perishable stuff of the everyday life which he
relishes is embodied with such warm resilience that the under-
tone of the menacing future which he expects reverberates far
more movingly than it would by means of any bare direct statement.

Where his dependence on oblique and symbolic images can
fail him is when they are not reinforced by sufficiently mature
experience. This is the trouble with the pictures of contemporary
man and woman near the end of the 'Eclogue from Iceland.' The
details by which they are presented do not bite deeply enough
into actuality, they are too private and trivial. The fact that this
can be the case in one of MacNeice's latest poems will be dis-
turbing to those readers who believe that the artist must progress
and offer with each new year a better-appointed model. But,
despite the clarification and firming of his social attitude, it cannot be said that MacNeice's graph has gone continually up-
ward. He seems to have remained on about the same level from
the time that he hit his individual stride five years ago, and he
may not yet have written a solider poem than the sardonic conversation between a city-dweller and a country-dweller, 'An
Eclogue for Christmas,' in 1933. It must also be added that in
spite of his realization, on the Iceland trip, that further travel
could be productive only of more souvenirs and 'copy,' 1937
found him, not following Grettir's advice, but in the Hebrides,

evolving another detached and sensitive descriptive poem about those islands.

It is undoubtedly true that MacNeice's conversational style is less socially useful to the needs of our day than the public speech that may be developed from Auden's exciting rhetoric. Nor does MacNeice possess the exuberance and inventiveness which Herbert Read believes Auden to have brought back into English poetry for the first time since Browning's death. On the other hand, MacNeice's richest resource is suggested in a curious remark which he made about Day Lewis, that he is an inferior poet to Auden 'perhaps because his vision is purer and more consistent.' He recognizes that Lewis, though doctrinally correct, can fall into both priggishness and diffuseness by his humorless preaching for the cause. MacNeice's own awareness that life 'is incorrigibly plural,' his deeper immersion in its complexities, his more unchecked reliance on the evidence of his senses, at times result in a vague softness. He does not have anything like the extraordinary range of technical dexterity with which Auden seemingly can take up or burlesque almost any kind of tradition from Skelton to Tennyson and Kipling. But MacNeice's control is far more matured, he rarely indulges in thin tours de force or slipshod virtuosity. And if the measurement is not by 'promise,' by brilliant passages standing out from obscurity, but by whole poems, which can be tested line for line and reread with accruing satisfaction, MacNeice's performance so far is ahead of that of his contemporaries.

*Partisan Review,* 1938

# A New York Childhood

Like Oedipus,
No one can go away from genesis,
From parents, early crime, and character,
Guilty or innocent!

FIVE years ago Delmore Schwartz's first book, *In Dreams Begin Responsibilities,* was greeted with more critical acclaim than has come to any other American poet of his generation, the generation since Auden. As a result Schwartz was placed in the hardest position for a young writer to sustain in a spotlighted age, a beginning poet with a reputation to live up to. When his short verse play, *Shenandoah,* seemed slight, it then became the fashion to declare that he had been overpraised and had not deserved his reputation in the first place. It is fortunate for both the poet and his readers that *Genesis* is a marked advance over all his previous work, and that it is impressive in a way that recent poetry has too seldom been—in the range of its subject matter.

As he says in his preface, Schwartz aims to be 'one more of the poets who seek to regain for Poetry the width of reference of prose without losing what the Symbolists discovered.' He bears out this aim by presenting a whole phase of our cultural history, the image of American life that was formed for and by the immigrants of the end of the nineteenth century, who came from Central Europe to survive or endure in New York. Their intentions were not political; their American dream was that of greater wealth. The most strikingly drawn character in Schwartz's narrative, Hershey Green's father, becomes a terrifying embodiment of our naked lusts. Running away from czarist Russia to

*Genesis: Book One* by Delmore Schwartz. New Directions.

join his older brother here, Jack Green soon gets his feet on the economic ladder. He climbs to being a successful dealer in real estate, and thus fulfills the intense feeling that he had brought with him from Europe, that 'the ownership of land was the greatest material thing.' His other passionate drive is for sensuality. His marriage with self-willed tactless Eva Newman is a succession of brutal scenes over his infidelities. ('Is not escape a major industry in North America?') At the time of the outbreak of the First World War, she is trying desperately to hold him by bearing him a son, and Jack Green feels proud and secure. Although the other lights may be going out in Europe, for him in America the radiance of making money surpassed them all in brilliance.

The form that Schwartz has devised for presenting his material is an alternating sequence of prose narrative and choric comment. The narrative consists of the compulsive reflections of sixteen-year-old Hershey Green as he lies sleepless one night and rages through all that he knows of his history, from his own memory and from family report. The chorus, a shadowy group of the dead, give their minds to discuss and explain, since, in the detachment of death, their sole desire is for clarification through full knowledge. The advantages for the author in such a chorus are obvious: he can gain thereby great density of reference. But the dangers are equally patent. Such commentators can overinterpret, and can then prove merely a distraction from the forward-moving story. And although the poet cites Hardy among the modern witnesses for a chorus, the example of The Dynasts is different in two crucial respects. For one thing, Hardy's various groups, such as the Spirits of the Pities and the Spirits Ironic, are characterized by a dramatic point of view, whereas Schwartz's succession of voices have no clear identity and often lose themselves in mere fluidity. What is even more important, the form of the choruses seems frequently too relaxed for full effectiveness. To be sure, Schwartz has stated that he has 'no wish to emulate Swinburne,' but that he seeks rather to approximate the flat accents of ordinary speech. But one of the most living delights of art is the surprise of contrast, and, as an offset to the prose narrative, the reader's ear often longs for more

of the resources of verse than Schwartz avails himself of, for
more formal stanzaic patterns, and for at least an occasional
tightening up by rhyme.

As it is, we are faced with the anomaly that the most lyrical
passages of the book are expressed in prose. An exquisite moment occurs when Hershey, coming downstairs for his sixth
Christmas and finding the bicycle for which he had longed,
wheels it over to the window and comes face to face with an
even more overpowering joy, the new snow, the deepest symbol
to him always of the mystery of release. Schwartz's writing is
masterly at such a juncture, and the chief reason why he can
convey the warmth of breathless emotion is that he has disciplined his narrative as he has not disciplined his choruses, by
stylizing his prose up to a tense rhythmical pattern. We have
traveled a curious distance from the lesson that Eliot and Pound
learned from Henry James, that poetry ought to be as well written as prose.

I may exaggerate this point, but the success of *Genesis* as-
suredly lies primarily in the accumulating richness of consciousness on the part of the growing boy. The narrative is thus a type
of *Bildungsroman,* and is a further addition to what seems to
have become about our most frequent modern genre since
*Buddenbrooks* and *Swann's Way* and the *Portrait of the Artist
as a Young Man.* But there is a peculiar freshness to Schwartz's
contribution to the genre, a freshness that is owing to his most
distinctive gift, irrespective of what medium he works in. He has
a fine capacity for combining lyric immediacy with philosophical
reflection, and can thus command both the particular and the
general. His great flair for observing all the surfaces of Hershey's
environment is not allowed to degenerate into the production of
mere décor, for Schwartz holds tenaciously to the poet's high
responsibility to intelligence. Thus the passage about the bicycle
and the snow—and here the chorus serves Schwartz well—widens
out into Aristotle's perception that motion 'is being's deepest
wish.' It is the same case with Hershey's other discoveries. The
street games of 'Buttons' and 'Picture Cards,' in which he so
delights, are seen as 'drunk with contingency and private property, the deepest motives that surrounded the playing boys.' The

Katzenjammer Kids who bore and perplex Hershey 'with their
endless destruction' are discerned as 'presenting the adult vision
of childhood,' the vision of the anarchy which adults 'yearned
for and could not have.' The narrative sections on Hershey's first
big league ball game and on his going to see Chaplin in *The
Kid* become, through similar broad handling, memorable passages of moral history.

The first book of *Genesis* takes Hershey up through Grade 4A
in school, and thereby gives occasion for a passage on Lincoln,
one of the most effectively unified of the choruses, which is
underscored with the belief that

> In fact, the North and South were losers both:
> —Capitalismus won the Civil War.

The narrative comes to a violent climax when Eva Green and
Hershey, out riding on a Sunday afternoon with friends, encounter Jack Green and his woman at a roadhouse:

> Childhood was ended here! or innocence
> —Henceforth suspicious of experience!

Hershey has already known for the first time what it is to be
scorned as a Jew; and talking to a Catholic boy, he begins to
have a sense of other mysteries. In continuing his story beyond
this point, Schwartz will have to be on his guard to avoid becoming involved in Hershey's adolescent self-pity. A related problem
for the form will be to devise some variation of the alternating
narrative and chorus, which has already become monotonously
expected by the end of this first book. But the deepening themes
of Schwartz's thought give great promise for what lies ahead in
Hershey Green's unfolding experience. For Schwartz's firm command of Marxist history has not prevented him from becoming
aware of the renewed urgency of religious issues. And his profound belief that Europe is 'the greatest thing in North America'
should prove one of the important forces for the renewal of our
culture in these days when we are continually threatened by a
recrudescence of narrow nationalism.

*Partisan Review,* 1943

# Four American Poets, 1944

YVOR Winters' *The Giant Weapon*, a collection of his verse from the past fifteen years, can serve to test the theories to which he recently gave his most considered expression in his critical study, *The Anatomy of Nonsense.* I admire Winters far less as a critic than, for instance, Ransom does. If the proof of the critic is his judgment, Winters would seem to have everything of a critic except the critical temper. His continued depreciation of Yeats, his long notorious remark that Elizabeth Daryush is 'the finest British poet since T. Sturge Moore,' have now been reinforced by the idiosyncratic statement that he would not have 'to strain his convictions greatly' to rank S. Foster Damon, Clayton Stafford, and J. V. Cunningham along with Hart Crane as 'among the major talents of our time.' Such shrill exaggerations, even though they spring from a generous concern for other underdogs, can do only disservice to the figures they attempt to exalt. Fortunately, however, when Winters gives up comparison and evaluation, for which he is so unfitted, and confines himself to the difficult task of articulating his conception of a poem, he is capable of furnishing a lucid and cogent standard against which to measure his own work.

His primary stress is on the rational concept, on the necessity for the poet to grasp his subject in coherent terms. He has

*The Giant Weapon* by Yvor Winters. New Directions.

*1 × 1* by E. E. Cummings. Henry Holt.

*Selected Poems* by Robert Penn Warren. Harcourt, Brace & Co.

*V-Letter* by Karl Shapiro. Reynal & Hitchcock.

In its original form this review, with the title 'American Poetry Now,' considered new books by seven writers. I have omitted three of these and have deleted some transitional phrases.—ED.

116

formulated his theory in a neat equation: 'The relationship, in the poem, between rational statement and feeling, is thus seen to be that of motive to emotion.' Most notable in that definition is its recognition of the indivisibility of understanding and feeling. It is the task of the poet to 'adjust feeling' precisely to the controlling motive and not to let his emotions run loose, nevertheless controlled emotion is what distinguishes poetical thought from the abstract statements of philosophy. Thus the keystone in Winters' defense of traditional meter is that 'verse permits the expression of more powerful feeling than is possible in prose.'

Faced with most of Winters' own verse, that is exactly what we do not find. In his essay on 'The Morality of Poetry' he spoke evocatively of a poem as 'an almost fluid complex,' but the majority of his own poems are stiff and dry. One reason would seem to be that too great a proportion of them are occasional poems for occasions that have been conceived too slightly. Remembering Gray's cat, one could not say that any occasion is too slight in itself, but the comparison with Winters' 'Elegy on A Young Airedale Bitch Lost Some Years Since in the Salt Marsh' reveals the latter's utter and devastating lack of humor. The school that Winters has fostered might well be called the Bookplate poets. For prominent among the few verses that the preceptor has singled out for praise from among the nonsense and obscurantism of the rest of modern degenerate art are several such decorous inscriptional pieces. Winters' own 'Dedication for a Book of Criticism' or 'On Teaching the Young' present the limitations of this type. They are carefully phrased and deftly wrought. There is no questioning the clarity of motive. But Winters himself provided the key for judging them when he said that 'some experiences offer very slight difficulties'; and that applies to both thought and expression.

Another of Winters' distinctions which helps us to place his own work is that between the conventional and the perceived. The lack of enough new and deep awareness in traditional situations reduces even some of his poems on the major occasions of death and birth into hardly more than exercises. Such is even the case with his 'Orpheus,' his memorial poem for Crane, where neither the potency of the legend nor the desperate chaos of the life have been more than remotely suggested. The giant weapon of Odysseus has dwindled into an academic pop-gun.

By the same standard, the poems of Winters which come closer to success are those where fresh perceptions stir the familiar verse pattern into new, personal movement. That is true of some of his descriptions of nature, particularly of 'A Summer Commentary,' where he permits himself a sensuous richness rare for him. This is even truer of some of his historical re-creations where he can depend on the tact of the scholar, as in his delicately felt 'On Rereading a Passage from John Muir,' or in such an expert literary poem as his 'Sir Gawaine and the Green Knight.' But he writes most movingly when he lays himself open to greater difficulties, when—still in his own terms—'more is implicated in the subject matter,' when he comes out of his world of formal occasions into touch with the tragic circumstances of our time. 'By the Road to the Air-Base,' 'Summer Noon' (1941), 'To A Military Rifle' (1942) still pose the ordered values of the scholar, the homely delights of the domestic man, but they pose them far more urgently through recognition of the violence by which all balance is now threatened. Yet his most memorable poem, 'Before Disaster,' was composed in the winter of 1933. Here he proved his contention that 'meter has moral significance,' that meter is not something laid on top of logical argument, but that in the true poem meter and meaning are interpenetrated. For here Winters' use of the octosyllabic couplet rises not from the correct mind alone. His line is truncated to seven syllables as if in response to the nervous movement of a precariously poised line of homeward traffic. The menace of death ever present in our mechanized world is so surely evoked in the first of the two ten-line stanzas that the broader application at the opening of the second to the ominously crowded 'ranks of nations' is made without a strain. Such an organic fusion between the personal and universal makes for the kind of poem that is rare for all except the few great poets—a fact which Winters would be the first to recognize. For however petulant he may be with his contemporaries, he is always patient and humble before his craft.

Cummings, whom Winters has long since rejected as showing 'little comprehension of poetry,' is still the experimentalist of one experiment. Ten years ago, following Blackmur's dissection of his language as a species of unvaried babytalk, he seemed likely to drop from the concern of a decade whose attention was upon social issues. But the turn of fashion's wheel has brought a renewed popularity to Cummings' belief that 'the single secret will still be man,' and Spencer, among others, has recently argued that we can see now that 'the emphasis on social issues, from which Cummings was so far removed, produced little good poetry.' That strikes me as a superficial view. Not only does it overlook that the best work so far of Auden's generation has sprung from such emphasis, but it also seems to confuse social issues with radical opinions, and to forget that a deepening preoccupation with society was what added stature to such different poets as Wallace Stevens and Eliot.

The fascinating thing about Cummings is that he is always talking about growth, and always remains the same. *1 × 1* finds him still against all his old enemies of the past quarter century, against advertisers ('a salesman is an it that stinks to please'), against war, against intellect, against 'unwish,' 'unself,' 'undream,' 'unshe,' against 'manunkind' and all the 'prodigies of un.' 'Mostpeople' are still 'snobs,' whereas 'the most who die, the more we live,' and 'there's nothing as something as one.'

Cummings is as concerned with and as incapable of the organic principle as Emerson was, and for surprisingly similar reasons. He insists that man and his work must continue to unfold and grow. He has rephrased here Emerson's doctrine of 'all in each': 'so isn't small one littlest why.' But he too is the son of a New England clergyman for whom 'life' consists entirely of inspired moments, and is thus without the basic requirement for growth—continuity. The mystery is how he has managed to defy nature by not changing and still keeping alive. The explanation lies again in Emerson's vein, in his capacity for exuberant renewal of the moment. In Cummings' case the phenomenon may best be described in linguistic terms, since his work is all a gay logomachy. As a romantic anarchist, a poem consists for him in a moment's breaking through the laws of syntax. He is against

nouns ('dull all nouns'), but even worse than nouns are probing
conjunctions, since doubting can turn men's 'faith to how, their
joy to why.' The sole principle of life is in the verb: the great I
AM. And so the moment can be created only by the glory of the
present indicative, and in one of his most brilliant displacements
the poet deplores the centuries of 'original soon.'

But a poem cannot be written entirely by conjugating the verb
to be, and, consequently, the device on which Cummings rings
every possible change to increase expectancy is the comparative:
'beauty is more now than dying's when.' Sometimes his special
use might be termed the extending comparative, since it loops
beyond one quality to another: 'heart was big / as the world
ain't square.' At others, the continuing comparative:

> love is a spring at which
> crazy they drink who've climbed
> steeper than hopes are fears . . .

There 'steeper' continues from the hill to the hopes and fears in
order to bring us closer to the unique essence. But always the
comparative aspires to be the superlative: 'purest than fear's
obscener.' And why not, since 'beautiful most is now'?

But the perpetually unique soon becomes solipsistic. Worse
still, for Cummings' values, it becomes expected. It might almost
be said that from the moment when he turned his first noun into
a verb ('but if a look should april me') he has been writing the
same poem. It is probably the first time on record that a complicated technique has been devised to say anything so basically
simple. The payoff is, unfortunately, monotony. After half a
dozen electric shocks in the penny arcade you begin to wonder
why the first was so thrilling. You are also not quite so sure that
it's most people who are snobs. But if Cummings' circus act was
once good enough to make people sit up, it is still just as 'won-
derful one times one.'

The poems I have considered so far bear witness to serious
concern with craftmanship, but to continuity in traditional modes
rather than to advance. Or, in Cummings' case, they still display
his remarkable playful joy that eludes any analysis. But in the

two remaining books at hand there is something else: the full maturity, after twenty years of development, of Robert Penn Warren; and the equally full confirmation of the promise of Karl Jay Shapiro. It is a token of the strength of these two poets that their most ambitious poems—Warren's 'Ballad of Billie Potts' and Shapiro's 'Elegy for A Dead Soldier'—are their best. But they work in such different veins that an examination of the talents that have come to masterful ripeness in these two long poems may also demonstrate the rich variety now possible in American poetry.

Warren has published two previous books of poems (in 1935 and 1942), but these had a very restricted circulation; and he has generally been placed as a minor figure in the school of Ransom and Tate, and is thus dismissed by Winters. His *Selected Poems: 1923–1943*, by separating his late work from his earlier, mark where he started and how far he has come. 'The Return: An Elegy,' eloquent as is its expression of undisseverable attraction and repulsion of a son for his mother, uses too many of Eliot's contrasts to be quite Warren's own. 'Kentucky Mountain Farm' expresses the particular and local concern with history of the Southern agrarian group, and yet Warren's resolution, his renewed emphasis on the will, his declaration that 'The act / Alone is pure' already carries his individual accent. The most striking poem in his first book, 'The Garden,' shows what it meant to have begun writing poetry in the era when the seventeenth-century metaphysicals had just been reassimilated for contemporary use. This poem and the somewhat later 'Love's Parable' are excellent instances of what Cleanth Brooks has called a structure of inclusion. They use an aristocratic and slightly archaic diction comparable to Ransom's, and they may have learned from him some of their suave irony. But, more essentially, they show how much a poet can still profit from Marvell. They are as different as possible from Cummings. Despite Cummings' distaste for abstraction, his lyrics hardly more than name the wonders of love and beauty, and thus, except for their eccentric syntax, are little thicker in texture than the songs of tin-pan alley. Warren, on the contrary, has devoted his whole attention to crowding his lines with the greatest specific gravity

they will bear, so that they will not merely assert the uniqueness
of an experience but will convey the actual burden of that experience, both as it has been felt and as it has been thought
about. 'Love's Parable' is as incapable of paraphrase as 'To His
Coy Mistress.' It could be reduced in prose to the statement that
love is perishable; and yet the poem, as constructed, contains
an impressive and absorbing range from sensuous delight to
somber reflection.

The title of Warren's second book, *Eleven Poems on the Same
Theme*, emphasizes the persistence of his dominant thoughts. It
also hints at the constricting limitations latent in such preoccupation. The theme detaches itself as one with which Tate has
been particularly concerned: a protest against the tendency of
our scientific age to reduce knowledge to abstraction, and to rob
experience of its religious tension by making sin meaningless.
Warren has not stated this theme in as explicitly philosophical
terms as Tate. His method, as in 'Picnic Remembered,' is to
present the apparently smooth surfaces of life in such an improved, amoral age, and then to suggest the violence and terror
ever lurking just beneath the enlightened consciousness. He portrays this as a nightmare stumbling past, or as a dim memory
of crime, or in quieter, but no less compelling terms, in 'End of
Season,' by an image which breaks through the effort to live in a
holiday timeless present: 'But the mail lurks in the box at the
house where you live.'

His frontal attack on the theme is carried out most thoroughly
in 'Terror,' 'Pursuit,' and 'Original Sin,' poems which are so
tightly organized through their successive images and which are
permitted such a minimum of generalization that the reader may
at first find them very obscure. Warren shares with Tate and with
some of the French symbolists a fondness for images of violent
disorder, and it sometimes becomes a question whether these
images rise inherently from his concept, or whether they are
manipulated too cerebrally upon it. His control is most decisive
in his demonstration that we are 'born to no adequate definition
of terror'; for here he makes, both at the beginning and at the
close of the poem, a functional repetition of the suggested figure
of Macbeth, the conscience-stricken man who sees the ghost of

his evil deed, whereas we simply crack nuts and 'see an empty chair.' The consequences of our shallow lack of implication in any moral struggle are imaged with telling violence when Warren notes that under such circumstances even war itself is meaningless, since

> Blood splashed on the terrorless intellect creates
> Corrosive fizzle like the spattered lime,
> And its enseamed stew but satiates
> Itself, in that lewd and faceless pantomime.

Warren is probably unaware of how often he poses our problem as one of definition: in 'Revelation,' 'In separateness only does love learn definition'; in 'Ransom,' 'Our courage needs, perhaps, new definition'; and in 'The Ballad of Billie Potts,' in a closer verbal echo than he probably intended, 'Our innocence needs, perhaps, new definition.' Such repetition may betray a static tightness, and some critics have found the texture of Warren's poems too uniformly dense. He seems finally to have come to some such conclusion himself, for the most exciting feature of his most recent poems is their breaking away from the intellectualized modes that have often become the mannerism of our generation. In 'Variation: Ode to Fear' he makes a far more loosely colloquial satiric statement of his theme. In 'Mexico is a Foreign Country: Five Studies in Naturalism' he introduces a hearty and humorous coarseness. And finally, in his 'Ballad,' he enters quite a new realm by accomplishing the fusion that Yeats urged between the poetry of the coteries and the poetry of the folk.

Warren's flair for drama was foreshadowed in his early 'Pondy Woods'—as well as by many passages in his novels—but here he has given it free rein for the first time in his poetry. He has handled his 'Ballad' on two levels. On one level he retells an old folk story of Western Kentucky about an outlaw innkeeper and his son. Little Billie, emulating his father's habit of practicing highway robbery on his guests, is caught in an attempted murder, and has to leave for the West. When he comes home ten years later, rich, he is murdered by his parents before they recognize him. The other level consists of the poet's philosophical

reflections on the story; and in such weaving back and forth
Warren reveals the almost inevitable influence of Eliot's *Quartets*. But only occasionally do Warren's meditations on time and
the timeless seem borrowed, and for the most part he is speaking
out of his own full mind. His verse has also learned something
of Eliot's later dangerous freedom in its frequent descents into
near prose, and some may find Warren's prosody too crude and
casual. Yet it increases his conversational effect.

The dramatic point of the story is the parents' horrified discovery of what they have done; but the reflective passages make
their contrast by concentrating on the role of the son. We cannot
escape going back to where we came from, as the son returns
to the father. But Warren's preoccupation, the preoccupation
of our generation, can hardly be with the Father of grace. We
have scarcely begun to understand even the grounds for salvation. We must first return to the old man, to an awareness of our
roots in erring humanity, and our first discovery must be the
blinding one of essential evil.

Shapiro, born in the year before the outbreak of the last war
and thus nearly a decade younger than Warren, has grown up
in a very different school. Instead of Vanderbilt, Yale, and Oxford in the late 'twenties, Shapiro had to survive the depression
and to piece out his education between jobs. Some of his earlier
work was a little drunk with Auden's flamboyant rhetoric, but
his satirical position, as seen in his poem about the University
of Virginia (from which he soon withdrew) was already poised
surely on his own feet: 'To hurt the Negro and avoid the Jew /
Is the curriculum.' His first collection of poems, in the New
Directions annual volume of *Five Young American Poets* for
1941, was called *Noun*, and thereby made explicit his recognition, so different again from Cummings', that a poem must be a
concrete substance, not just verbal tricks. His prefatory note said
that he wanted to start with recording experience rather than
any language experiment. He also added: 'The reader will see
that I write about myself, my house, my street, and my city, and
not about "America," the word that is the chief enemy of mod-

ern poetry.' His first full-length volume in the following year underscored that intention through its title of *Person, Place and Thing*.

When that book came out, Shapiro was already 'somewhere in the Pacific,' and although his introduction to *V-Letter* says that ever since the war began he has 'tried to be on guard against becoming a "war poet," ' the fact that he was drafted the better part of a year before Pearl Harbor means that a great deal of his experience has already been that of a soldier. He speaks of that life in ambivalent terms: in one sentence as 'the peculiarly enlivening circumstances of soldiering'; in another of how he does not want to dwell on 'the private psychological tragedy,' nor on 'the commonplace of suffering,' but on 'the spiritual progress or retrogression of the man in war, the increase or decrease in his knowledge of beauty, government and religion.' He has learned that war has no particular reference to 'values,' and finally, that 'if war can teach anything it can teach humility; if it can test anything it can test externality against the soul.'

The dominant tone of his new book is far from the apathetic misery he noted in his peacetime 'Conscription Camp.' But his method of writing a poem is still the one prefigured by his earlier titles. Those of Place, such as 'Melbourne' and 'New Guinea,' are often the most casual, like the travelogues of Auden and Mac-Neice. Yet in 'Troop Train' his alert camera-eye has embraced a human scene in its complexity, and in the swift anapests of 'Sydney Bridge' he has caught not only the outflung beauty of its structure, but also its function: 'You are marxist and sweaty! You grind for the labor of days!'.

These two poems are representative examples of his prosody. His fondness for the brassy anapest—which in 'Sydney Bridge' he introduces into the pattern of the sonnet and on other occasions into the rhyme scheme of *terza rima*—denotes that his music is lively rather than subtle, and that itself is an event of some novelty in modern poetry. Yet he is by no means a poet of one tune: the cumulatively terrifying repetition of the word 'death' in the last stanza of 'Troop Train' is testimony to another kind of mastered control:

Trains lead to ships and ships to death or trains,
And trains to death or trucks, and trucks to death,
Or trucks lead to the march, the march to death,
Or that survival which is all our hope;
And death leads back to trucks and trains and ships,
But life leads to the march, O flag! at last
The place of life found after trains and death
—Nightfall of nations brilliant after war.

Among the Things which he now presents in their varied amplitude are 'Piano,' 'The Gun,' 'Public Library,' 'The Synagogue,' and 'The Bed'; but both his method and his attitude are to be seen at their most searching in his Persons. 'Nigger' is typical of his best. It builds up through a series of staccato notations from the lives and dilemmas of many different black men:

When you boxed that hun, when you raped that
trash that you didn't rape,
When you caught that slug with a belly of fire and
a face of gray . . .

Shapiro aims to arrive thus at his generalization in the only way that he believes authentic, through the massed evidence of gritty details. The social attitude to which he gives allegiance may be amplified from some of his other portraits. 'Jefferson' expresses his veneration for our past, and yet his acute knowledge of what a tremendous problem we are faced with in maintaining living continuity with such a sanguine tradition. 'Jew' recognizes his own problem, but with no self-pity.

One of the hopeful signs for a diversified culture in America is the number of our recent poets who are Jews: among them Kenneth Fearing, with his nervous and more shallow satire; Delmore Schwartz, with his sensitive evocations of his city boyhood; and now Shapiro, who has given voice to a more robust vitality. He has exorcised the dangers of his temperament in 'The Intellectual,' with its startling variation on Wordsworth:

I'd rather be
A milkman walking in his sleep at dawn,
Bearing fat quarts of cream, and so be free . . .

And in 'The Bed' he has affirmed his delight in physical rankness.

The weakness latent in his method is that it may become a
formula. Moreover, Shapiro's particular way of piling up details
risks turning some of his pictures into composite portraits. His
soundest means of avoiding that blurring of features is to be
sure of the point of view from which he is approaching his subjects. But sometimes a too-self-conscious desire for detachment
almost robs him of the social convictions that are his strongest
asset. He is certainly ambiguous in repudiating all 'the stock
attitudes of the last generation, the stance of the political intellectual, the proletarian, the expert, the salesman, the world-
traveler, the pundit-poet.' There are great differences in value
among these attitudes, and divested of all of them, the poet
would no longer be man thinking. He would be the passionless
observer of whom we have had far too many examples in our
non-political genteel tradition.

The salutary limits of detachment are reached in 'Elegy for A
Dead Soldier,' where Shapiro makes his thoughtful tribute to
another kind of American, an American far more typical of our
army than the poet serving as a medical sergeant:

> No history deceived him, for he knew
> Little of times and armies not his own;
> He never felt that peace was but a loan,
> Had never questioned the idea of gain.
> Beyond the headlines once or twice he saw
> The gathering of a power by the few
> But could not tell their names; he cast his vote,
> Distrusting all the elected but not law.
> He laughed at socialism: *on mourrait*
> *Pour les industriels?* He shed his coat
> And not for brotherhood, but for his pay.
> To him the red flag marked the sewer main.

That single stanza indicates how much character Shapiro can
pack in by means of his carefully selected objectivity. As he proceeds with his recital of the qualities of this man who 'belonged
to church but never spoke of God,' whose 'laugh was real,'
whose 'manners were home made,' and who yet took interest 'in
a gang-war like a game' and who 'hated other races, south or
east,' we have a rarely mature balance between fondness for the

American soldier's humanity and lucid perception of its savage and staggering limitations. Such recognition, implicated as well as detached, is the essence of moral judgment in poetry. This elegy is in the tradition of Yeats' tribute to Major Robert Gregory, but Shapiro's structure is as freshly devised as the original rhyme scheme to which he holds through all his eleven stanzas. The poem ends with a brief 'Epitaph' which may seem weakly inconclusive since all it urges to posterity is that

> if you can lift your eyes
> Upon a peace kept by a human creed,
> Know that one soldier has not died in vain.

But the inconclusiveness would seem the only honest response to the evidence Shapiro has presented. His satirical 'Geographers' concluded that 'War cannot change the shape of continents.' No more likely are the shapes of nations to be changed if our soldiers know only the enemy they are fighting against, and so little positively what they are fighting for. Shapiro's response to the moral temper of our era reveals, like Warren's, the depth of awareness, on the part of our best younger poets, of the grave and menacing future into which we are all walking.

*Kenyon Review,* 1944

## Fragmentary and Whole:
## Williams, Aiken, Tate

'EVEN the chips of it are invaluable,' says Williams, voicing once again the poetic faith of an imagist. To be sure, he has never been confined to the restricted subject matter of most of the imagists, which Aiken stigmatized long ago as 'the semi-precious in experience.' By contrast Williams has followed the Whitman tradition in opening up ever fresh material from common existence. He defines poetry here as 'the exceptional truth of ordinary people,' and finds a characteristic image of beauty in

> a cylindrical tank fresh silvered
> upended on the sidewalk to advertise
> some plumber's shop.

He has said that imagism failed because it did not master 'structural necessity,' and he reaffirms now the belief shared by Whitman and Thoreau that a poem must grow organically out of physical life. But the dangers in that principle, as Whitman proved far too often, are that the poet can become so happily absorbed in the immediate concrete details that he mistakes their life for the structure of his poem. Such is the case with most of Williams' poems in this book. None of them shows the formal invention that made 'The Yachts' or 'The Catholic Bells' into sustained wholes. The best are those that depend on the intimate knowledge of humanity that Williams has gained as a doctor to

*The Wedge* by William Carlos Williams. Cummington Press.
*The Soldier* by Conrad Aiken. New Directions.
*The Winter Sea* by Allen Tate. Cummington Press.

129

working people in an industrial town. Like Lawrence, he has wedged deep into the mingled gentleness and violence of love. He can also demonstrate the validity of his axiom 'No ideas but in things!' by creating unforgettable pictures of ditch-diggers in a sewer or of a woman facing him with the demand for an abortion. But he never presents these with the grimness of the naturalistic novelist. From first to last Williams' great quality has been gusto. That carries him through the best, if one of the shortest, poems here, 'The Dance,' which celebrates how the big-bellied men and women still

> prance as they dance
> in Breughel's great picture, The Kermess.

Though his poems do not deal with the war, Williams felt the necessity of beginning his preface by saying that they too are part of it, 'merely a different sector of the field.' Such a need to identify himself with the war has operated more compulsively on Aiken. His last book, *Brownstone Eclogues* (1942), was marked by his turning away from his too persistent theme that 'the maelstrom holds us all,' and by a consequent access of new perceptions and of more energetic rhythms. *The Soldier* is another departure, a meditation on the course of history: 'Dark is our past, secret and dark our future.' Its theme may have been suggested in part by Eliot's *Quartets*, but Aiken's own delicately modulated music is, as always, the chief sign by which we know him. The line just quoted suggests the kind of interweaving from the past that he makes here. It is a paraphrase from some Anglo-Saxon gnomic verse, and there are similar allusions to Widsith, to an ancient Chinese poet, to Suetonius, Leonardo, Napoleon, and others.

His grave account of mankind's migrant course becomes unsatisfactory only as it is brought near the present war. Then its weaknesses are the two that generally beset war poetry by a civilian. Aiken either delivers the too easy statement that 'we are all soldiers,' when we know very well that ours is not their sacrifice, or he concocts an equally facile justification of all wars as 'true culture-bearers.' True as that may be for the anthropologist, such cool detachment has the effect of making present

suffering remote and unreal. Such is hardly the function of a
poet, and Aiken's real subject is heroic struggle of the kind he
understands and also interweaves—that of Beethoven facing
deafness, or of Keats facing certain death with the remark that
he feels like 'a soldier marching against a battery.' Five years
hence, Aiken's references to *The Infantry Journal* will seem even
more adventitious and superficial than they do now.

The tensions between good and evil, so slurred over by Aiken's
detachment, form the substance of Tate's best poetry. In the
eight years since his *Selected Poems* he has written quantita-
tively little, but, as his poem to the memory of Yeats reveals, he
has learned from that master deliberately to loosen his style. He
too has tried, like Robert Penn Warren recently, to bridge the
gap between the poetry of the coteries and that of the folk. One
result is his experiment with a ballad refrain in 'Jubilo'; another
is his conversational piece, 'Eclogue of the Liberal and the Poet.'
In 'Ode to Our Young Proconsuls of the Air' he engages in topical
satire, but though he has a fine dry irony against those who hold
that 'Proust caused the fall of France,' it is harder, as with the
Southern agrarians generally, to know what he takes his stand
politically for, and not merely against.

Tate is most effective as a poet of religious sensibility who
finds very difficult any sure affirmation of faith. 'More Sonnets
at Christmas' continues his debate with himself, and expresses
more compellingly than his directly political poems his misgiv-
ings as to the international role we are likely to play so long as
we are complacently superior and possessed with

> a faith not personal
> As follows: The American people fully armed
> With assurance policies, righteous and harmed,
> Battle the world of which they're not at all.

The most ambitious work here is 'Seasons of the Soul.' This
sequence is steeped in Dante, as Eliot has been, but Tate has
worked out a very personal effect in his ten-line trimeter stanzas
mounting to a refrain. It is characteristic of him that the two
somber seasons yield the best poetry. 'Autumn' embodies the
hallucinated dread that Tate has expressed before, notably in

'The Wolves.' It conveys the atmosphere of nightmare, as the poet, caught at the bottom of a pit, confronts fragments of his past. It reminds us of what Tate meant by saying: 'I often think of my poems as commentaries on those human situations from which there is no escape.' The most integrated whole, and one of the most impressive of recent poems, is 'Winter.' An invocation to the Goddess of Love to return to our time of dead faith, it builds its structure through the antiphonal contrast of its refrain. 'The livid wound of love' is what we know all too much about in our lust and violence. What the poet prays for is its transformation to 'the living wound of love.' The rich texture of this poem depends on the bold interpenetration of sexual and sacred imagery. It is further commentary on our strange reading habits that at a moment when any bad novel can sell by the thousands, such poetry has to be issued in a limited edition, at a prohibitive price.

*New Republic,* 1945

## *Music on the Fingerboard: Marshall Schacht*

INTRODUCING this first collection of poems by Marshall Schacht, I am deprived of the phrase usual to such occasions. This is not a promising book.

American literature, in our time especially, has known far too many first books of showily forced growth for the quick return, whose promise was all in the store window. What is unusual now is to find someone who has been quietly cultivating his talent for over twenty years, undistracted and undisturbed by the absence of any visible audience. One of the compensations for the harsh fact that it is virtually impossible to make a living out of poetry is that the poet's work, unlike that of the novelist or play-wright, runs no risk of being corrupted by the market. If he can survive at all, the poet can come at last to real maturity. Like the author of *Fingerboard* he can slowly master his forms to the point that they will release a considered view of experience that commands consideration from the reader.

The view of this poet is that of the city man, along East 24th Street. The daily objects which engage his tender attention are not the fringed gentian, nor the katydid, nor the ovenbird, but chalk marks on a wall. Like most artists in our fragmentary society he is the observer, not the participant. In the lonely wilderness of New York this can create a special problem for the artist: he becomes so habitually the outsider staring through plate glass that he is almost forced into a museum-goer's atti-tude toward life. Poems resulting from this attitude may be hardly more than travelogues, which, despite the sharp bright vocabulary of *The New Yorker,* after a swift glide over exciting surfaces leave us about where we started.

When Mr. Schacht escapes this dilemma, it is because he realizes that the worst enemies of the artist are the sophisticated, 'the fancy people.' His closest knowledge is of the slums, of 'the thin walls of the poor.' He also possesses, by the accident of background, a knowledge of another region, the New England in which he grew up and went to college, and where his brother is a Unitarian minister.

Many of his poems are engaged with spanning from his pres-ent to his past. He is aware that he is scarcely a New Englander any longer, that he is not 'single as Thoreau.' Nature in his eyes is cold and impersonal. He now sees it at a distance, as through a lens. When he goes back home, he feels like an 'overnight guest,' since he knows that he has not come to stay. He suggests this divided awareness in one of his controlling title-images: 'the train in the meadow.'

This may seem to suggest again the limitations of the trave-logue, but the test of a poet is never his subject matter but what he can say through it. 'How To Say Oranges' is a sample of this poet's method. Its subject is a Gauguin still life, but just as that painter's 'expert childish eye saw oranges,' so this poet, by his

full response to what made one work of art, has produced another. His medium is one of the rewards that have come to him
through practicing his craft at a time when Yeats, Frost, and
Eliot, no matter how diverse their other aims, have all been
devoted to bringing back into poetry the colloquial speech which
the poets of the previous half century mainly allowed to fall into
disuse. Despite the conventional impression that modern poetry
has been needlessly difficult, its masters have combined to perfect a language that is no longer special, as was that of the sono-
rous and ornate late nineteenth century, but endowed with the
timbre and resilience of the most flexible conversation, capable
both of formality and informality.

A share in this language is Mr. Schacht's most valuable resource, as he himself knows, for he tells us 'not to forget Miss
Dickinson.' His range of command in it is impressive. At one
extreme is the jauntily unexpected twisting of a phrase, in presenting the denizen of 'Hall Bedroom': 'He looks at trees in
stores, his cows / Come home in magazines.' At the other is the
controlled simplicity, in the final stanza of 'Cancer Home,' which
can convey better than any heightened devices of rhetoric the
depths of his feeling for his father.

But language alone is not enough. If you want to see how
long and lovingly Mr. Schacht has meditated over what it takes
to compose a poem, read the second of his 'Two Reviews,' or
more particularly 'The Fiddle's Body,' the poem which gives
this book its title. He believes that the poet is 'the farmer farm-
ing self in a few home fields,' that the last question for him to be
concerned with is whether he is 'major' or 'minor,' that the only
question is whether what he is expressing is authentic to his own
vision. But it will not become authentic by his merely saying so,
nor by any direct promulgation, no matter how vigorous or 'important' his ideas. Mr. Schacht suggests the necessary process
through his title. Poetry, according to his conception, is not a
spontaneous gushing forth of either ideas or words. It is the last
act of an endless discipline, the long calculated and yet incalculable moment when the finger exercises finally merge into
music on the fingerboard.

As a player of the violin Mr. Schacht makes his poetry not

only that of the speaking voice, but of the trained ear. His stanza forms are for the most part the simplest. But he is at his best in making much of little. He may have learned from Frost, who is not generally recognized to be the chief American master of the sonnet, how to modulate and vary this form so that we are hardly aware he is using it, because it is exactly, delicately right for what he wants it to say. Oranges, for instance.

For him the city is 'the house of man,' and 'the doors lead out.' But he plays a variation on this theme. They lead us also out of the city, back to the land, but if, as feeling and thinking beings, we are to possess what we have experienced, they lead us most essentially back to contemplation of ourselves. This is the sense in which Mr. Schacht is a 'farmer.' His estimate of his crop is very modest. He says he has 'regulated' his life 'to make it possible to have the experience of poetry.' In our age of rapid and superficial reading we are in constant danger of losing touch altogether with that richest experience that reading can yield. Mr. Schacht brings us back to it in a flash in another of his controlling images: 'a green stroke.' Poetry will not come for the calling, and

> Comes seldom. If it comes, it comes like thunder,
> A green stroke welding man and sky and tree.

*Fingerboard,* 1949

# The Alienation of the Writer

THE 'thirties seem in retrospect a more coherent if more limited period of expression than the 'twenties. And the 'forties? It comes as a shock to realize that they are nearly at an end, for they have witnessed no new figures with anything like the weight of production of any of the leading novelists of the 'thirties. There has also been much less production by the novelists already known. Dos Passos has not written an important novel for a dozen years. Hemingway has not yet written any novel since *For Whom the Bell Tolls* in 1940. Faulkner, Farrell, Steinbeck have hardly increased their range since then.

What are the reasons for this break? The big and obvious one is the war, and yet when we recall the First World War, the situation was very different. Many writers were emerging just before 1914, some of them too old for military service and so continuing to write through 1918, and others began to emerge at the war's end. One heavily altered factor is the length of time during which America was involved in the recent war. Yet even before then, by the end of the 'thirties, there began to be a collapse of the novel of social protest, not because the issues were not still grave, but because they had become so much graver, so much harder to handle.

In a time increasingly flooded with rival propagandas, we have come to a still greater awareness of the distance between the official and the actual. In the years just before, and now after the war, there has been a special importance in the little magazine for the experimental writer who found that what he had to say did not fit into the mode of the slick magazines, and who

This passage is from Matthiessen's Benjamin Franklin Lecture, delivered in 1948 at the University of Pennsylvania.—ED.

136

needed to strike out anew. What he had to say did not fit into the conventional mode because it was often agonizing. It was often an acute conflict between the outer and the inner, which came to expression not in a sustained form but in a short story.

Some deep awareness of that conflict also formed the common denominator between the older writers who have impressed our most recent beginners in fiction. The vogue, especially among readers under thirty, of authors of such diverse value as Henry James and Kafka, Henry Miller and Anais Nin, bespeaks their common concern with escape, not from the real, but from the monstrously unreal.

Some of the most recent short story writers from the little magazines are now beginning to appear in volume form, most notably J. F. Powers and Peter Taylor. But their work, though excellent in quality, is still a little too limited to support generalizations. More certain comparisons may be based upon the work of the best-known writer for the theater to have appeared in the 'forties. The plays of Tennessee Williams reveal the decade's particular awareness of the tensions between the inner and the outer life. Like O'Neill and Odets, he too is engaged with the disinherited, but his portrayal of them is characteristically of the case histories of fevered sufferers driven in upon themselves or escaping only in fantasy.

In mentioning the names of the newest writers, one must be even more conscious of the tentativeness of his judgments, especially since the work of the war generation, the generation of John Burns and Norman Mailer, is still mainly ahead. But whatever the case may prove to be in the 'fifties, the 'forties have been a time when it was hard for the writer to possess enough steadiness or enough coherence for creative renewal . . .

In *Winesburg, Ohio,* probing beneath the flat, starved surfaces that Lewis caricatured so effectively, Anderson found the still unspent sources of love. One of his characters, reflecting on the bitter fact that 'men coming out of Europe and given millions of square miles of black, fertile land, mines, and forests, have failed in the challenge given them by fate and have produced out of the stately order of nature only the sordid disorder of man,' cried out: 'There is a curse on my country. Everyone has come here for gain, to grow rich, to achieve. Suppose they should begin to want to live here?' Facing that question, Anderson set himself, like his own Windy McPherson's son, to the task of 'understanding those other lives in love.' He wanted to awaken his readers to 'the thing beyond words, beyond passion—the fellowship in living, the fellowship in life.'

That seems immeasurably harder now than in the mood of promise in which Anderson shared at the end of the First World War. Such a mood cannot be evoked at will or without rededication to the extension of economic and social democracy at home and abroad. But such a rededication is essential if our writers are to escape from their pervasive sense of alienation, if their worlds are not to remain private, if they are to repossess, as Anderson did, the central core in Whitman's meaning—his unshakable belief in solidarity with the common life.

*Changing Patterns in American Civilization,* 1949

# IV.   THE AWARENESS OF THE CRITIC

# A *Classic Study of America: Tocqueville*

A CENTURY after its appearance Tocqueville's analysis of our society is still unique, in that it can be read equally profitably in two ways. His close observation of the effect of our institutions upon our customs can still help us to understand the age in and about which he was writing. His rare gift for, and even rarer control of, penetrating generalization can serve to light up anew the problems that continue to threaten any democracy. This double grounding in fact and philosophy was what caused President Wilson to perceive Tocqueville's superiority to Bryce's more purely descriptive *American Commonwealth.* It now causes Harold Laski to state that here 'is, perhaps, the greatest work ever written on one country by the citizen of another.' The reasons for such superlative estimates are substantially documented in Phillips Bradley's long introduction to the revised translation that he offers. The first reissue of this classic in thirty years, the only one with full scholarly equipment, Professor Bradley's edition should remain the standard one for our time.

As a student of government Professor Bradley is chiefly and thoughtfully concerned with Tocqueville's 'sociological insights.' But it is a tribute to the fertility of Tocqueville's work that although it is properly classified as a contribution to political theory, it is remarkably illuminating of our cultural and intellectual history as well. In the first volume (1835) he was largely taken up with the structure of our government as he had studied it in action. But five years later he added his matured reflections concerning the influence of democracy on the American mind.

*Democracy in America* by Alexis de Tocqueville, edited by Phillips Bradley. Alfred A. Knopf, Inc.

His chapter explaining 'why the Americans show more aptitude and taste for general ideas than their forefathers, the English' is offset by the related explanation 'why American writers and orators often use an inflated style.' When Tocqueville had visited the United States in 1831–1832, Walt Whitman was a boy of twelve, but I know of no more perceptive account than Tocqueville's of the peculiar cultural climate that was to produce *Leaves of Grass*.

He noted how our people seemed to 'care but little for what has been, but they are haunted by visions of what will be; in this direction their unbounded imagination grows and dilates beyond all measure.' That suggests the afflatus in Whitman's prefaces, as other remarks in Tocqueville's discussion of potential 'sources of poetry among democracies' suggest some of the vistas that were to stretch out in the 'Song of the Open Road.' The Frenchman's belief that 'the general similitude' of people in a democracy would force a poet from the treatment of individuals to that of man falls in with Whitman's projection of what he called 'stock personality' that could typify all men as brothers. Furthermore, Tocqueville's remarks on how 'democratic nations are passionately addicted to generic terms and abstract expressions' are borne out by Whitman's habit of soaring at one bound from the concrete detail to the vaguest generalization. Tocqueville's whole chapter on how 'the inhabitants of the United States frequently intermingle phraseology in the strangest manner' could also be used as an introduction to Mencken's masterly investigation of the American language.

What a pioneer Tocqueville was in discerning the drift of our society is illustrated by the fact that he even had to coin a new word, *individualisme*—'a novel expression to which a novel idea has given birth'—in order to describe us. It is almost impossible now to realize that that term, which many hold to be the most descriptive of our way of life, did not exist in English until adapted by the first translator of Tocqueville in 1840. That may shock us into an awareness both of how recently individualism came to be our primary assumption, and of how different a world from the present that assumption sprang from.

For Tocqueville's America was primarily an agricultural country wherein he could envisage the town meeting as the healthy center of our institutions. We were still mainly 'the descendants of a common stock.' There were 'few wealthy persons,' religion was believed 'without discussion,' and violence was 'rare.' Like Jefferson, Tocqueville conceived a deep threat to the permanence of democracy in the growth of big cities. (The New York that he saw had a population of 200,000.) Unlike Emerson, the first of whose sanguine essays appeared the year after the first volume of the *Democracy,* Tocqueville was more struck by the restless and melancholy tendencies in the American character. He noted how a condition of equality could isolate men from one another instead of bringing them together, how it could concentrate 'every man's attention upon himself,' and how this in turn could 'lay open the soul to an inordinate love of material gratification.'

The very fact that Tocqueville was a reluctant rather than an enthusiastic equalitarian can make his main thesis very instructive for our present needs. There has probably never been a time when we have had a looser use of the word 'freedom' than we have right now. We hear much about 'free men' in a 'free world' of 'free enterprise,' but we see little evidence that these slogans have any other basis than that of their utterers' emotions. Tocqueville also described himself as an ardent lover of freedom, but he knew where its possibility lay. An aristocrat who yet could discern the central tendency of his age, he reached the conclusion that there could be no real freedom in the modern state unless it was based on equality.

That conclusion led him to study the United States where 'equality of condition' was 'the fundamental fact' upon which the thesis of his long work revolved. He accepted the sovereignty of the people, his observations convinced him that equality gives men a natural taste for free institutions. But he was never blind to the dangers, and when he recognizes that if equality can lead to freedom, it can also lead to despotism, we become most aware of how much he has to say to us now. He feared the 'possible tyranny of the majority,' and thought that we had 'inadequate securities' against it. He also foresaw that if 'local liberties' yielded to the centralization of government, we might end up

with the despotism of one man. On that ground he wished that
the President might be ineligible for re-election.

But unlike the drifting liberals of his time (or of ours) he
accepted as 'both necessary and desirable that the government
of a democratic people should be active and powerful.' He did
not want a weak administration. He simply wanted to prevent
it from abusing the strength, and he believed that the only effectual check to any threat of executive dictatorship was through
active popular participation in all the processes of government,
from the grass roots. For those who find the natural continuation of the world of Walt Whitman in the world of Henry
Wallace, that seems still to talk our language.

Tocqueville foresaw other dangers that might be even graver
than an excessively centralized administration. Such a one could
be the presence of a large army in peacetime. He was also anxious about the vulgarization and degradation that could result
from the people's excessive concern with nothing but material
ends. He did not believe that a democracy could endure without
a renewed concern with its foundations in Christian ethics, the
source for fraternity as well as for equality. In one short chapter
on the nascent 'growth of manufacturers,' he gave, as Professor
Bradley notes, a brilliant piece of pre-Marxist analysis of that
new source of 'harshest' inequality. He was sure that the most
formidable of all the threats to our future lay in the race question, that 'if ever America undergoes great revolutions, they will
be brought about by the presence of the black race on the soil
. . . that is to say they will owe their origin not to the equality
but to the inequality of the condition.'

As a nineteenth-century analyst Tocqueville ended each of his
volumes with a peroration. His final words were: 'The nations of
our time cannot prevent the conditions of men from becoming
equal, but it depends upon themselves whether the principle of
equality is to lead them to servitude or freedom, to knowledge
or barbarism, to prosperity or wretchedness.' The conclusion of
his first volume has another and unexpected relevance. There
he put side by side the two great nations of the future, the
American and the Russian, each of whom seemed marked out
'to sway the destinies of half the globe.' The contrast that

Tocqueville saw between the freedom of the one people and the servitude of the other no longer prevails. In the intervening century we have learned some of the cruel lessons of the inequalities of industrial and finance capitalism; and during the past generation the Russians have made the first thoroughgoing attempt to root out the economic bases of such inequalities. At a time when many people in our country and much of our press hold that the Russians' equality means the loss of freedom, we should pay the most careful heed to Tocqueville's other peroration as well.

*The New York Times Book Review*, 1945

## Margaret Fuller as Critic

T HE limitation of Mason Wade's recent biography of Margaret Fuller was that it gave hardly any living sense of her ideas or of the cultural ferment of which she was part. Though his subtitle was 'the whetstone of genius,' his mildly popular account failed to show wherein she performed that function. But now, by making available a comprehensive selection of her works, he has presented the evidence upon which the reader can judge for himself. He has included the bulk of *Summer on the Lakes* (1844) and *Woman in the Nineteenth Century* (1845). The first of these two books, opening with Margaret's approbation of Niagara as 'the one object in the world that would not disappoint,' belongs to the same genre of travel books as Thoreau's *Week on the Concord and Merrimack Rivers*, a genre which demanded his concentrated genius to salvage it from mere passing interest. Her tract on 'the sphere, condition and duties of woman,' was, as Mr. Wade notes, 'a landmark in the history of

The Writings of Margaret Fuller, edited by Mason Wade. The Viking Press.

feminism,' but its style is no less turgid than ardent, and makes the point that her friends were always repeating, how she was much more brilliant in conversation than in print. Her essays from Europe on Italy and the Roman Revolution (1848–1849) reveal her growth in conviction and clarity. She was disgusted with the way that most of the American art colony failed to make any contact with the life around them, and after risking her life in months of activity for the revolutionary cause, she declared, shortly before sailing for home on her fateful voyage: 'I have become an enthusiastic Socialist; elsewhere is no comfort, no solution for the problems of the times.'

This declaration of faith is from one of the two dozen previously unpublished letters that the editor has found. But the heart of the volume, as of Margaret Fuller's work, is her criticism. Mr. Wade has sensibly limited his selection to her discussion of literature, since her essays on painting and sculpture, though of great value in awaking her New England contemporaries to richer resources than their ancestors had permitted, are more full of emotion than light, as is her imaginary letter to Beethoven. Many of her tastes ran parallel to Emerson's, especially her devotion to the metaphysical poets of the seventeenth century, as witnessed by her dialogue between George Herbert and his brother, Lord Herbert of Cherbury. But her appreciation of art was more inclusive than that of any of the Concord philosophers. She said that the three authors who had most impressed her early youth were Shakespeare, Cervantes, and Molière, and they had prepared her to find Dr. Channing, however noble in his thought, 'not well acquainted with man on the impulsive and passionate side of his nature.' Such passion and impulse were what she celebrated in Goethe against the strictures of more timid ministers. Against the objections that he was 'not an idealist,' she answered proudly, in the preface to her translation of his conversations with Eckermann, that Goethe 'thought not so much of what might be as what is. He did not seek to alter or exalt Nature, but merely to select from her rich stores.'

Her own refusal to fall into the most common error of her surroundings, the mistaking of idealism for art, gave penetration and solidity to many of the judgments in her long essay on the prospects of American literature (1846). She recognized both the subtle beauty and the insubstantiality of Emerson's poetry. She had no doubts, even before *The Scarlet Letter,* that Hawthorne was 'the best writer of the day.' She could see quite through the enormous vogue of Longfellow; his ethical reflections had 'a hollow, second-hand' ring, but his elegance and sweetness, though 'imitative,' were not 'mechanical,' and 'if not allowed to supersede what is better, may promote a taste for good poetry.' And her few observations on Lowell were definitive: 'His interest in the moral questions of the day has supplied the want of vitality in himself; his great facility at versification has enabled him to fill the ear with a copious stream of pleasant sound. But his verse is stereotyped; his thoughts sound no depth; and posterity will not remember him.' Even when Margaret Fuller loses this incisiveness in her many rhapsodic flights or in the hastily written pages of the transcendental hack-writer, she gives the sense that she is fulfilling a major obligation of the critic, in that she possesses what she had responded to in her masters, their 'deep and steady sympathy with all that is human.'

*New Republic,* 1941

## *Moses Coit Tyler*

THE primary interest in the biography of Moses Coit Tyler consists in the light that it throws on the composition of his two great histories—*A History of American Literature, 1607–1765,* which was published in 1878, when its author was forty-three,

*The Life of Moses Coit Tyler* by Howard Mumford Jones: based upon an unpublished dissertation from original sources by Thomas Edgar Casady. The University of Michigan Press.

and *The Literary History of the American Revolution,* which
was not finished until nineteen years later. Up until the time
that his mind focused on the production of the first of these,
Tyler's life had revealed no marks of great distinction. Born in
Connecticut, he was taken as an infant to Michigan, where his
pioneering father was hopeful of a fortune that never materi-
alized; indeed, it was only through the assistance of well-to-do
cousins that young Tyler was later enabled to return East to go
to Yale. Graduating in 1857, he was thus in the same class with
Cyrus Northrop, who was to be president of the University of
Minnesota (though not, as Professor Jones states, with the
destined president of Cornell, Andrew D. White, who was actually four years ahead of him). As an undergraduate Tyler
was an active member of various societies, but a persevering
rather than a brilliant student, and was just barely elected to
Phi Beta Kappa. Uncertain in his mind as to what career he
should pursue, he spent a year in the Yale Divinity School and
another at the Andover Seminary; with the result that he was
ordained as minister of the Congregational church at Owego,
New York, just after his twenty-fourth birthday.

The next year he was called to a much larger congregation at
Poughkeepsie, but this period seems to have been the most conflicting and doubtful of Tyler's whole life. His diaries show him
to have shared to the end of his days in the spiritual restlessness
of his era, harassed by doubt, and yet driven on by the necessity
of faith. At this juncture, however, his health gave way under
the strain, and he resigned his pastorate in 1862. There followed
an episode that was so much of his age that it is hard for a later
time to make it seem other than fantastic. In the effort to regain
his strength he began to practice a new system of 'musical
gymnastics' that had been developed by Dr. Dio Lewis, of
Boston. More than that, he grew so impressed by its salutary
effect upon him that he became an apostle, and set out the next
year to found a school of physical culture in London. Put in
these bald terms, it makes nothing seem less likely than that
such a man would be the first distinguished historian of American letters. But Tyler's school did not seem exotic to the contemporary English preachers of 'muscular Christianity'; he was

invited to speak before doctors and scientists as well as before literary societies. He soon began also to lecture on some of his other interests, on 'The Pilgrim Fathers' and 'American Humor,' and was presently being advertised as 'the great American orator.'

Yet Tyler's real career can not be considered to have started until after his return to America and his appointment as professor of rhetoric and English at the University of Michigan in 1867. He was from the outset a memorable teacher, and introduced almost at once a revolutionary innovation—which unfortunately has not even yet been everywhere adopted—that of devoting his lectures to the direct study of literary masterpieces, instead of to the accessories of literature, to grammatical dissection, or to textbook 'background.' Soon he suggested to the regents an even more revolutionary idea: the teaching of our own literature, which in 1872 had not yet been included in any university curriculum, though Professor J. S. Hart of Princeton was to break the way in the following year.

At about this time Tyler was also beginning to discover the one thing he desired to do. As late as 1869 he could write: 'The problem of my life-work, though my life is probably half gone, is yet unsolved'; but already he had confided to his journal, 'As a literary and philosophical servant of American society, I might be first rate.' He embarked on an ever wider course of reading, not only of literature and American history, but also of political economy and law in order that he might be able to understand social processes. Burke, in a certain wide sense, was his model. Tyler aspired to something akin to his combination of learning, philosophical penetration, taste, and style: 'I would follow him— even though afar off.' Soon, however, the reading of Buckle provided him with a more definite goal and challenge:

He obsessed me for weeks together. No sentence could I shun [slur?] over in reading. He shall be one of my friends for life. As a historical writer he indicates nobly, in many respects, the path to be taken by every other historical writer—the exhaustive preparation; the recognition of a spirit of the age as ruling the evolution of the events of the age, and using kings, presidents, statesmen, warriors, as the tide uses the chips that are carried upon its top; the necessity, therefore, of finding for each period and for each people the hidden law of progress.

Tyler now felt that he had grasped the essence of history in a way that Bancroft and Palfrey had not been able to reveal it. He set himself to the task of discovering the law of American development. 'I have,' he wrote in August, 1871, 'at last really found my work.' He had not yet settled upon his exact subject, but was at this time contemplating 'a history of the United States, beginning with Washington's administration.' He was shortly to be distracted from his pursuit by a period of editing the *Christian Union*, as well as by lecture tours and miscellaneous journalism. But beneath all these surfaces deflections, and between repeated intervals of uncertainty as to whether he perhaps ought not return to being a preacher, from now on he continued to have an aim.

His critical dissatisfaction with the way that American history had been written was steadily mounting:

If, however, early American history has seemed dry and provincial, and its social life helplessly petty, it must also be owned that a considerable part of this impression has been due, in the main, to the imperfect art of the American writers who have hitherto handled their topics . . . American history still reserves its charms for the presence of a genius corresponding in that sphere to the greatness of Longfellow and Hawthorne in poetry and romance.

When he came to read Sparks, Tyler noted that he 'describes better than he narrates. His story lacks action. He fails to present the *flow* of events, to state with clearness the sequence of essential details, and to exhibit all the moving life of the story . . . How stupidly is this History written from beginning to end.'

While Tyler was thus developing his ideas on historical method, and reflecting that 'every fact of American history for the last century has now to be re-examined,' the stimulus that he had received from Buckle was driven into channels more closely allied to his own interests and preoccupations by a reading of Sainte-Beuve. In an essay written in 1873 he declared that in the pages of this French master 'every literary critic of this generation must search for the costliest secrets of his craft.' The

secret beyond all others that Tyler learned from him was 'that
in literature the producer must be studied as well as the thing
produced.' His whole mind responded with conviction to Sainte-
Beuve's statement of principle:

I can relish a work; but it is difficult for me to judge it without a
knowledge of the man himself. The literary study leads me naturally
to the moral study.

Upon this principle Tyler reflected:

It will connect criticism with biography. It will make the study
of letters a study of human nature. It will indicate that there is a
relation between living and thinking, and that the conduct of phrase
is a part of the conduct of life. It will also select authors, and not
books merely, as the texts for literary discourse.

The formula for his own literary history had now been evolved;
and this series of glimpses that Tyler's words have given us into
the process of this evolution enable us to place his own statement of that formula in full perspective. We are now in a position to recognize the various strands that combined to produce
the opening paragraph of his history of colonial literature:

There is but one thing more interesting than the intellectual history of a man, and that is the intellectual history of a nation. The
American people, starting into life in the early part of the seventeenth
century, have been busy ever since in recording their intellectual
history in laws, manners, institutions, in battles with man and beast
and nature, in highways, excavations, edifices, in pictures, in statues,
in written words. It is in written words that this people, from the
very beginning, have made the most confidential and explicit record
of their minds. It is in these written words, therefore, that we shall
now search for that record.

The most valuable pages in Professor Jones' study are those
devoted to evaluating the fruits of Tyler's search, to pointing out
the thoroughness of his reading, the balanced judgment that
determined most of his selection and organization (his omission
of Thomas Morton on grounds of moral disapproval is one of
the very rare blots), the dramatic skill of his outstanding portraits, such as those of Edward Johnson and John Wise, the

latter figure being one of Tyler's principal 'discoveries.' Tyler
stated the simple truth when he wrote: 'I have studied, as I believe, every American writer of the colonial time, in his extant
writings'; and Professor Jones indicates to how great an extent
that study meant the exploration of unknown territory; that ' he
found little in the way of a purely literary or intellectual history
of the country to guide him, and was compelled to blast a Roman
road through the wilderness with such aid as the historians and
bibliographers might furnish.'

The method of approach to literature that Tyler had evolved
was especially fruitful in dealing with the particular subject he
had chosen. Aesthetic evaluation alone could hardly be of primary service in bringing to life the writings of the colonial age,
for as Tyler wrote:

> Literature as a fine art, literature as the voice and ministress of
> aesthetic delight, they had perhaps little skill in and little regard for;
> but literature as an instrument of humane and immediate utility, they
> honored, and at this they wrought with all the earnestness that was
> born in their blood. They wrote books not because they cared to write
> books, but because by writing books they could accomplish certain
> other things which they did care for.

Such an account of literature as an instrument may overlook
the aspirations of a poet like Anne Bradstreet, but it is an exact
description of the more prevailing desire, as represented by
Edward Johnson, to 'handle the pen as he did the sword and the
broadaxe—to accomplish something with it.' Consequently Tyler
was on the broadest and solidest ground in not trying to write
literary criticism, but intellectual history as presented by a series
of biographies of minds in action.

The long span of years that separated Tyler's two master-
works was marked by his being called to Cornell, in 1881, to fill
the first professorship of American history ever to be established;
by his final conversion, to which he devoted great meditation,
to the Episcopal church; by his excellently balanced biography of
Patrick Henry, in 1887; and by his *Three Men of Letters,* 1895,
which is devoted to three 'Yale Worthies,' Bishop Berkeley,
Timothy Dwight, and Joel Barlow. Any differences in method

that distinguished *The Literary History of the American Revolution* from the colonial history are only those called forth by differences in the subject matter. For as Professor Jones puts it: 'The first History had surveyed one hundred and fifty-eight years of intellectual development; the second was confined to eighteen . . . The first work had traced the unfolding of the American mind; the second rehearsed a drama, a conflict of views.' But this change of focus simply affects Tyler's method of presentation by giving it a closer unity; his chief preoccupations remain the same. He is still absorbed in the desire to relive the past; in his search for the fundamental principle in history, he still believes that he finds it in the primacy of ideas. His sense of proportion is thrown into even clearer light than before by the equal way in which he allows both Tories and Whigs to speak for themselves. His chapters have been wrought with the same great care; Professor Jones gives an interesting example of Tyler's way of writing by tracing the long course of the various revisions of the section on Francis Hopkinson. The style, except for occasional heavy pages which begin to show exhaustion, still keeps Tyler's personal touch. It is a style fully marked by its time; still very readable today, it now appears somewhat fulsome, showing throughout both works Tyler's taste for old-fashioned rhetoric.

It is unfortunate that such substantial services to our literary history did not win Tyler a more expertly written biography. Professor Jones' work is characterized here as always by the vigor of investigation which makes him one of the few really challenging present-day scholars of American culture; but in his highly commendable effort to relate Tyler's boyhood to its background, instead of adequately assimilating what he has read of early Michigan history to his present purpose, he seems often to have poured into this volume the contents of his notebooks, with the result that, in the opening chapters in particular, facts in the text that have only the slightest conceivable bearing on Tyler's life are backed up by more facts in the barrage of notes that have no bearing at all, and the reader is constantly distracted from any attention to the subject. As the book continues, an even worse flaw is revealed in the way that the style veers to and fro between the sober vein of a heavily documented dissertation and an attempt at following the modes of popularized biography. This may perhaps be owing to the circumstances of composition, to the fact that Professor Jones was working with a thesis that had been left unpublished by the death of its author, T. E. Casady. But whatever the cause, the efforts at 'lively writing' are almost uniformly disastrous. At best they lead to such clichés as: 'Young Tyler was in love. The lady in the case was Jeanette Hull Gilbert'; at their worst they fall into the ejaculatory vein which has been with us now for more than a decade of abortive imitations of the final paragraphs of Strachey's *Queen Victoria:* 'Ah! that earlier time! The Beecher's Bibles and the Divinity School, and Owego and Poughkeepsie, and the Civil War! How far away it all seemed!' But the worst lapse of all is reserved for the last page, where, after describing the bearded figure of history in the memorial window to Tyler in the Cornell chapel, the author concludes: 'Was not Tyler's generation the bearded generation?' That clumsy attempt at a 'light touch' establishes, I submit, a new low for a final sentence to a serious biography.

*The New England Quarterly,* 1934

# Sherman and Huneker

I N every phase of his life Stuart Sherman was characteristically American. Born in Anita, Iowa, he passed a good part of his boyhood in California, and at the age of twelve, after eight months in an Arizona mining camp, he got lost while cross-

*Life and Letters of Stuart P. Sherman* by Jacob Zeitlin and Homer Woodbridge. Farrar and Rinehart.
*Essays by James Huneker,* selected with an introduction by H. L. Mencken. Charles Scribner's Sons.

ing the desert with only the mine-owner's wife and her baby, and came within an ace of dying before they finally reached water. Thereafter he returned to his family's original home in Vermont, went to high school, where he played on the football team, suddenly awoke to a passionate interest in books and devoted himself to learning Greek, helped earn his way through Williams by waiting on table at his mother's boardinghouse for students, wrote the Class Poem of 1903, and continued his education at the Harvard graduate school. After he had saturated himself in Elizabethan drama and had turned out one of the few doctoral dissertations on record which possessed a feeling for literature, and was writing essays and letters in a somewhat painfully elaborate Stevensonian manner, it might have seemed the natural thing for him to stay in New England. But it was no accident that caused him to spend his whole teaching career in the Middle West. He believed in the state university as an ideal: that was part of his democratic notion that American life should taste equally good at all points.

And this belief in democracy became in turn an integral part of his critical theory. It was not an expansive or unreflecting belief: he pointed out that even Mark Twain had in his later years begun 'to emerge from the great romantic illusion about the average man, namely that liberty or equality or any kind of political recognition . . . or even economic independence can make him a happy or a glorious being.' On the other hand, Sherman refused to accept the current bitter disillusionment with democracy; rather, he followed the sober argument of *Democratic Vistas* that we may as well embrace this faith because it is going to be tried whether we like it or not. He held staunchly as his central principle 'the duty of bringing the whole body of the people to the fullest and fairest human life of which they are capable.'

The role that he thought scholarship and letters should play in effecting our national reintegration was 'to connect us with the great traditions and to inspire us with the confidence and power which result from such a connection.' In this conception of the importance of tradition we strike the main fiber of his critical purpose. Unlike the uncurious academic critics who paid

little serious attention to America, and even more unlike the
metropolitan journalists who stated that America had no civilized
cultural atmosphere worth mentioning, Sherman believed that
in our consciousness of such figures as Emerson, Whitman, and
Thoreau we possessed a heritage that deserved to be cherished.
What he meant by this is revealed in his essays in *Americans,*
where he winds into his subjects from every angle, isolates the
very essence of each, and indicates in what sense each is an unspent force with some vital energy to communicate to the modern spirit. What is gained by tradition, what constitutes the perpetual appeal of the masters,

is a kind of innermost poise and serenity, tragic in Sophocles, heroic
in Michelangelo, skeptical in Montaigne, idyllic in Sidney, ironic in
Fielding. This enviable tranquility reigns only in a mind that, looking
before and after, feels itself the representative of something outlasting
time, some national ideal, some religious faith, some permanent
human experience, some endless quest.

In his first book, *On Contemporary Literature* (1917), which
was a direct product of the fine discipline of Irving Babbitt,
Sherman was chiefly engaged in waging the battle of humanism
against naturalism. It was not until after the war, with two books
printed in 1923, *Americans* and *The Genius of America,* that he
found the angle which was to be more specially his own. By that
time he had turned partly away from both his early masters,
sensing, in spite of all his admiration, a grave defect in Mr.
Babbitt's air of universal condemnation, and in the chilling
aloofness of Mr. More, and declaring that they both kept too far
from the scene of action. He had grown to consider the central
position in American criticism to be occupied by W. C. Brownell,
who stood in direct succession from Emerson and Matthew
Arnold. He took great satisfaction in Brownell's dictum that 'the
business of intelligent criticism is to be in touch with everything'; and yet he felt that even Brownell was perhaps too purely
intellectual, too cool.

About the time that he had reached this point in his reflections, Sherman resigned his professorship and came to New
York. The significance of that move is to be read in his journals,

for they reveal the heartening picture of a man of forty-three not content to stop where he is, but sensing that there is something he has missed, and eager to go farther and attain it. He realizes that he has been too wrapped up with the ethical contours of experience, that he has not grasped it in its full color and taste and odor. He no longer wishes to judge, but to understand. He notes: 'Unfold, leaf by leaf. Become more and more intimate with life . . . Study all things with docility, seeking their principle of beauty. Consider whether it is better to change and be living than to be unchanged and dead.' In this spirit he turns his attention more fully than ever before to the contemporary scene, believing that the only service the critic can do for those 'who are moving, lies in calling attention to that part of their motion which seems to be forward.' In this upwelling desire for life, his old standards are inevitably relaxed, and he runs the danger of blurring all the edges of his distinctions; and by giving a good deal of time to wholly unimportant books, he threatens to become, in his own words, an efficient 'critical cheer leader,' a kind of Mark Sullivan of literature, with no finely balanced scale of values, but a glowing enthusiasm for everything simply because it exists. As a result the essays of three years, *Critical Woodcuts* and *The Main Stream,* have probably no lasting value; but they seem to point the way to a further period when Sherman's mind will again contract its energies and reap the benefits of this rich time of expansion. The importance of his awakening sympathy with the modern world was strongly emphasized by a critic who previously had not thought much of Sherman's work, Mr. Van Wyck Brooks:

Sherman is the only critic in America today who writes of the past and the present with equal relish. Of the past he writes with relish and authority. Is he going to command the modern world with the same genial assurance? He has only to take one further step to make his position unique in American literature.

Before that step could be taken Sherman was dead, literally killing himself, it appears, by overwork. Consequently his achievement is as characteristically American as his life: it is uncertain, too diffuse, lacking in any final form. Mr. More frequently pointed out to Sherman that his thought was 'indecisive': it was both sharp and confused at the same time, constantly aware of the need of final definitions, but never, except in some of the essays in *Americans,* quite attaining them. The reason for his failure is, however, perhaps what gives most interest to his work. For he was not content to abide by too abstract standards: his constant movement was towards a greater awareness of what life actually is.

It is only in his last phase that there is a link between Sherman and Huneker. The two approached life from entirely different backgrounds. Before Sherman was born, Huneker was listening to music in Bayreuth, talking with French painters, and catching a glimpse of Flaubert in the streets of Paris. And while Sherman was lecturing to students on the Illinois prairies, Huneker was pouring out his mellowed impressions in a rich, intricate flow. He was our one real apostle of the 'nineties, doing in a sense for America what Anatole France and Lemaître did for the French, and Arthur Symons for England. He had adventured widely among masterpieces little known in this country before he wrote about them: Villiers de l'Isle-Adam, Laforgue, Huysmans, Strindberg, and Hauptmann are only a few of his discoveries. He believed that the critic's aim should be 'to spill his own soul'; and so he wrote enthusiastically, rapturously of all his devotions, and especially of his first and last love, Chopin. His pages are crowded with information, with good gossip of all sorts, and he certainly creates a desire in his reader to go and experience the masterpiece for himself. Once that has been done, Huneker's function is at an end. His essays then appear rather like disjointed passages of conversation, still full of charm and gusto, playing gaily over the surfaces, but communicating very little of exactly what quality distinguishes one work from another, and defining almost nothing. They have served as important pioneers in pointing the way to a fuller culture; but to state that Sherman's work seems the more permanently valuable is not to start again the quarrel of ten years ago in which, although Sherman's manners remained better than Mr. Mencken's, he often fell into an uncomfortable schoolmasterly tone. For it is not that Sherman's way is right and Huneker's wrong; it is simply that Sherman had more elements of good criticism at his command. His appreciation was possibly not so sensitive as Huneker's, but in addition to the impressionist's animation he possessed other gifts: a firmer intellectual grasp, a more solid sense of structure, a deeper perception of the relation of art to life in all its phases. These were the qualities which, at his best, enabled him not simply to describe the effect made upon his spirit by a work of art, but to illuminate its essential nature.

*New Republic,* 1929

# Axel's Castle

F OR several years now Edmund Wilson has been a critic whose importance has been greater than his published work. Reading his essays in *The New Republic,* one has increasingly felt that, slowly and patiently, and with a degree of thoroughness unequaled by anyone else in his generation, he has been equipping himself for the task of interpreting modern literature. He has not only steeped himself in every aspect of present-day writing and examined the immediate roots from which it has sprung, he seems also gradually to have extended his mastery of the culture of the past, and still to have kept his mind in touch with contemporary movements in science and metaphysics.

The promise of his development has not been betrayed in this book. His individual essays may not always be satisfactory; particularly in dealing with the poets he seems to become so absorbed in his descriptions of the evolution of Yeats' ideas, or of

*Axel's Castle: A Study in the Imaginative Literature of 1870–1930* by Edmund Wilson. Charles Scribner's Sons.

Eliot's significant debts to French symbolism, that he does not succeed in giving us rounded estimates of the power of their poetry. But his studies of Proust and Joyce show his method at its best, and are the heart of the volume. Mr. Wilson writes such a packed and relevant account of the vast structures of *A la Recherche du Temps Perdu* and of *Ulysses*, he is so illuminating in his analysis of Proust's effort to reintegrate the whole of his experience in a work of art, and of Joyce's intention to create in his book the illusion of an actual living social organism, that we emerge from the reading of *Axel's Castle* with a deepened understanding of just why these two authors, beyond any others who have written in the twentieth century, are able to make us feel the actual quality and passage of life. As Mr. Wilson brilliantly indicates, Proust has embodied in a novel the world of relativity; in Joyce's world, as in that of Whitehead or Einstein, events are always changing as they are 'perceived by different observers and by them at different times.'

Even more searching than these excellent studies are Mr. Wilson's reflections concerning the whole nature of modern literature. It is useful to be reminded that our strange and difficult explorations of the individual soul are not so new as we generally assume, that, for instance, the kind of disillusionment expressed in Rimbaud's *Une Saison en Enfer* is not very different from that found in *The Waste Land* fifty years later. Mr. Wilson is emphatic in his declaration that the writers whom he is discussing stand at the end and not at the beginning of a tendency. Part of their great attraction for us today lies in the fact that, in the general disintegration of society since the war, we have lost our faith in the possibilities of action, and are consequently 'peculiarly hospitable to a literature indifferent to action and unconcerned with the group.' But it becomes increasingly apparent that nothing more is to be gained by following further the course taken in 1890 by the hero of Villiers de l'Isle-Adam's *Axel*, who, abandoning the ordinary objective world, retired utterly into the life of his mind. Axel is of the same lineage as Roderick Usher and Huysmans' Des Esseintes, a stock which reaches its most extreme and certainly final representative in the neurotic central figure of Proust's narrative. For beyond his tor-

tured depths of introspective suffering, in spite of the rare beauty
with which Proust has invested them, it seems both futile and
dangerous to go. As Mr. Wilson states, we have probed the
world of the private imagination in isolation from the life of society to the furthest degree that seems at present either wise or
possible. As we move farther away from the war, the insistent
question that presents itself again is 'whether it is possible to
make a practical success of human society, and whether, if we
continue to fail, a few masterpieces, however profound or noble,
will be able to make life worth living even for the few people in
a position to enjoy them.' In asking this question so forcefully,
Mr. Wilson has proved his supreme value as a critic. Absorbed
in the present, he is not lost in its flux; he can indicate both its
weakness and its grandeur.

*Yale Review,* 1931

# *Irving Babbitt*

T HE tributes to Babbitt from forty of his students and associates do not compose a very rewarding type of book. Centering as they do on memories of his personality and conversation, they inevitably traverse the same ground again and again.
You begin keeping score on how many of them compare Babbitt
with Dr. Johnson; and you are sorry that Boswell's gifts have
been so rare. But the fullness of testimony leaves you in no
doubt as to the quality of the teacher, for as T. S. Eliot says

*Irving Babbitt: Man and Teacher,* edited by Frederick Manchester and
Odell Shepard. G. P. Putnam's Sons.
*Spanish Character and Other Essays* by Irving Babbitt, edited by Frederick
Manchester, Rachel Giese, and William F. Giese. Houghton Mifflin Co.

here, no one who 'was ever deeply impressed by Babbitt, can ever speak of him with that mild tenderness one feels towards something one has outgrown.'

In the face of the solidity of Babbitt's contribution to the criticism of ideas, you tend to forget now that his first book, *Literature and the American College,* was not published until he was past forty; and it is well to recall that the narrow conception of 'productive scholarship' which is still so damaging to the development of the humanities was arrayed to the full against him. As Paul Elmer More says, weighing his words with care, this 'very great teacher, perhaps even the greatest this country has ever produced . . . had to force his way up against resistance and through protracted depreciation. There was a moment in his mid-career when it was even touch and go whether he would not be dropped altogether.'

The chief value of this volume of appreciation—which notably does *not* come from Harvard—lies in the scattered materials it furnishes for the assessment that is still to be made of Babbitt's place in our intellectual history. One striking feature that is corroborated by all those who knew him longest is the extraordinarily early age at which his mature position took shape. William Giese remembers how Babbitt was deeply immersed in Buddhism while still an undergraduate. Frank Jewett Mather, whose intimacy dated from Babbitt's late twenties, observes that the humanist's doctrine was then already militant, and adds the useful particular that the immediate forces conditioning that doctrine were the writings of Arnold and the strong personal influence of Charles Eliot Norton. Emerson also played an important if elusive role in teaching Babbitt how to enunciate such startling maxims as 'The function of books is to teach us to despise them,' and how to become Man Thinking. Norman Foerster, in suggesting Babbitt's relation to the American background, finds in him 'the intuitive flexibility of an Emerson' combined with 'the logical firmness of a Jonathan Edwards.'

The two most comprehensive essays are those by George Roy Elliott and Paul Elmer More. Elliott gives the most rounded intellectual portrait. He has been able to evoke Babbitt's acrid humor no less than his vigor. He is also amused at his excesses—

though it remained for another contributor, who attended Babbitt's lectures in Paris, to overhear the exact note of French incomprehension: '*Mais que diable veut-il dire par ce "inner check?"*' Elliott has remembered such a significant statement from Babbitt's later years as 'I have had to live at a time when all the ideas which I know to be most vital for man have more and more declined.' His skill in definition has enabled him to characterize Babbitt's career as 'a restless campaign against American restlessness.' But More alone undertook any fresh evaluation of Babbitt's work. Agreeing with many others that Babbitt was much more effective as a talker than as a writer, he put his finger on a central defect in his style. It was the defect of a mind every aspect of whose system was so clear to it that instead of finishing one link in an argument and proceeding to the next, it would tend to crowd its 'whole thesis, at least implicitly, into each single paragraph,' with the result that any of his books, 'despite the inexhaustible variety of his illustrations, gives the impression of endless repetition.' More's most penetrating pages are those in which he analyzes why Babbitt felt it a prime necessity to rehabilitate the thought of the Orient for Western civilization, and why, unlike More himself, Babbitt found his deepest kinship in Buddha's denial 'of anything corresponding to Grace, in his insistence on the complete moral responsibility of the individual.'

Odell Shepard never will forget the somber conviction with which Babbitt once told him that he believed the modern world to be 'treading very near the edge of sudden disaster.' But among all this group of admirers, only Brooks Otis departs from academic assurance far enough to examine the relation of Babbitt's thought to the American world since 1930. Most of the others seem satisfied with Babbitt's version of the saving remnant, with his challenge to his fellow humanists that 'if the best men want to rescue themselves they will have to come together, support each other, preach a gospel.' Otis knows that the analogy with Edwards holds, not merely in Babbitt's courage before the grimmest facts and in his cutting through the easy optimistic solutions 'of lesser and more comfortable men,' but likewise in that both thinkers 'were contending for a faith without a future.'

Otis finds the 'atomic individualism' of the new humanism 'very frail in the chaos of immense social forces.' He recognizes that much of Babbitt's political thinking was reactionary. But he also knows that Babbitt was attacking the right things, that in laying bare the weaknesses of romanticism he has shown us the falseness of any antisocial aesthetic, that he has warned us, as strongly as anyone could, against the disasters of being either sheltered academics or shallow liberals.

The fourteen essays now collected together under the title *Spanish Character* range from 1898 to 1932, and so span virtually the whole of their writer's career. The editors have also provided a very useful subject index to his collected work, which runs to nearly a hundred pages. The essays group around the familiar centers of his other books. Four of them deal with French literature, with Pascal, with Racine and the antiromantic reaction, with the bicentenary of Diderot, with George Sand and Flaubert. Two are concerned with interpreting India to the West. An extended review of Stuart Sherman's book on Arnold gave Babbitt the opportunity to make his fullest statement of the relation of his own thought to that source. In another characteristic piece, 'Are the English Critical?' he answered a gusty 'No' while bearing down upon the superficial amenities of Saintsbury's history, at that time (1912) a bible to most professors of literature.

A more significant title-essay, instead of the early one containing the impressions he had absorbed during several months' walking through Spain, would have been the latest he wrote, his address to the American Academy of Arts and Letters in the autumn of 1932, 'The Problem of Style in a Democracy.' This raises, as do those on 'Humanist and Specialist' (1926) and 'President Eliot and American Education' (1929), many of the crucial questions that still face us. They add nothing to what Babbitt had already said elsewhere; but they remind us of many things which our educators now again like to slur over. Babbitt insisted on re-examining what was involved by President Eliot's substitution for the traditional training for culture and character of—in Eliot's own phrase—'training for service and power.' Bab-

bitt found Eliot so lacking in any capacity to understand evil
as not even to perceive how his phrase could boil down to what
European countries had long remarked, how 'we are altruistic
in our feelings about ourselves and imperialistic in our practice.'
When he was writing about Arnold, in 1917, Babbitt noted that
'democracy is now going forth on a crusade against imperialism.'
But he profoundly distrusted the bases of Wilsonian idealism,
and thought that our miscellaneous expansiveness could easily
become engulfed in the direct opposite of true democracy, the
lust for world domination.

Against that danger Babbitt posed, as always, the aristocratic
principle, the discipline of the mind and of the will. About all
he had to say for what I would hold to be the chief strength in
our American tradition was that 'the cult of the common man
that the equalitarian democrat encourages, is hard to distinguish
from commonness.' To any statement that the best bulwark
against imperialism consists in the continual extension of our
democracy through the socialization of our resources, he would
have turned a deaf ear, or rather, he would have charged in
full belligerence. But no matter how inadequate the whole drift
of a book like *Democracy and Leadership* may seem to our social complexity, or how frequently Babbitt's lack of sympathy
for our common life may seem to play into the hands of those
who would damn democracy as wasteful and undisciplined, his
words always bring us back to the phrase from Arnold he liked
to quote: 'the imperious lonely thinking power.' He demonstrated in his own practice the cardinal importance for any
civilization of a man's retaining his hold 'on the truths of the
inner life.' In a period of prophets and confessors he refused to
be either. He fulfilled the function of the critic, bleak though
his isolation often was.

*The New England Quarterly,* 1942

# Study Out the Land: T. K. Whipple

THESE essays by the late T. K. Whipple span the decade
from his earlier book *Spokesmen* (1928) to the year before
his death in 1939. The bent of his later development makes us
realize now the greatness of our critical loss, an impression that
is heightened by Edmund Wilson's prefatory memoir. Wilson,
who had known Whipple when both were students at Princeton,
produces here one of his most resilient portraits in the genre he
has inherited from Sainte-Beuve. The picture he presents is that
of a man slowly getting rid of the handicaps of conventional
scholarship and finding his real voice through the intensity of
his devotion to the equalitarian strain in our democracy. By the
time of *Spokesmen* such an evolution was well under way, even
though that study of 'modern writers and American life' was
marked by no particular originality. It responded to the challenge of Van Wyck Brooks' earlier thesis of our cultural 'failure'
by presenting the counterevidence, in a series of workmanlike
discussions of ten writers from Henry Adams to Eugene O'Neill.
Its virtues were those of solid fairness, and its concluding chapter, 'The American Situation,' made no exaggerated claims for
our promise.

The earliest essays in this present book start with some of the
same preoccupations. Whipple was still using many of Brooks'
terms. He was arguing that modern literature had largely failed
to be a literature of power, except on its lowbrow levels. He
seemed to regret that our writers had found Henry James more
interesting than Jesse, and in 'American Sagas' and 'The Myth
of the Old West' he advanced the position that in the 'crude

*Study Out The Land* by T. K. Whipple. University of California Press.

epic stories' of Zane Grey we have our nearest equivalent of *Beowulf* and the Norse skalds.

By the middle of the nineteen-thirties he was thinking more searchingly in his own terms. 'The American Predicament' is the best example both of the range of his concern and of his method. It gives a brief and simple statement of the problem created by the successive projection of new men against our new land. Its simplicity is deceptive, since Whipple had thought not only about 'the winning of the West,' but likewise about geography and anthropology and economics. He realized that environment could transform character in such a way that the second and third generations were often less civilized than the original immigrants. And he stressed how the initial equation, the relation between the enormously varied races and the varied kinds of land, had been rendered far more complicated by the introduction of a third factor, the overnight development of imported industrialism. In a companion essay, 'The American Land,' he made an indictment of the destructive and sterile role played by the exploiter.

Against such a background Whipple surveyed again the literature of the two decades between 1910 and 1930. He saw that that renaissance, like so many other renaissances in history, really marked a culmination rather than a beginning. He pointed out that most of its leading figures, like Frost, Lindsay, and Sherwood Anderson, had been born in the eighteen-seventies, and that their lives had been conditioned by two main forces, by the older agrarian tradition and by the cultural individualism attendant upon such a mode of existence. He believed that the literary scene at the end of the nineteen-thirties was much less rich than it had been twenty years before, and that the reason lay in the decay of those two forces, coincident with the end of the free land. He knew that if our literature was now 'in the doldrums,' the new equatorial line we must all cross is that 'which divides the individualist world from the collective.' He took for granted, as any acute observer today must, that the social processes in an industrialized civilization have already crossed that line. But he was equally aware that in America 'the corresponding transit of individuals' minds has barely begun.'

Whipple was sure that the preponderance of forces was, ultimately, on the radicals' side, but our literature told him how
far the battle was from being won. He now looked at our lowbrow successes with less complacence. He saw the dangers in
our cult of power and force, in the glorification of 'blood-think-
ing.' He saw that if there was such a thing as the 'fascist unconscious'—and he was afraid there was—'it is the product and
property of the lower middle class, and Jack London shared it.'
When Whipple turned to our most serious literature of the
'thirties, he could also make a mature diagnosis of Dos Passos'
weaknesses as a novelist. Noting the fact that the biographical
portraits are the most living parts of USA, Whipple realized how
that argued that Dos Passos' creation of his own characters is
incomplete. He found one clue in the autobiographical 'camera
eye,' where the author is so 'sensitive to impressions and so
amazingly devoid of anything else' that most of these sections
are spineless. The root cause of the general banality, indeed of
the almost pathological inertness of life in Dos Passos' books,
lies in his failure to grasp the dynamic relations of social change:
'Society is hardly just rotting away and drifting apart; the destructive forces are tremendously powerful and well organized,
and so are the creative ones.'

Such was Whipple's theme again in 'The American Way,' and
in the concluding essay of his book, 'Literature as Action.' He
stressed the continually renewed necessity of squaring freedom
with equality of opportunity. He pointed to the dangers that can
result from 'harboring individualist principles of action in a collective age,' and accepted the inevitability of drastic and even
fundamental social change. No more than Jefferson had been
was he disturbed by the word 'revolution.' The breadth of his
demands for a literature adequate to the needs of such an age
had emerged at the close of his discussion of USA: 'Dos Passos
does not call himself a Marxist; if he were more of one, he
might have written a better novel.' Whipple went on to eluci-
date what he meant. He wanted no mechanical simplification of
life. He argued, on the contrary, that the biographical portraits
are 'the most nearly Marxist' since they show 'the dynamic contradictions of our time in the only way they can be shown,

namely, as they occur in the minds and lives of whole men.' Whipple's concluding sentence is eloquent of his own aims: 'Nothing will do, in the end, but the whole man.'

*American Literature,* 1944

# The Scholarly Profession: Hardin Craig

IN scrutinizing the profession that he has practiced in half a dozen universities throughout the country, Hardin Craig has also given us a portrait of the literary scholar in action during the first half of the twentieth century. His victories may seem slight to the general public, his defeats and frustrations many; but Professor Craig has inherited from Bacon the firm belief that 'the pleasure and delight of knowledge and learning, it far surpasseth all other in nature.'

This vintage of the American scholar is also a rationalist with a hearty respect for Bishop Butler. But unlike the general run of rationalists he is not suspicious of the imagination, and devotes one of his chapters to urging its 'exact and vivid' cultivation. He knows that 'man's cultural life is one,' and that humanists neglect science and social science at great peril. He recognizes no hopeless gap between scholarship and literary interpretation, but insists that scholarship cannot afford to be as specialized as it became during the past generation. He is particularly effective in demonstrating the barrenness that resulted from the now hopefully obsolescent practice of literary scholars' restricting themselves to the arbitrary confines of a single century in a single country.

*Literary Study and the Scholarly Profession* by Hardin Craig. University of Washington Press.

He speaks of himself as a Crocean in his belief that it is the critic's role to repossess the works of any age for contemporary appreciation. But if he respects the aesthetic approach, his own best work, as in *The Enchanted Glass: The Elizabethan Mind in Literature,* has shown him as an historian of ideas. Though his chief attention has been devoted to Renaissance studies, he has fertile suggestions for further research, ranging from 'the liturgical basis of almost all medieval literature' to 'the popular life and culture of the eighteenth century.' He mentions Parrington—at whose university these lectures were delivered—as one great model in the American field, and indicates by so doing that, unlike many intellectual historians, he is not concerned merely with the abstract pattern of ideas, but with their truth. He follows Bacon and Butler in his desire to advance learning 'by way of the discovery of truth in terms of probability and proof.'

Two ideas that he holds to are those forming the double basis for democracy: 'the rights of man, which is an idea from the region of moral philosophy' and 'the dignity of man, which is a religious idea.' When he tests our educational institutions by the effectiveness with which they have propagated those ideas, he finds that the traditional small college has often been our most coherent cultural community. He holds that our period of immense expansion after the last war was 'an era of brick and stone and of intellectual defeat.' He lays no flattering unction to the souls of university administrators now priding themselves on their 'war-service' courses. For he knows that so far as the humanities in wartime are involved, the collapse of responsible concern has been little short of disgraceful.

Looking back over his long experience with universities, he sees a great danger in the gradual loss of power on the part of their faculties. For he believes that 'men of learning should control higher education and historically have always done so.' He quite rightly fears the autocracy that exists so incongruously in so many institutions of a democracy. But he seems not yet aware of the latest phase by which autocracy carries out its ends: through 'the managerial revolution' which has already overtaken many of our universities, and has spawned what Jacques Barzun has called 'Deans within Deans.'

Professor Craig has expressed doubt in his preface whether this record of his opinions was 'worth doing' as a book, and it must be freely admitted that trenchant as many of his observations are, the form in which he has cast them here is hardly more than shop-talk of a high level. He is sententious, discursive, and hortatory by turns, and the reader outside the shop will often find him dry. Yet some of his ideas about literature have a bearing on our immediate lives. When he reflects, as a longtime student of drama, that 'tragedy is in the nature of things, and comedy only an aspect,' we have a useful sentence with which to confront our horizon, ringed as it is with storms on every side.

*Saturday Review of Literature,* 1945

# Classic Models for Modern Critics

AN ingenious way of evaluating the aims and accomplishments of modern criticism was to induce several of our critics to undertake the task of re-evaluating some of the great critics of the past. Such was the function of a recent symposium at Johns Hopkins, though you might never guess the timeliness of the discourse from the neutral title of the resulting volume.

All criticism moves between the poles of abstract formulation and application to the concrete instance. In his introduction, Huntington Cairns laments the continued absence of a system-

*Lectures in Criticism* by R. P. Blackmur, Benedetto Croce, Henri Peyre, John Crowe Ransom, Herbert Read, Allen Tate, with an introduction by Huntington Cairns. Pantheon Books.

atic theory of criticism, but the more experienced practitioners
in the arts usually recognize, like Allen Tate, that: 'The permanent critics do not answer questions. They compel us to ask them
again.' For the general reader the first question to be posed
might seem to be that in Henri Peyre's piece on 'The Criticism
of Contemporary Writing.' Peyre, taking what he calls a French
view of the American scene, holds that 'one probably does not
understand the past aright if one fails to understand the present.'
This proposition is borne out, with a fascinating reverse twist,
by the particular re-evaluations. In every case the liveliest
thought is called forth by those aspects of the past having most
kinship to the present writer.

Ransom starts off by saying that his account of Aristotle might
well be subtitled 'the literary criticism of a man of letters who
had become a pedagogue, and of an idealist who had become a
naturalist.' Though the Senior Fellow of the Kenyon School is far
too modest ever to have thought of a parallel between himself
and the author of the *Poetics,* the quotation is a more exact description of Ransom's own career. Both he and Tate are concerned with 'appropriate structure,' with 'linguistic analysis,' with
'ambiguity,' and they may recall that at the Kenyon School last
summer I suggested the fine of a nickel for anyone who used the
word 'strategy' at the breakfast table again. Tate's consideration
of Longinus enables him appropriately to bring into play all
these key terms of the modern craftsman. It will be especially
offensive to specialists, since Tate remarks that he has just reread Longinus for the first time in twenty years. But this candor
underscores the fact that Longinus has seldom reached the common reader in our time. By letting this reader share in his observations as he makes them, Tate demonstrates how fundamental the questions are that Longinus compels us to reformu-
late. In addition, Longinus has stimulated him to one of his best
generalizations, on the theme that 'Style does not create the
subject; it discovers it.'

The arbitrary leap in this symposium from classical antiquity
to Coleridge is again characteristic of contemporary taste. And
no more symptomatic contemporary exists than Herbert Read,
whose chief critical role during the past thirty years has been as

the generous explorer of each successive new movement. It should not be surprising in view of his previous tracing of the roots of surrealism to the nineteenth-century romantics, that the Coleridge who absorbs him is the philosopher with kindred preoccupations to those of the existentialists. It may be more surprising, and pardonable only in the light of his advanced age, that Croce, invited to write on DeSanctis, treats him exclusively as the precursor of 'the principle of intuition' developed in Croce's own work.

Since Gide was unable, at the last moment, either to come or to send a paper, Peyre filled in for him, and took upon himself the responsibility of raising some of the wider questions for contemporary America. He is struck, as the European almost always is, by the peculiar isolation of the American writer. Concerning criticism in particular, he reflects upon the sad anomaly that 'the two richest nations in the modern world, the United States and Great Britain, are the only ones in which critical talent must starve or be stifled.' He knows how our leading magazines have altered for the worse even since the days of Howells, and observes that 'no future historian of American letters between 1919 and 1949 will find in *Harper's* or *The Atlantic Monthly* an accurate picture of the literary life of those crucial years.' I'm sorry to say that he also adds that the common reader, who used to find the new issues 'touched upon in *The New Republic* or in *The Nation* of twenty years ago, nowadays has to resign himself to living in a critical desert.'

Peyre's leading desire is for a greater play of taste, but he reveals curious lapses in his own. He lumps together Babbitt and Spingarn, who were at opposite poles, and makes a sweeping dismissal of the serious criticism of our time that has been produced under the aegis of Eliot and Richards. In this he receives odd support from Blackmur's paper, 'A Burden for Critics.' As a painstaking practitioner in 'the new criticism,' Blackmur has always been at his best when he has stayed closest to textual analysis. But now in his consciousness of the limitations in that method, he denies it too much. Aware that it has sprung out of our renewed concern with the English metaphysicals and the French symbolists, he falls into a broad misstatement when he says that it is therefore 'useless for Dante, Chaucer, Goethe, or Racine.' What one finds in the 'structure' and 'texture' of a poem (to use Ransom's terms) naturally varies with the poet at hand. But resilient attention to language, the primary resource of every poet, can always come up with new treasure—as, for example, Martin Turnell, one of the *Scrutiny* critics, has just been demonstrating in the case of Racine.

Peyre goes even farther astray in lamenting that the critics in the little magazines have reserved their praise for the less 'energetic' talents. It could easily be documented that much of the pioneering work in developing a wider public for, say, Joyce, Kafka, or Faulkner has gone on in the pages of such periodicals. But the central dilemma remains in the widening gap between the blurb writing that passes for reviewing in the organs of mass circulation, and the criticism that often becomes too serious in the wrong sense from the consciousness, on the part of writers in the little magazines, that they may have a fit audience but far too few. It would be illuminating to see what would happen if a periodical with the circulation, for instance, of the *Saturday Review* set itself to give its readers essays and reviews of a consistently exacting standard. Certainly anyone now in touch with the big postwar classes in our universities can realize that thousands are graduating each spring with an alert desire to hold together their knowledge of the present and the past. Is it impossible to provide a supply for this demand?

*New Republic,* 1949

# Selfless Devotion to the Arts: Paul Rosenfeld

THIS unusual book came into being because Jerome Mellquist possesses the same kind of selfless devotion to the arts that Paul Rosenfeld possessed. At the time of Rosenfeld's death in his mid-fifties, two summers ago, Mellquist was shocked by the hasty unawareness of what had been lost, by the callous shortness of memory that makes it so hard for us in this country to feel a really living sense of tradition. So he and Lucie Wiese conceived that the best way to remind us of Rosenfeld's value as a critic was to ask as many of the subjects of his criticism as possible, musicians and artists and writers, to say what his work had meant to them.

Lewis Mumford has sketched the essential history of Rosenfeld's association with *The Seven Arts* and *The Dial*, and Alfred Kreymborg has recounted in greater detail his tireless collaboration on *The American Caravan*. These periodicals mark the time of Rosenfeld's flourishing, but it comes as a shock to note that eight of his nine books appeared within the span of the nineteen-twenties. Yet Rosenfeld's spirit contributed to the hopeful buoyancy of that period, not to its other moods of cynicism and escape. 'For the first time among these modern men and women,' he wrote in *Port of New York*, 'I found myself in an America where it was good to be.'

In the best essay in the volume Edmund Wilson has provided a portrait of Rosenfeld's mind and temperament in the disciplined and deft tradition of Sainte-Beuve. Wilson makes the same point that Mellquist does in his introductory essay: that Rosenfeld really began where James Huneker left off, that he

*Paul Rosenfeld: Voyager in the Arts*, edited by Jerome Mellquist and Lucie Wiese. Creative Age Press.

175

brought something of the same impressionistic gusto, but that he turned his attention, as Huneker had not, to the American scene, and that he conceived it his primary function to encourage his contemporaries through what he called 'disinterested companionship in art.' Wallace Stevens has a grateful epithet for that function. He calls Rosenfeld a 'shaper': 'he was shaping, helping to give shape, to those to whom that meant becoming choate.' Waldo Frank has another. He states that even before Rosenfeld found his chief role as a critic of music, he 'was already, in his literary tastes, not a seer, not a thinker, but a *listener*.'

Rosenfeld once remarked that someone ought to see to it that every young musician got a hearing, and then added, with the modesty that struck everyone who knew him, he guessed that was his particular responsibility. To anyone who ever watched him looking at paintings, the word 'listener' must seem just as apt for the absolutely absorbed attentiveness that he brought to each new canvas.

Again and again the half a hundred contributors here recur to the theme enunciated by Mumford: 'I know of no other critic in our time who has approached the creations of other artists with so little envy and with so much love.' Allen Tate phrases it in Rosenfeld's own conviction that 'the best attack on the bad is the loving understanding and exposition of the good.' Louise Bogan underscores it when she says that Rosenfeld felt 'privileged' to respond to the works of his own age. When so much criticism is written by intellectuals without love, that sense of privilege gives a lift to the air.

What this meant to many artists, especially musicians, is attested by the varied statements from William Schuman, Carlos Chavez, Elliott Carter, Charles Ives, Aaron Copland, Charles Mills, Ernest Bloch, Edgar Varèse, Roy Harris, David Diamond, and Lehman Engel. Among the most interesting passages are those where the younger composers describe their experiences when Rosenfeld asked them to play for him, and recount the helpful questions he asked and the kind of encouragement he offered.

Harold Weston quotes some of the remarks that made such a critic invaluable to a painter. Robert Penn Warren tells how

Rosenfeld, in search of new writers for *The Caravan,* first prompted him to experiment with fiction. E. E. Cummings, Kenneth Patchen, and John Marin each contributes a memorial poem, all of them too slight or too personal to convey very much. Amid the wealth of these testimonials it is unfortunate that someone did not undertake a more systematic account of Rosenfeld's published work as a whole. There are many obiter dicta, which tend to go over and over the same ground, but except for Joseph Warren Beach's brief analysis, there is too little attention paid even to the qualities and defects of Rosenfeld's elaborately impressionistic style.

The most trenchant psychological formulation of what happened to Rosenfeld's career, of why he came to consider himself a 'failure,' is made by Gerald Sykes. In placing Rosenfeld among the 'sons' rather than among the 'fathers,' Sykes suggests both his eagerness and his helplessness before the inexorable history of our time. Yet his latest book, *Discoveries of a Music Critic* (1936), would seem to be a solid advance over his *Musical Portraits* and *Musical Chronicle* of the decade before. And though as a Jew of German ancestry he grew increasingly appalled by the Nazis' destruction of the Germany he loved, toward the end of the war he quickened to several new projects, among them an extended study of the various literary genres.

His last completed work was the introduction to his posthumous *Sherwood Anderson Reader.* The letters from Anderson to Rosenfeld make the most moving tribute of all those gathered here. For Anderson, while recognizing how different his aims in writing were from those of Rosenfeld's 'jeweled' prose, felt nevertheless a deep kinship with him. He wrote once: 'Whenever I am in any creative work, I go to your work and draw from it something I need.' He also asked: 'Does the tendency we both felt in the life about us to feel life a bit clearer and sweeter in America remain?'

*The New York Times Book Review,* 1948

# V. THE EFFORT TO REPOSSESS THE PAST

# New Standards in American Criticism, 1929

I T is time for the history of American literature to be rewritten. For fifty years our manuals have been divided into sections on political and geographic lines: we have spoken of the periods of our literature as the Colonial, First National, and Second National; of its groups as the New England and the Knickerbocker—just as if (Norman Foerster remarks) our subjects were banks. We have thus wholly obscured the two interrelating factors essential to any real comprehension of our literature: the implications of American life, and the organic relation of our thought to that of Europe. On the one hand, there has never been any adequate account of the significant part played either by our Puritan background or by the symbol of the frontier in forming our most characteristic American minds; on the other, such things as romanticism and realism have invariably been charted simply as ways of writing, instead of as inevitable reactions to the spirit of their times, here as well as abroad. Literature has been studied in a vacuum without relation to anything but itself, a genealogy of printed works, one book begetting another.

Its new historian must take into account every side of American culture: the effect of our religion and education in forming it (although anything like a complete study of either of these forces has still to be written), the increasing ease of communication and travel, the movies and cartoons, the Ford, and the radio, the significance of the fact that the village reads Whittier and Longfellow, and the city, Whitman and James. In brief, he must

The Reinterpretation of American Literature, edited by Norman Foerster. Harcourt, Brace & Co.
American Criticism by Norman Foerster. Houghton Mifflin Co.

follow the impressive lead of historians like Turner, Andrews, Adams, and Beard, who have given us a new vision of the forces dominant in our political and social past. But he must not lose himself in his background, or forget that he is dealing primarily with literature. He must remember that his real quarry is aesthetic values, and that perhaps one does not have to master the importance of Jacksonian democracy to read intelligently 'Rappaccini's Daughter.' Above all, he must be aware that the imperative thing for American scholarship today is not so much the accumulation of small facts as a sensitive interpretation of them.

Before any such literary historian can arise—and this is the main point of *The Reinterpretation of American Literature,* edited by Mr. Foerster—many incisive monographs must be produced. The various contributors to this volume, who include such distinguished scholars as Howard Mumford Jones, Vernon L. Parrington, and A. M. Schlesinger, are united in their efforts to point out suitable fields for such studies. Mr. Foerster's own book on *American Criticism* is an illustration of what they think should be done. His exhaustive analyses of the four principal critical minds in our nineteenth century throw many important details into a new light. The reason for Poe's enormous influence on poets of the magnitude of Baudelaire and Verlaine and for his comparative neglect at home has never emerged so clearly as in this elaboration of his theory of art: the metallic brittleness of his conception of beauty, his insistence on a brief unity, his fine sense of restraint, his artful creation of the strange— all these qualities are much closer to French sympathies than to ours. It is also of supreme importance to be reminded that Whitman was a critic in the sense that Wordsworth was, that he believed great literature must be an organic expression of its age and nation, and so set out to define what he conceived to be the fundamental implications of a democratic nation, and an age of science. Whitman has too often been considered the poet of random generality and vagueness. It can be hoped that Mr. Foerster's essay will cause more readers to discover that *Democratic Vistas* is packed with acute observations on the trend of American life.

The essay on Emerson is an equally useful synthesis, but in that on Lowell one is conscious of the limitations of Mr. Foerster's work. His scholarship there gets the better of his critical sense: by laboriously codifying Lowell's abundant comments on literature he has produced a critical theory of greater weight than any that Lowell's writings actually possess. The fact is that Lowell's essays are too diffuse and too purely literary to have stood the test of time, and so when Mr. Foerster makes Lowell's criticism seem important, he has been working in the very vacuum we have been warned against. This is even more seriously true about Mr. Foerster's concluding section on the twentieth century. For there, instead of an analysis of individual critics, he states the creed he thinks our contemporary literature should follow, a brand of modern humanism. This doctrine, even in the work of its most sinewy-minded exponent, Mr. Irving Babbitt, seems increasingly arid, for it insists too blindly on what ought to be, without any view of the actual. Wise standards are the greatest need in American life and literature today, but they will never be achieved through scholars pointing them out already created for us in Plato and Aristotle. We shall have to create them for ourselves in relation not only to the literature of the past but to the demands of our own environment. To this end the efforts of such writers as Mr. T. S. Eliot and Mr. Edmund Wilson, although more uncertain and experimental, seem far more fertile than those of Mr. Foerster.

*Yale Review,* 1929

## An Excited Debater

THIS book is the first full-length survey of American literature from a Marxian point of view, and as such has been accorded respectful attention. The early reviews agreed for the most part in regarding it as a significant piece of vigorous pioneering. Mr. Harry Elmer Barnes went further in stating that as a radical interpretation of our literature it deserved to rank with the late Vernon Parrington's interpretation from a liberal angle.

Building on the thesis that America has been the great bourgeois experiment as Soviet Russia is today the great proletarian experiment, Mr. Calverton gives, in the latter portions of his work, a forceful description of the gradual disintegration of our nineteenth-century middle-class individualism as measured by the change in our writers from the confident optimism of 'Self-Reliance' and the 'Song of the Open Road' to the widespread disillusion and despair of the present. His conclusion is that we have now reached the impasse where our artists, for the most part the product of middle-class culture, can no longer find meaning in the ideals of that culture, and consequently, no longer possessing an adequate standard of values, are unable to perform the highest function of art, interpretation of life. From such an impasse he finds one highroad to liberation in a new integration of the individual with society, or in his own words: the nineteenth-century 'belief in the common man was a belief in him as a petty bourgeois individualist; our belief must be in him as proletarian collectivist.'

Unfortunately for the value of Mr. Calverton's book, this

*The Liberation of American Literature* by V. F. Calverton. Charles Scribner's Sons.

184

thesis is only one of the many which he develops and then compels to interlock with the mechanical rigidity of an intricate system of cogwheels. His opening chapter is devoted to what he calls the colonial complex. Starting on the basis that no country can have a national literature until it is established economically as a world power, and that America was hardly such a power in any full sense until after 1914, he argues that therefore there was no real American literature until the twentieth century. His determination to prove our complete cultural dependence up to that time leads him into many novel statements. The work of Cooper and Hawthorne was scarcely less English in spirit than that of their British contemporaries, though precisely which contemporaries is not indicated, the proof offered being that *The Scarlet Letter* reads more like 'a romantic legend than a realistic fiction,' and that Cooper's Natty Bumppo was 'nothing more than an Anglicized red man'—a view of the Leatherstocking's color no more unique than that of the subservience of his creator to a European culture of which he was as forthright and clear-eyed a critic as any writer living today. Emerson patterned his style on Carlyle's; Lathrop's remark that Hawthorne's creations were 'statuesquely molded like Goethe's' is taken as a proof of their having been derived from him; the early readers of 'Thanatopsis' were carried away because they were reminded of Shelley and Keats, a difficult feat, for it was written in 1811, before either of these poets had started to publish. These views all find illustration within the compass of two sample pages, although, to be sure, they are sufficiently amplified elsewhere in the book.

Apparently the initial fact that 'we took over the language of the mother country' instead of immediately evolving one of our own was a large factor in preventing our development of a native quality (Mr. Calverton at one point calls it 'nativity'); so that one can speak of the 'Russianness' of Dostoevsky, the 'Frenchness' of Anatole France, but can find no developed pattern of 'Americannesses' in Thoreau. (The compound words are Mr. Calverton's.) On the other hand, Mac Leisch's *New Foundland* (both the author and title being thus spelt on page 35) possesses such 'Americanness' in 'daring form,' which makes it hard to see on what ground Mr. Calverton is basing his distinctions, because

Mr. MacLeish has obviously been far more affected by foreign
cultures than Thoreau was. And the way in which he develops
such distinctions indicates a curious blindness to the necessity of
the constant fertilization of the thought of one country by another, and the convenient vacuum in which a good deal of his
argument takes place.

Mr. Calverton fares no better when he proceeds in his second
chapter to argue away the 'Puritan myth' as less fundamental in
the explanation of the development of American culture than the
struggle between the upper and the lower bourgeois. For although it is of great importance to stress the middle-class dominance that has existed in America from the start, Mr. Calverton
again applies his abstractions in such a mechanical way as to
simplify the pattern out of all recognition. Anne Bradstreet, for
example, was 'scarcely more than a feminine counterpart of
Michael Wigglesworth,' and 'imitative in every line, her stanzas
show all the unfortunate effects of that synthesis of the colonial
complex and the petty bourgeois philosophy of life.' Waiving the
question of the lack of discrimination involved in grouping together two writers so unlike not only in their intentions but in
the whole quality of their thought and spirit, by what accuracy
can the label of petty bourgeois be given to the daughter of
Governor Dudley who had been brought up at Tattersall Castle,
where her father was the Earl of Lincoln's steward before emi-
grating to America, especially when Thomas Morton is described
a few pages later as 'an aristocrat in both psychology and
origin'? Also what possible meaning can the 'colonial complex'
have in relation to a well-educated young woman who was
eighteen years old before she came to this country, whose early
writing shows everywhere the mark of her enthusiastic readings
of Du Bartas then at the height of his popularity, but who gradually, as her life ripened into maturity in America, found a lyrical
expression, fragile and tentative, but no longer imitative and
unmistakably her own?

Similar distortions appear throughout, owing in about equal
share to the way in which Mr. Calverton hypostatizes his abstractions, and to his utter inability to make a measured statement.
Thus Jonathan Edwards' dismissal by his congregation is not

only a symbol of the 'overthrowal' of the petty by the upper bourgeoisie, but also marks the last stand of religious idealism, for with Edwards' defeat 'every trace of that idealism disappeared,' and 'religion speedily became—what it is today—the personification of a yes-man in social and economic life'—a generous ignoring of the main development of religious idealism from Edwards through the whole transcendental movement. In such a quotation as this last one is made clear Mr. Calverton's addiction to current jargon, his ready substitution of cliché for thought, as well as his fatally easy simplifications of society, and, most damaging for a sociological critic, his lack of an historical sense. It is set solemnly down in reproach that 'laissez faire economics . . . and the modern democratic conception of society, were not defended by the ruling class in the Bay Colony.' As to Hawthorne, 'at best he had little of the sansculotte about him.'

Such looseness of both thought and writing vitiates the value of even those limited portions of the book where Mr. Calverton seems to have adequate knowledge of what he is talking about, as in his energetic account of the shaping force of the frontier, or in his penetrating remarks on the society that has formed Eugene O'Neill and Robinson Jeffers. The principal objection to his book is not that it is written on a series of oversimplified theses, frequently damaging as those have been shown to be, but that he constantly shifts his ground like an excited debater. At one moment, upper middle-class Puritanism 'never reached these shores,' but only the lower middle-class elements of the Dissenters; yet, shortly after, the American Puritan is described as representing 'in his whole ideology the unresting zeal of a merchant class which had to bend all its energy to fight the domination of the landed class'—a landed class the very existence of which in America he has already frequently denied. When it suits his convenience the whole moral attitude of the nineteenth century was merely weak and shallow hypocrisy, thinly masking the vital preoccupations of the time; on the other hand, as a result of the strength of this same moral attitude 'our literature for several generations to come was emasculated of all claim to vigor and veracity,' a statement which overlooks the existence of Whitman and Melville, but such an oversight is not difficult when one is as eager as Mr. Calverton to prove a point. Especially when he comes to contemporary literature, he betrays this constant shifting in his approach. Whereas Cooper was merely an American Scott, nothing foreign is to be found in Dreiser, except 'a trace' of Zola; and it is with Upton Sinclair that we come to 'the first signs of radical culture in this country,' a remark that makes it clear that he has missed the essential note of revolt and protest that has been in our literature from the start.

Thus the question is raised on nearly every page of exactly how much of the literature he is discussing Mr. Calverton has actually read, how much he has simply examined from the point of view of fitting it into his theses. The quality of his ignorance is frequently naive. The *Bay Psalm Book* was a Bible; Anne Bradstreet and Thomas Godfry [*sic*] are grouped together as contemporaries though one hundred and twenty-five years separated their births—an error resulting largely, one suspects, from the fact that selections from their poems follow each other in certain anthologies. Dunbar was 'nothing more than a negro prototype of Longfellow,' which leaves the reader to choose whether Mr. Calverton has again mixed his chronology or is unaware of the meaning of prototype. But it is hardly worth while to multiply instances of small errors in a book so filled with large ones, other than to remark that such things as the slovenly grammar, the wrong tenses, the obvious misquotations and misspellings all witness not only to the author's haste, but to an inexcusable carelessness on the part of a reputable publishing house.

That this book has been praised as a pioneering work must, therefore, be set down to a similar carelessness and haste on the part of a lamentably large number of our critics. For although there is especial value today in the insistence that literature is organically related to the society that produces it, it has been apparent for some time to others than Marxians that the movement of our culture has been from the center outwards, that our most powerful individuals have again and again been dangerously isolated from or opposed to society as a whole, and that the construction of a society in which both the individual and the group can have some measure of full development is the gravest problem with which we are faced. The service of the Marxian critic could lie not in the constant repetition of the catchwords, bourgeois and proletarian, but in some at least tentative definition of the meaning of these terms in relation to American society; not in emotional proclamations of an unexamined faith, but in coming to grips with the problem of what the virtues and defects of a proletarian culture in America might really be. The pioneering Marxian critic, unlike Mr. Calverton, will have to have a solid knowledge of American history and literature, and a resiliency of mind that is not content to warp all materials to fit his theories. But Mr. Calverton, in spite of his energy and enthusiasm, is clearly more interested in saying the timely thing than in making sure that what he says is true.

*The New England Quarterly*, 1933

## The Great Tradition: A Counterstatement

BY making the first comprehensive analysis of our literature since the Civil War which throws all of its various tendencies into a logical pattern, Granville Hicks has written a very valuable book. Heretofore, except for the brilliant chapters in Vernon Parrington's unfinished *Development of Critical Realism*, we have had only the usual handbook method of writing literary history by listing the names and achievements of every possible author. There has been no sustained effort to relate the full sweep of our literature during these seventy years to the basic forces in American history, nor to interpret it from a coherent

*The Great Tradition: An Interpretation of American Literature Since the Civil War* by Granville Hicks. Macmillan.

point of view. Mr. Hicks' point of view is Marxian, and he has succeeded in his pioneering effort where V. F. Calverton's *Liberation of American Literature* almost entirely failed, since he has not fallen into that author's facile theorizing, but has gained a mastery of his subject by very wide reading, and has reflected penetratingly on what he has read.

His test of the value of an author is: to what extent do his books reveal the actual economic forces at work in the life of his time? After an opening chapter which stresses how the development of industrialism began rapidly to separate American life from the assumptions of the generation of Emerson, Mr. Hicks asks that question in turn of successive groups. He starts by probing the shortcomings of the sectionalists of the 'seventies and 'eighties: the way in which they finally wasted their talents in overemphasis of surface differences of dialect between their regions, instead of realizing that the clue to understanding any region lay in perceiving its relation to the general patterns that were shaping the country as a whole. But the full pertinency of his question is particularly demonstrated when he comes to the first efforts to write realistic novels of politics or labor, to Henry Adams' *Democracy* or John Hay's *Breadwinners*. The reasons for the relative inadequacy and emptiness of those books have never been so sharply apparent: in spite of their wide contacts, neither author had sufficient imaginative insight into the significance of the events he was describing to enable him to create a living picture. It was not enough for Hay to state, in the later reissue of his novel, that he had not intended to give a typical account of conditions, nor to attack the working class or even trade unions; or to maintain that he had simply made use of certain actual events that had come to his attention. For, as Mr. Hicks points out:

It was impossible to describe even 'a commonplace soldier with a large property,' if one refused to take into consideration the economic processes of the time. It was impossible to describe even 'a little society, organized for his own ends by a criminal,' if one paid no attention to the real grievances of the workers, the actual mechanism of strikes, and the extent and ideals of labor associations.

Mr. Hicks does not make the mistake of the doctrinaire of applying a more severe standard to authors with whose social attitude he has little sympathy; he is just as exacting with Jack London and Upton Sinclair as he is with Adams or Hay. He has a searching paragraph on what a socialist novelist might be expected to accomplish, indicating how such a writer's approach should enable him to perceive a unifying thread in the seemingly disparate complexities of the surface of events, and thus to make an interpretation of the whole. But Mr. Hicks is aware that neither of these two novelists arrived at such a goal. He remarks astutely that 'their work, unfortunately, shows that official allegiance to a theory and the development of a way of looking at life are two different things.' London, an avowed apostle of the Revolution, was able to furnish his wide audience with a romantic escape from their own drab surroundings, but not at all to help them to understand those surroundings and thus to suggest ways of transforming them. Sinclair's novels have failed of a fully rounded development, not because they are propaganda— indeed, in the strict sense of attempting to extend belief in a doctrine, much great art has been propaganda, as Dante or Milton could illustrate as well as *Walden* or *Leaves of Grass*. But Mr. Hicks has laid his finger on Sinclair's weakness: although he possesses really notable gifts for collecting a wide diversity of material, he has been unable for the most part fully to assimilate it, and has thus remained an investigator, and not an artist in any full degree.

So far I have illustrated Mr. Hicks' method mainly from his approach to various aspects of the development of the social novel, and, indeed, it is on such ground that he makes his solidest observations. But throughout the other portions of his book, as well, he reveals the power and clarity that the critic gains by consistently held principles of evaluation. Each individual work is seen in some perspective; instead of the general inconclusive blurring by which most literary history reduces the recent period in particular to a formless mass, the achievement of each author is measured against a defined standard. Equipped thus, Mr. Hicks can suggest reasons for the fundamental incoherence of Eugene O'Neill, that both his expression of frustration and despair, and his less frequent celebration of life, as in *Lazarus Laughed*, moving though they often are at the theatrical moment, are upon reflection 'somehow beside the point.' That is to say, in Mr. Hicks' estimate, they possess a certain air of unreality owing to their partial lack of correspondence with the really central elements that are struggling in contemporary society. On similar grounds Mr. Hicks can make an able analysis of the shortcomings of Robinson Jeffers, simply by showing how his heaped-up horrors take us so far from ordinary experience that in the end 'neither his terrible themes nor his desperately violent style can create in us an effect more enduring than the brief trembling that follows an evil dream.'

The sharp conclusiveness of Mr. Hicks' book makes it the challenge which criticism should be. In his view the great tradition of our literature from Emerson to Dos Passos is in the voice of protest against abuses and of revolution to transform them. In his final pages he sums up the course which this tradition has taken since the Civil War. It found a spokesman in Howells, who, in such a book as *A Traveler from Altruria*, 'taught himself to think in terms of a new order, and he and Bellamy tried to create, in imagination and in fact, a better world. Garland and Norris denounced oppression; Herrick and Phillips worked for reform; Sinclair and London called themselves socialists. This is the great tradition of American literature.'

That list is significant in its omission of the three names which the ordinary reader would probably consider those of the principal figures in our late nineteenth century, Mark Twain, Henry James, and Emily Dickinson. The omission is deliberate, and clearly defines the limits of Mr. Hicks' conception of the nature of literature. For him literature is inevitably a form of action; and it has been one of the great services of Marxian criticism that it has brought to the fore the principle that 'art not only expresses something, but also does something.' There are, however, various ways of defining what it does. There is, for instance, the form of action expressed by the political pamphlet, of which the writings of Thomas Paine are still our most effective example; and this is kindred to the form of action in the problem novel which focuses its whole attention on presenting the consequences of specific wrongs, and by the very strength of its recreation of them serves as a weapon in their destruction. But if art is to be adequately described as a form of action, it must be realized that action can not mean simply the immediate righting of wrongs. The greatest art performs its most characteristic action in more subtle ways; it 'does something,' in the novels of Fielding or Proust, by bringing its reader a new understanding or a fresh insight into the full meaning of existence. It thus acts on life by giving it release and fulfillment.

Two principal ways in which art has achieved fulfillment in America are by means of poetry and humor; and it is notable that Mr. Hicks does scant justice to both of them. Although he mentions in his bibliography Constance Rourke's excellent *American Humor: A Study of the National Character,* he does not himself seem to consider the prevalence of humor to be a factor of much import in our tradition. There are no smiles in his treatment of Mark Twain, who, partly following Van Wyck Brooks, he regards as a writer who did a good deal less than he had given promise of doing. Joel Chandler Harris is mentioned in a clause among the minor group of local colorists; and there is no mention at all of Ring Lardner, which is particularly surprising, since his rare combination of sardonic wit and quick understanding gave him the kind of closeness to actual American life which Mr. Hicks is repeatedly seeking in more professedly serious writers. As to the value of the creator of Uncle Remus, Mr. Hicks was again blinded perhaps by a seeming lack of important purpose. Harris did not simply 'preserve the folklore of the Negro'; he created a small world, the very fantasy of which is an accurate mirror of many elements of existence, and which is certainly comparable in its value to the world created by Sarah Orne Jewett, whom Mr. Hicks estimates very justly.

Perhaps a certain misconception of how an artist creates his world is at the root of Mr. Hicks' lack of a full appreciation of what is accomplished by poetry. He is entirely aware that the developed artist does so create a world, which is simply another way of saying that he gives full order and coherence to his material by means of a sustained vision of life. In fact, it is pre-

cisely owing to such creation that Miss Jewett, in Mr. Hicks'
view, ranks apart from and above the other regionalists of her
time.

Elsewhere, however, he is not always so successful in perceiving the value of this function of the artist. The point can be
illustrated by one of his remarks on Henry James, whom he discusses, with Sarah Jewett and Emily Dickinson, in a chapter
called 'Fugitives.' He has great respect for James' skill, but his
final quarrel with him and the reason why he thinks the majority
of readers are wise to reject him is summed up in this question:
'Why should one read a novel if it does not give him a sense that
he is moving, with enhanced powers of perception and a greater
certainty as to direction, through the strange world of which he
is part?' There is obviously only one answer; but before you can
be sure that James does not give you that sense, you must examine what you mean by 'world.' In Mr. Hicks' opinion, both the
settings and preoccupations of James' characters are so remote
from ordinary American existence, and his handling of them so
selected and specialized that his work amounts merely to an
elaborate technical game. But surely for an artist to be able to
give the reader an increased sense of the 'world of which he is
part' does not demand that he take for his material only the
surface details of the kind of life with which the reader is most
familiar, for in that case any reader's comprehension of art would
be restricted to the realistic novel of his own day and circumstance.

The use of the word 'world' here is ambiguous: the artist may
or may not give an exact picture of everyday life; what he must
give is a heightened sense of reality, a feeling on the reader's
part that he understands certain aspects of the human problem
more fully for having read this book. That Henry James' 'world'
was limited is increasingly apparent as the years go on; but the
point to be noted is that within these limits he came closer to
creating fully projected complex characters than any other American writer of his time. Mr. Hicks objects that 'some knowledge
of economic processes is obviously essential to the interpretation
not only of America but also of England'; and, to be sure, James'
people often seem to be moving on an unsupported plateau. But

granting all the restrictions of his scope of knowledge which prevented him from being one of the very few absolutely major novelists, a Balzac or a Dostoevsky, are not his most completely realized individuals sufficiently part of the 'world,' even in Mr. Hicks' sense, to make their fates lastingly moving? Although we are not given any detailed account of how Christopher Newman or Lambert Strether made their money, the inadequacy of the society which produced them is written large over their characters. The Marxian critic is beyond doubt increasingly justified in his desire to wipe out such laws as permit Isabel Archer to possess her large inheritance; but that should not prevent his seeing that the intricately suggestive portrayal here of the impact of sophistication upon idealistic ignorance enables such a character to suggest permanent attributes of humanity beyond the confines of any given milieu.

This matter is fundamental enough to try to put in another way. It is Mr. Hicks' assumption that literature does not speak to man directly unless it grows out of and deals with his own immediate material preoccupations. Mr. Hicks establishes this conception at the outset in accounting for the lack of interest in Melville in the period after the Civil War; and it is throughout one of his standards of measurement. As a result he can find little satisfaction in our poetry. He opposes the admirers of Robinson who contend 'that he concerns himself with the eternal problems,' for Mr. Hicks maintains that the 'only problems we really know are those posed by our own age.' But how do we know them? When I mentioned above that one of the principal ways in which art in America had achieved fulfillment had been through poetry, what I had in mind was the strain of affirmation of the ideal that runs from the seventeenth century to the twentieth, sometimes ecstatic, sometimes somber, not necessarily taking form in verse, but running through Jonathan Edwards to Emerson and Emily Dickinson, from John Woolman to Whitman, throbbing at the heart of Thoreau's discoveries in *Walden,* finding its most tragic voice in the darker passages of *Moby Dick,* often coming to articulation in only a minor key, but still being our principal expression of the aspiration of the individual spirit. To that strain Robinson relates. Far from not concerning himself with the problems of his age, in his most searching poem, 'The Man Against the Sky,' he has examined all the soaring assumptions that his generation inherited from transcendentalism, and has shown where they ended, that the gleam was dying down, that what was left for a man in that tradition was, as has been said, simply 'a quiet curbing of despair.' Such a probing analysis of the tragic position of the individual in a world where nineteenth-century individualism no longer looked bright would seem to me the very way in which the poet, by his sensitive insight, penetrates beneath the surface flux of his age, and thus sounds its deepest voice.

For Mr. Hicks, however, the poet learns fully to know his age only by coming to grips with its dominant economic forces. On such grounds Robert Frost is dismissed as belonging to a moribund tradition. He possesses great talents, but he can not be a 'mature and satisfying poet,' for he writes of the countryside, largely as it has been for generations, instead of coping directly with the violent new industrial cities. But the clearest illustration of the sharp limits which Mr. Hicks puts upon the poet's way of gaining relevant knowledge is furnished by his passing remark that Dos Passos was less 'drugged' than the other young Harvard poets 'by Baudelaire, Petronius, and the Old Howard.' Mr. Hicks seems to have no suspicion that reading *Les Fleurs du Mal* might be anything more than an unheeding escape from reality by means of a variety show. He does not perceive that Baudelaire's pages provide the very evidence which he finds wanting in Frost of the immediate tragic impact of the modern city upon the individual, and are thus capable of bringing their twentieth-century reader into direct lyric contact with reality by articulating what he has himself often felt.

But any such conception of the function of the poet is hardly visualized by Mr. Hicks. In his definition of the way in which the poet should transform society as well as expressing it, a great premium is put upon hopeful optimism. He holds to the proposition that dismay and doubt sap the vitality of the artist's imagination, a proposition not to be verified by *Hamlet* or the satires of Jonathan Swift; nor indeed by the tragic intensity that lies beneath the light surface of many of the lyrics of Emily Dickinson, whom Mr. Hicks inevitably thinks lacking in the vigor which would have come to her if she had been more fully a part of the society of her time. Mr. Hicks does not seem to realize that doubt and dismay, difficult though they may be for the individual and often tragic in their implications, are an integral part of human life; and that the service of the poet can lie in resolving them by full expression. As a result he misses entirely the value of T. S. Eliot, whom he groups curiously in a five-page subsection along with the humanists and Thornton Wilder. For Mr. Hicks the futility of Eliot's development is sufficiently proved by the fact that, in *Ash Wednesday,* 'he can now speak neither as poet of faith nor as poet of doubt.' He is unaware that the richness of that series of poems depends on the very precision with which Eliot suggests the almost impalpable alternations of the mind between skepticism and belief. For he is equally unaware that the lyric poet is at the vanguard of his time not in the same way as the political orator; that it is not the poet's main function, though one he may sometimes fulfill incidentally, to define and proclaim a new program of action; but rather to give the most accurate account he can of the particular quality of life as he has discovered it to be by means of his mind and senses. The poet is thus, in F. R. Leavis' phrase, 'at the most conscious point of the race in his time,' in direct proportion to the extent to which he makes articulate what his contemporaries feel. And the chief value of Eliot's poetry, which gives it greater substance than would seem to be indicated by its somewhat narrow range, has lain in the uncompromising integrity with which he has striven for and achieved the exact expression of the complexity that he knows to inhere in any mood.

Enough has been written in the latter part of this essay to suggest some of the shortcomings that are inevitable for the critic if the nature of literature is conceived too narrowly. For Mr. Hicks it is a weapon in the class war which is becoming increasingly the central fact in American life. Consequently his final call to action to the present inheritors of the great tradition is on the ground that 'the issue is now so clearly drawn that evasion is almost impossible: on the one hand lies repudiation of

the best in the American literary past; on the other the fulfillment of all that was dreamed and worked for in the past and
the beginning of struggle for more than the past ever hoped.'
I have a good deal of both respect and sympathy for Mr. Hicks'
political position; but in such a passage he seems to me to draw
such a close analogy between politics and literature as to blur
the essential distinctions between them. When he talks about
'the fulfillment of all that was dreamed' in our tradition, he is
thinking almost entirely in terms of the social novel of revolt; as
I have tried to indicate, he is leaving out of account what have
been some of the most fertile springs for our art.

The spirit of protest and revolution has been a fundamental
element in American life since the seventeenth century, and Mr.
Hicks is thoroughly sound in insisting on the great importance
of the contemporary manifestation of that strain. My quarrel
with him is that in his insistence he is blind to the value of less
obvious but equally pervasive American traits; that as far as his
account of our literature is concerned, he so underestimates as
almost to reject some of the most ripely human elements that
have actually come to expression. It is perhaps worth passing
notice that the one conspicuous place where he falls into an
inadequately examined cliché of Marxian criticism is when he
looks forward in a glowing if somewhat undefined fashion to
'the literature of a classless society.' If that day should arrive,
the tradition of social protest would presumably no longer be
very necessary; and without that tradition, art, as Mr. Hicks
defines it, would have little function.

The trouble with Mr. Hicks' great tradition is that it is too
thin. He envisages a theoretical ideal state for the future, but
he is not fully enough aware of the part which art can actually
play in enriching human life. His desire for 'a genuine proletarian literature' is perhaps conceived in too abstract terms to
allow him to see the full qualifications, say, of *Huckleberry Finn*
as just such a piece of literature in terms of American life, in
the way that it has spoken intimately to a whole people. Mr.
Hicks' limitations as a critic are owing to his lack of understanding not only that art is a richer experience, but also that it
possesses more varied uses than he perceives. Its role is not only

that of revolt, but the counterbalancing one of realization. And owing to the very roots of American life having sprung from the forces of the Reformation, so much emphasis has been thrown on the protesting strain that it is doubly important that whatever full-created affirmation there has been, not of life as a future dream, but of life itself as it has been lived, should not be allowed to be lost sight of. Consequently for any American future it is essential to preserve by wise evaluation far more elements than Mr. Hicks stresses, since only thus can an individual find revealed in the past of our country the complexity which he knows to compose life.

*The New England Quarterly,* 1934

## The Flowering of New England

VAN Wyck Brooks has evolved a very individual method of writing literary history. Having read capaciously in memoirs, letters, and journals, he has incorporated passages from them, as well as from the principal authors, directly into his own text in the effort to suggest as intimately as possible the milieu in which the New England renaissance took place. The ordonnance of his materials is frequently brilliant. There could hardly have been a happier conception than that which led him to call his opening chapter 'The Boston of Gilbert Stuart,' and so to group therein many of the worthies of the Revolution who sat for that florid brush and who still set the tone for New England in 1815. John Adams reading each year *De Senectute,* Colonel William Prescott, the hero of Bunker Hill, returning like Cincinnatus to his farm at Pepperell, the younger Josiah Quincy

*The Flowering of New England* by Van Wyck Brooks. E. P. Dutton.

seeing his father's career mirrored in Pope's Homer—such figures might equally well have been chiseled as Roman busts or have had their lives written by Plutarch. And in adumbrating so deftly their classical qualities, their solid devotion to their land, their notion of public duty as sharply cut as their profiles, their belief in themselves and their descendants, Mr. Brooks has made clearer than ever before why Daniel Webster's periods could fall so naturally into the mode of a Roman senator's, and why the Greek revival in architecture became so integrally our national style.

In his second chapter, 'Harvard College in 1815,' and later on when he follows the *Wanderjahre* of George Ticknor and Edward Everett, he begins to suggest the stirrings of a new age that are best symbolized in the awakening power of Dr. Channing. By the time his narrative reaches 1837, the moment when Emerson has published *Nature* and delivered his address on 'The American Scholar,' when Prescott's *Ferdinand and Isabella,* just out, is causing its instantaneous sensation, and when Longfellow is settling into Craigie House, Mr. Brooks has made lucid the reasons for this efflorescence. Quoting Tolstoy's remark in *Anna Karenina* that 'the only nations which have ever come to be called historic are those which recognize the importance and worth of their own institutions,' he has described how the historians and orators of the new nation had fulfilled their function in creating such a mood of self-confidence. In addition, he has singled out the common strain that runs through so many authors of the period that it can be said to bind widely diverse talents into a distinct cultural group and thus justify the word 'renaissance.'

Mr. Brooks first hints at the nature of this strain in a sensitive paragraph that sketches the physical surroundings of a child growing up in early nineteenth-century New England. Such sights and sounds as he enumerates are the homeliest facts of the Yankee world: the bobolink and katydid, the sea booming on the distant rocks, the washing-day, the dinner-bell, the blacksmith and the oysterman. No wonder that the poets who used these for their material came to be known as the 'household poets.' The richest notes of Longfellow rise from such spontaneous nativism. They come from the Longfellow who while traveling in Europe recalled the yellow pumpkins of the New England cornfields, who, even when adapting Scandinavian verse forms, was sharing in the century's wide revival of folk material, since he was able to sense, if only faintly, a genuine kinship between the Vikings and the child of Maine for whom the sea and the forest kept their 'unfailing magic.' Such poetic creation followed the resolve that Americans should make their own country 'classic to themselves,' a phrase of Robert Bartlett's, the Plymouth tutor, for Emerson was by no mean alone in preaching 'Self-Reliance' to the younger generation of the 'thirties and 'forties. Lowell struck his one autochthonous vein when, remarking that 'the tongue of the people in the mouth of the scholar' was the right motto for poets, he produced *The Biglow Papers*. This work, as Mr. Brooks rightly asserts, is 'almost a folk-creation,' since Lowell's one moment of radical sympathies enabled him to recognize that Parson Wilbur and Hosea Biglow were brothers under their skins, that literate and illiterate New England could unite in their common feeling 'on essential matters, religious and political alike . . . their regard for human rights, their hatred of war and false ideas of empire.' * Like closeness on the part of other authors to the life they were describing resulted in Whittier's *Legends of New England* and Dana's *Two Years Before the Mast*, Thompson's *Green Mountain Boys* and Mrs. Stowe's *Old-town Folks*, all of which were seasoned with the salt of everyday occupations.

Mr. Brooks' emphasis on this common native strain constitutes the most perceptive and fresh element in his book. His method for the most part is biographical and descriptive; he devotes the major part of his effort to establishing the ambient atmosphere in which the writers did their work. With a sustained delicate mastery of detail he draws the very likeness of Longfellow's 'Heidelberg in Cambridge': the lovely yard of lilacs and syringas, the poet's embroidered waistcoats, the wines in his cellar as *gemütlich* as the flowing conversation with Agassiz and Fel-

* The distance that Mr. Brooks has advanced in his feeling for our culture in the twenty-one years since *America's Coming of Age* can be noted by recalling that then he took these very two characters in Lowell's poem as a symbol of 'the unbridgeable chasm between literate and illiterate America,' of our disastrous division into 'highbrow' and 'lowbrow.' F. O. M.

ton. Or Mr. Brooks is equally vivid in summoning up the Boston
of Prescott: the opulent household with its magnificent library,
the historian's abundant stock of buoyant spirits in spite of his
near blindness, his extravagant delight in gay parties, while all
the time he was thinking out the composition of his long episodes,
sometimes on horseback, sometimes pacing round and round
the cherry tree in his garden at Nahant.

But as the evocative chapters cumulate, often with only
oblique mention of the works which these writers were producing, one begins to wonder exactly what Mr. Brooks implies in
stating that his 'subject is the New England mind.' A comparison with Parrington's sections given to the same theme reveals
striking differences in treatment. For example, the bulk of Mr.
Brooks' pages on Webster are occupied in painting the portrait
of the robust squire of Marshfield, as he forms the Bunker Hill
oration word by word while wading up the river with his trout-
rod, Old Killall, in hand. His range is demarcated from that of
Burke in the brilliant *aperçu* that while he 'had a feeling for the
sublime, he had little feeling for the beautiful,' but beyond that
there is hardly anything about the orations themselves, and none
of Parrington's analysis of Webster's leading ideas, either in relation to their conditioning by Boston Federalism, or in their der-
ivation from Montesquieu and Harrington. In fact, Mr. Brooks
deals at no point very directly with ideas themselves. He sketches
Andrews Norton, 'the tyrant of the Cambridge Parnassus,' with
his methodical list of American authors that included Emerson
and Hawthorne as minor figures in the second fifty. He presents
Emerson's talent flowering unhurriedly in the soft air of Concord. But he gives no hint of the long slow battle that is revealed
in the first three volumes of Emerson's *Journals* before the young
thinker had found his own secure direction. Nor does Mr. Brooks
even mention Norton's famous onslaught upon 'The Divinity
School Address,' and thus loses a chance to let his readers share
in the immediacy of the issues involved in that utter cleavage
of faiths which gave the new generation its particular tone of
excited release and discovery.

Perhaps one reason why he missed this opportunity is that Mr.

Brooks is frequently weak in his handling of the religious thought. In all the generous range of his gallery there is no canvas centering on Theodore Parker, whom Mr. Commager has recently demonstrated to be the principal transcendentalist in action, the very epitome of the movement's social and economic convictions. Mr. Brooks may have felt that Parker's activity lay outside the field of literature proper, though his omission of Parker's narrative of his 'Experience as a Minister,' which Mr. Commager characterized as 'the most satisfactory intellectual history' on record of the Boston of the 'forties and 'fifties,* is hard to make consistent with Mr. Brooks' own valuable discovery that Orestes Brownson's *The Convert* 'is the best account that has ever been written of the spiritual cross-currents' of those very decades.

Or again, Mr. Brooks may have concluded that others had dealt adequately in defining the drift from Unitarianism to transcendentalism, and that he wanted to bring out the more specifically literary elements in Channing's interest. Nevertheless, when one turns to his treatment of the few major artists, one is forced to ask what Mr. Brooks conceives to be the scope of literary history. He devotes almost fifty pages to Thoreau, not all in one block, but, in accordance with his original scheme of interweaving the careers of the various authors, he portrays him in one chapter in the years of the *Dial*, four chapters later at Walden, and returns again to relate him to the general current of 'Concord in the Fifties.' But in all this space there is literally no analysis of *The Week* or of *Walden* as works of art. The book *Walden* is mentioned specifically in four passing sentences, though there is repeated reference to it as a pond. It is not as if Mr. Brooks was holding himself to the narrowest conception of literary history, believing that his role was to present the successive books in the order of their appearance, and to eschew all judgments of value. For he is not loath to recall such neglected facts as that New England had produced no other biography that could be placed beside Ticknor's *Life of Prescott;* or to affirm that the few aesthetically trained eyes of the day, those of the sculptor Horatio Greenough and Jarves the art col-

---

* My own opinion would be that Emerson's 'Historic Notes of Life and Letters in New England' is even more comprehensive. F. O. M.

lector,* in being the first to insist on the clipper ship as a work
of art, anticipated the later vogue of the 'functional' theory of
beauty. Such rediscovery of Greenough's forgotten lectures on
American architecture makes me regret the more that Mr. Brooks
did not bring their doctrines into relation with Emerson's and
Thoreau's conception that style in writing also must be based
organically on nature.

Perhaps Mr. Brooks feels that the value of *Walden* can be
taken for granted, though one would hardly expect him of all
writers to fall into that academic pit, since the critic knows that
any understanding of the subtle principle of life inherent in a
work of art can be attained only by tenacious awareness. It is
rather the case that the limitations of Mr. Brooks' method of
presentation are disclosed here most sharply. He has believed
that he could distill the essence of Thoreau by following his own
words as closely as possible. But with the vast range of the
*Journals* to draw upon, he has been betrayed on the one hand
into discursiveness, and on the other into paraphrasing. And
nothing could be less wise than tampering with that particular
style, since every change means some loss of its full-bodied,
nutty ripeness. The net result of Mr. Brooks' abandonment of
the critic's tools of analysis and discrimination in favor of a
flowing evocation of his author's 'personality' is that none of
Thoreau's thoughts ring with quite their own hard clarity. He
appears a fascinating if wistful figure, but no one would ever
suspect that he was one of the few great masters of concrete
sensuous language ever to have been born in America.

If Mr. Brooks has diluted Thoreau so that it is hard to tell
him from Bronson Alcott, he has practically dismissed the problem of wrestling with Hawthorne. One knows from *America's
Coming of Age* that Mr. Brooks possesses great admiration for

* Mr. Brooks' thumbnail sketches of these men are so illuminating that one
wishes that he had also included the painter William Morris Hunt and the
poet and art-historian H. T. Tuckerman. But it would be unfair to quarrel at
all with the inclusiveness of Mr. Brooks' range, since probably the most remarkable quality of his volume is owing to the very number of neglected figures that he has brought back to life. Especially useful is the way he demonstrates the importance to the total cultural pattern of such masterpieces of
the practical intellect as Nathaniel Bowditch's work on navigation or George
Perkins Marsh's contribution to human geography.  F. O. M.

the 'shining purity' of Hawthorne's talent, but the implications
of that talent are allowed here to seem altogether too mild. In
a volume that gives room to more than a dozen thoughtful pages
of fairly close examination of the contradictions involved in
Lowell's work, and that formulates impressively 'the larger
meaning' of Motley's histories by pointing out the type of men
whom he repeatedly chose as his heroes—men of action who
would have felt at home with Abbott Lawrence—it is particularly
disconcerting to watch *The Scarlet Letter* and *The House of the
Seven Gables* slip by in a single page of graceful praise. And
the note of that praise bears only tangential relation to the
fundamental elements in Hawthorne. When Mr. Brooks concludes that the story of the latter novel 'moved in a soft September light, melting like a happy dream of Shakespeare,' one
is conscious that he has missed the brooding darkness. Nowhere
does Mr. Brooks make more than fragmentary reckoning with
what should be a focal center in any exploration of the New
England mind: Hawthorne's rare understanding of the problem
of evil.

Indeed, there is no discussion of the nature of tragedy in this
volume, which can perhaps be accounted for when one notices
that there is little recognition by Mr. Brooks of any tragic factors
in the actual life of the times. The New England that he dwells
on so charmingly clusters its associations around spacious houses
or across the lovely surface of the land. He is able to create very
winningly the church sociable atmosphere of Brook Farm, but
he does not sense enough of the clash and struggle of ordinary
human existence. Otherwise he would never have made the remark that 'there were not wanting well-informed observers who
were to assert, in later years, that from the farm had sprung
the movement of organized labor in New England and throughout the nation.' He would not have had to go any further than
Professor Ware's *The Industrial Worker: 1840–1860* to find the
record of far more central grapplings with this problem, such
as can be read in the realistic resolution of the Laborers Union
of South Boston in 1845: 'That as practical laborers who have
not the means or the inclination to withdraw from society, we

deem it incumbent on us to use all the means in our power to remove existing evils from the present state of society.'

It is curious to note that Mr. Brooks' earlier stringent dissatisfaction with the deficiencies of our civilization has now yielded to a mood of celebration. One welcomes the warmth of his affirmation of the virtues of our past, yet still regrets the *tone* of such a sentence in his conclusion about the writers in general: 'They stood for good faith and fair play and all that was generous and hopeful in the life of their time.' That seems again to put the dark searchings of Hawthorne at a discount, to ignore the satire of 'The Celestial Railroad,' to rob Thoreau of the realistic instinct that prompted his anarchistic protest against many of the basic assumptions of his age. Mr. Brooks is too lavish in his creation of plaster busts. His sympathetic desire to mold flattering likenesses of Alcott and Margaret Fuller has caused him to slur over all but the more smiling aspects in the flow of gossip about them by their contemporaries. It is true, as Mr. Brooks says, that Emerson loved Alcott 'for his copious peacefulness and for the mountain landscape of his mind.' But Emerson also set down, on the candid level of the understanding, that Alcott was 'a tedious archangel' and 'a pail without any bottom,' and such gritty details are needful to make Mr. Brooks' saintly image give any sensation of flesh and blood. So too with the spice of Hawthorne's observations about Miss Fuller and the transcendental heifer. But it is much more serious to have Rufus Choate mentioned solely for the nobility of his feeling for the origins and greatness of New England, and to have no indication of the narrow plutocratic bias that conditioned his dismissal of Jefferson's Declaration as 'glittering and sounding generalities.' At this point Mr. Brooks could have taken with advantage several leaves from the volumes of Becker and Beard.

For the chief limitation of his criticism is that it lacks third dimension. He ends a chapter on Prescott with the remark that 'One might well ask for different things, but one could scarcely ask for anything better.' But that is precisely what one could do; one could ask for, and presently get, Parkman. And recognition of the later writer's more sensitive skill serves to throw into relief Prescott's contribution. If it causes much of his drama to

seem rhetorical tour de force, it likewise emphasizes the importance of the vigorous narrative method that he devised, since
Parkman's volumes would hardly have been possible without this
work before him. And if Mr. Brooks had been willing to consider why different things were asked for, on what grounds, for
instance, Margaret Fuller and Parker attacked Prescott so strenuously, he would have probed deeper into the kind of conflict
that constitutes the real life of any age. For if Miss Fuller's objections that Prescott had no 'great leading views, or discernment as to the motives of action and the spirit of an era' seem
rather airy, Parker's two solid essays leave no doubt as to the
democratic core of the transcendentalists' conception of history.
For the historian 'must tell us of the social state of the people,
the relation of the cultivator to the soil, the relation of class to
class. It is well to know what songs the peasant sung.' In the
light of such a philosophy of history Prescott's work is characterized as that of a superficial and frivolous aristocrat. It is not
necessary to accept all Parker's strictures, and it is possible to
show many of them naive, but bringing them to bear instead
of waving them aside with a defensive remark would have given
Mr. Brooks' estimate more of the quality of being inside his
material, of growing from a more dense intellectual nexus.

But Mr. Brooks' criticism has always been extremely personal
in the bias of its emotional intensity. Indeed, his greatest vir-
tue, the awakening power that has made his role in the revival
of American literature since 1912 something akin to that of
Channing's a century before, has depended upon his insistence
on the value of a deeply individual approach to life in opposition to all standardization. The defect of his quality has lain
in its subjective distortions. Near the close of this volume, after
his wholehearted praise of many minor talents, one is bewildered
to find that Mr. Brooks keeps his old prejudice against Henry
James, whose 'furtive apology' for America he contrasts un-
favorably with the unself-conscious confidence of the earlier day.
If he had read James more temperately, he would know that
that novelist's admirable characters are nearly always his Americans, that it is Christopher Newman, Isabel Archer, and Milly
Theale who are marked for their courage, loyalty, and self-

sacrifice, and that James was occupied with moral values as profoundly as the Hawthorne whom Mr. Brooks has not probed. His loose generalizations miss the essential kinship between our two major novelists, and thus blur anything significant that can be meant by speaking of an American tradition.

If I have held Mr. Brooks to the most absolute standards in pointing out some of the weaknesses of his method, it is because this is a book that no one else could have written. His tone may be too elegiac; instead of showing rigorously the very form and pressure of the time, he may have made it appear too like a piece of glowing brocade that he has unfolded from the drawer of a highboy. But he is steeped in his material as one could be only after long familiarity; and when he refers to the European literature of the time, as in his brief remarks on what Fichte or Schelling meant to New England, his accent is equally one of ripe cultivation. His style is more resilient than it ever has been, an enheartening contrast with the rather flat thinness of the biography of Emerson. New England's past has brought him a resurgence of life, and he in turn has brought to it both generosity and wit. I would have quoted some examples of the latter if Mr. Brooks' way of borrowing directly from his authors had not left me uncertain just when the words were his and when they were those of the Autocrat.

*The New England Quarterly,* 1936

# Nathaniel Hawthorne

IN his incisive, closely packed study of Hawthorne, Mr. Arvin has also written an important comment on the chief problem of American life, the problem of how the individual can adjust himself to society. As he observes, our most characteristic achievements have been those of the isolated spirit: Emily Dickinson in her lonely room, Melville restlessly wandering the seas, the pioneer of a hundred years ago, and the captain of industry today—all have won their victories by turning their backs on society, by denying its claims or escaping from them. Ever since the voyage of Columbus, our movement has been a constant expansion from the center outwards, and in the peculiarly detached career and genius of Hawthorne lies an essential illustration of the results of such a movement.

As you read through Hawthorne's notebooks, you become aware of the distinct cleavage between the two worlds in which he lived: the solid, actual world of Salem, and the fugitive, evanescent world of his fancy. Observations from both are set down side by side: a conversation with a crippled soap-maker at North Adams; the reminder, 'To make a story of all strange and impossible things—as the Salamander, the Phoenix.' The former type of material seems invariably more vivid and racy, but it was from the latter that the great mass of his writing was to spring. For, whether owing to the thinness he felt in his surroundings or to the extreme reserve of his nature, he gradually grew to be almost completely separated from outside experience, and devoted himself to fathoming a purely subjective reality. The result was that he plunged more deeply into the realms of personality than any American had done before, and

*Hawthorne* by Newton Arvin. Little, Brown & Co.

made the first universal exposure of our philosophy of easy optimism.

But his inability to get out of himself, or to compel his imagination to take hold of externals and transform them, cost him very dearly. Instead of building a world out of what he found at hand, as Fielding or Balzac had done, he took refuge in allegory, the weakest form of literary escape. He was aware of his own defection, for he wrote of his days in the Custom House, in the preface to *The Scarlet Letter:* 'A better book than I shall ever write was there; leaf after leaf presenting itself to me, just as it was written out by the reality of the flitting hour, and vanishing as fast as written, only because my brain wanted the insight and my hand the cunning to transcribe it.'

He knew that his books were 'too remote, too shadowy and unsubstantial,' and, strangely enough, it is partly owing to this knowledge that his seemingly pale representations are filled with so much intensity. For the theme of nearly all his work is guilt, an obsession that has generally been ascribed to his Puritan ancestry, and has caused him to be called a Puritan critic of Puritanism. The insufficiency of this explanation becomes apparent in the light of Mr. Arvin's sharp analysis, which demonstrates that the guilt which Hawthorne broods over rises invariably out of isolation, that its most sinister aspect is that it separates man from ordinary life. The tragedies of Ethan Brand, Rappaccini, and Roger Chillingworth are all owing to the fact that they have lost their grasp of the central human elements, and have drifted dangerously away from the center. They no longer feel any bond with society, and, as a consequence, they are no longer individuals, but restless burning exaggerations of a single quality. And the reason why Hawthorne, in spite of all his stiff self-consciousness and the flimsiness of his allegory, could suggest so hauntingly the dark recesses of their fate was that he knew it to be his own. He realized in his imagination that he had failed to meet life squarely, that that was the great failure of America. There seemed to be no alternative to a ruthless individualism which preyed upon itself until the individual was destroyed, no normal society, but only a lifeless standardization which drove the sensitive man farther back into himself. Both

Hawthorne's life and his work are fatally marked with the limitations of such a condition, but his enduring importance lies in the fact that, although one-sided himself, he had the strength not to accept what he knew to be false, and to embody in his quiet prose a searing criticism of what was, then as now, the dominant direction of American life.

These are only a few of the reflections that rise directly out of Mr. Arvin's book. He has done a great service to our letters by reiterating Hawthorne's significance, by revealing that beneath a surface which so often seems to modern readers disappointingly thin, is contained an essence which we cannot afford to forget. This is the third biography of Hawthorne in as many years, and it is evidence of the present overproduction of books that it renders both of the others unnecessary. Mr. Lloyd Morris' *The Rebellious Puritan* (1927) was in the Maurois pattern, which means that, although considerably longer than Mr. Arvin's study, it made no evaluation of Hawthorne's writings, a singularly unfruitful venture in this case. Mr. Herbert Gorman's *Hawthorne: A Study in Solitude* (1927) was a brief piece of hackwork for the Murray Hill biographies, which simply compressed the chief facts of its subject's life from the far more fertile volumes of Julian Hawthorne, and added nothing to a critical estimate that had not already been better said by Henry James, Woodberry, or Brownell.

It is not Mr. Arvin's highest praise that he transcends such work, but that what he has written goes right to the top of contemporary literary biography, and stands with Lewis Mumford's *Melville* as the rich, many-sided type of criticism which we should have. His style is perhaps somewhat level and monotonous, as is his addiction to the academic habit of long series of rhetorical questions and exclamations; it also seems that after his climax, the impressive section in which he sums up the nature of Hawthorne's genius, he might have applied more sensitively his otherwise admirable principle of selection in bringing his book to a more rapid close. The defects, however, are slight, and he has presented an absorbing picture of Hawthorne's tragedy, and America's.

*New Republic,* 1930

# Thoreau: A Relaxed Chronicle

OF the three phases of Thoreau which command the greatest interest—as the amateur naturalist, the political and social philosopher of 'Civil Disobedience,' the master of language—Mr. Canby's biography is most adequate on the first. He has observed that *Walden*, the second and last of Thoreau's books to be published during his lifetime, was substantially finished by 1850, though not in print until four years later. He has given, therefore, the second of the two divisions of his biography to examining the consequences of the fact that not until 1850, though for the remaining dozen years of Thoreau's life, nature study became his chief concern. Mr. Canby does not repeat the mistake of some earlier biographers by making any claim for the scientific value of Thoreau's work. He knows that the saunterer in the woods possessed none of the necessary equipment of exact instruments. In addition he regards it as unfortunate that the first professional scientist with whom Thoreau came into contact, Agassiz, was a classificationist, a collector of examples as a means of establishing identities. For Thoreau's needs were quite other—to arrive at some synthesis between science and transcendentalism. Following a hint from Professor F. S. C. Northrop, Mr. Canby has noted how Locke's principle of experiment through the senses, which Thoreau would have been taught at Harvard, 'survived, with complete metaphysical inconsistency, his conversion to truth by intuition,' and thus produced a lifelong conflict in him. Mr. Canby argues that had Thoreau begun his serious nature study a decade later, under the aegis, say, of Darwin, he would at least have been provided with a philosophy that could have given direction to his accumu-

*Thoreau* by Henry Seidel Canby. Houghton Mifflin Co.

lation of facts. As it was, he bogged down in them increasingly, as witnessed by the final ten or twelve volumes of his journal. Mr. Canby suggests that a perceptive editor might still winnow from these another book of the stature of *The Maine Woods*, the book of the seasons which Alcott looked forward to as Thoreau's 'Atlas of Concord.'

Little other valuable harvest is to be gleaned from this biography. Mr. Canby's main concern with 'Civil Disobedience' and 'Life Without Principle' is to try to prophesy what Thoreau's attitude would have been toward 'dictatorship' and 'the totalitarian state.' Such isolation of Thoreau's ideas from their original context obscures any chance of getting at their real meaning. The more fruitful way to start would be to relate Thoreau to the background of native American anarchism, as Eunice Shuster has done in a study which Mr. Canby ignores. For, in order to understand the content of Thoreau's radicalism, it is necessary to know the exact forces against which he was protesting. In briefest form, these were the narrow standards of a society dominated by mercantilism. These had stifled all richness of cultural development, and consequently when Thoreau takes his stand against them, it is not for himself, the free individual, alone, as Mr. Canby seems to think. For he argues in *Walden* for more adequate expenditure on such resources of the community as the lyceum and the library, and backs it up with a sentence that needs to be pondered, since it runs counter to nearly all Mr. Canby's drift: 'To act collectively is according to the spirit of our institutions.'

Mr. Canby is even less penetrating into the nature of the gift that seems destined to make Thoreau's stature more solidly enduring than Emerson's. He quotes their author's remark, 'You have the best of me in my books,' and then proceeds to give one chapter out of twenty-eight to a consideration of the *Week* and *Walden* together. Nor are his obiter dicta very useful when he loosely ranks Thoreau as a maker of sentences with Bacon, Shakespeare, Pope, Dr. Johnson, and Franklin; or when he delivers the more interesting remark, though without the necessary substantiation, that Thoreau 'excels all moderns'—whomever these may include—in his 'control over metaphor.' Close comparison with the nearest master at hand, with Melville, would at least have served to make clear what Mr. Canby meant, though it would probably have caused him to change his statement.

That he has not left himself space for adequate criticism is owing to his acceptance of the arbitrary division between it and biography. This is particularly damaging in the treatment of a life whose ideas and words were not divorced from its acts. What this book thus, for the most part, amounts to is a relaxed chronicle of minor events plus a diluted Freudianism in dealing with Thoreau's sex life. The author's exploitation of this latter technique seems peculiarly unrewarding here, since Mr. Canby does not maintain that the abnormality of Thoreau's lifelong chastity left any distorting mark on his writing, which, indeed, it did not, except in restricting its range. Nearly all the relevant material boils down to Thoreau's tender expressions in letters to older women, upon which Mr. Canby erects a preposterous romance of a marriage proposal from Margaret Fuller, who was in Italy at the time, largely on the shaky foundation that the biographer 'hopes' that an unidentified woman was she. But beyond all specific defects, and granting that I have not cited enough minor virtues which spring from Mr. Canby's unquestioned devotion to his subject, the most unfortunate feature of this book is its prevailing tone. For its effect is mild and polite, neither of which Thoreau was.

*Yale Review*, 1939

# Whitman: Sanguine Confused American

O N his opening page Newton Arvin sets himself a single question, the degree to which Whitman may be regarded as a socialist poet, and devotes his volume to a detailed and searching answer. His structure consists of successive chapters on Whitman's politics, his economics, his views on science, philosophy, and religion, with a final synthesis which gives a more thorough grounding of the poet's thoughts in the matrix of his time than we have heretofore possessed for any American writer. Arvin has utilized every available kind of material, ranging from the early random journalism, which during the last few years Holloway and others have shown to be more extensive than used to be assumed, down to the interminable conversations with Traubel and the other disciples who tried to draw the old man out on any conceivable subject. In weaving through this mass Arvin has demonstrated how impossible it is to give any one answer to what views Whitman held.

It is not merely that the young admirer of William Leggett, the adherent of left-wing Jacksonianism, is inevitably different from the admirer of Grant and Carnegie, who nevertheless becomes enthusiastic about free trade under Cleveland and looks out hopefully to internationalism. For, in addition, within any given period, Whitman's complacent acceptance of the circumstances immediately surrounding him was always capable of the most paradoxical contrasts. The radical affirmer of humanity was at times by no means clear on abolition or unprejudiced about the Negro; even more unexpected, the writer of *Democratic Vistas* and of notes on 'The Tramp and Strike Questions,' who, in the light of the panics of the 'seventies, discerned the grow-

*Whitman* by Newton Arvin. Macmillan.

ing portent of 'vast crops of poor, desperate, dissatisfied, miserably waged populations,' could yet turn around and declare to a
reporter his belief that 'things in our time . . . all are going on
as well as possibly could be.' Many of his pronouncements, written to fill a column or expounded to live up to the role of
prophet, carry no very high voltage; and few claims can be
advanced for his power on the level of conscious thought. Yet,
through the very blur of his inconsistencies, there finally emerges
a curiously typical image of the sanguine confused American
who belonged in youth to the world of the small farmer and
artisan; who was aware of the economic needs of plain people
and yet, sustained by an ingenuous idealism, was still too hopeful of the future to be moved by Brisbane's utopian socialism;
who, in the period of the great plunder, still kept his Jacksonian
distrust of inequality, but was nevertheless excited by the spec-
tacle of the triumphant march of industry.

An acute problem is where to put your emphasis in charting
the drift of such flux, and, even with all Arvin's skill and tenacity,
it cannot be wholly resolved. For the Whitman who at the close
of the chapter on 'Wealth and Illth' is moving to a solider
enunciation of socialist principles is, in the next chapter, shown
to have been drifting at the very same time to a looser faith in
the unseen and life beyond. Arvin is aware of the necessity at
every juncture of distinguishing between Whitman's superficial
complacencies and the deeper loyalty to his instincts, but the
pages which deal with Whitman's religion seem to be the one
occasion when his own firm materialism causes him to desire a
kind of scientific poet who could not possibly have produced
'Song of Myself.' He makes the keen observation that one factor
which prevented Whitman from soaring so far into the transcendental void as Emerson was his early debt to the clear-
sighted rationalism of Paine and Frances Wright. But it seems
futile to regret that as a boy Whitman was equally stirred by the
'obscurantism' of Elias Hicks. For one thing unmistakable from
the first accents of *Leaves of Grass* is that Whitman, in his celebration of the solid glories of the earth, is moved to that desire
by a mystical intuition that finds the formulas of 'the age of
reason' shallow and inadequate. Without that vibrant response

to what he considered the inner light, he could not have written his kind of poetry at all.

In stating my demur in such brief compass, I have done injustice to the careful qualifications with which Arvin supports his position; and there can be nothing but praise for the discernment and restrained eloquence with which, in his closing section, he affirms Whitman's significance. The figure to whom he wants to draw his reader's attention is the man who 'did more than all but a few other writers to domesticate the modern sensibility in its natural setting,' who could embrace so much of the common life of his times, not as a romantic gesture, but 'because he was himself quite literally one of the people,' who could say unaffectedly, 'I have imagined a life which should be that of the average man in average circumstances, and still grand, heroic.'

My one misgiving about Arvin's critical approach lies in his acceptance of the current simplified conception of 'the usable past.' He believes Whitman to have a special claim upon a socialist audience, 'to be the real "ancestor" of our generation and of the future,' because he voices the healthy, forward-moving, progressive life of his time. He holds that Whitman's optimism was 'an intrinsically more creative attitude' than 'the repudiation of it by men like Poe and Melville.' At this point serious questions obtrude themselves, questions which can scarcely be answered here, but may be briefly brought to focus by the remark in Yeats' *Autobiography* that Emerson and Whitman 'have begun to seem superficial precisely because they lack the Vision of Evil.' Is the availability of a poet to be made to correspond to the degree in which his opinions chime in with our hopes? Is it not rather the function of the artist to bring to concentrated expression every major phase of human experience, its doubts and anguish and tortured defeats as well as its cheerful confidence? Indeed, is not one measure of the great artist his refusal to yield us any innocent simplification, his presentation of an account of life as intricate in its harsh tragic matching of good and evil, as complex in its necessities of constant struggle as the life that we ourselves know? Will any less dense past correspond to our usages as mature human beings?

*New Republic,* 1938

# Whitman: His Poetry and Prose

AN anthology of a well-known author is always a lively stimulus to our reading. It serves to make us see him with fresh eyes, as we compare our own former choices with new findings. Our minimum demand of the editor is that he add enough to our comprehension to justify his name being added to the title page.

Last fall Samuel Sillen selected Whitman with the strictly political aim of presenting him 'as a living force in the war against fascist barbarism.' Now Mark Van Doren contributes to the useful Viking Portable Library a far larger selection, with the interesting feature of devoting a little over half its pages to the poet's much less known prose. But his one criterion of choice is that of literary excellence, and as a lyric poet himself he is more sensitive to Whitman's lyricism than to his political and social implications.

He has concluded that Whitman's arrangement of *Leaves of Grass* under classifying headings is less meaningful than simple chronology, and the result is to throw unexpected highlights upon several poems. Thus the poetry begins here, not with the customary 'One's-Self I Sing,' but with 'Europe, the Seventy-second and Seventy-third Years of These States'—that is to say, with Whitman's ardent response to the defeated revolutions of 1848, his denunciation of the restored reactionaries, and his enfolding sympathy for the 'aching close of exiled patriots' lives.' With such an opening it is too bad that the editor did not drive home the opportunity of showing where *Leaves of Grass* started by including 'Blood-Money,' an even earlier experiment with

*The Portable Walt Whitman,* selected and with notes by Mark Van Doren. The Viking Press.

218

free verse in that same spring of 1850. For Whitman's portrayal of Christ as the betrayed deliverer of the poor reveals the indissoluble connection between the poet's social and religious convictions and makes clear what he meant by saying much later that he could not 'have written a word of the "Leaves" without its religious root-ground.'

But by including eight of the dozen poems that made up the first slim volume of the *Leaves* in 1855, Van Doren has let us see most of the other sources of Whitman's initial impulse. 'Song of Myself' was, of course, by far the most notable of these poems, but it is well to be reminded that 'A Song for Occupations' was also there from the start. And although *Children of Adam*, which so distressed Emerson, did not make its appearance until the third issue of 1860, 'I Sing the Body Electric' was among the initial dozen. So also was 'The Sleepers,' in which Whitman plunged deeply into his dream-life and wrote more compulsively from his subconscious than he was ever quite to do again.

The main additions in the second (1856) issue were the long 'Song'—'of the Open Road,' 'of the Broad-Axe,' 'of the Rolling Earth'—and 'Crossing Brooklyn Ferry.' But another poem that takes on particular significance by appearing in the order of its composition is 'This Compost.' For therein Whitman, the celebrator of life, began to show the basis upon which he could later celebrate also 'sane and sacred' death in his tribute to Lincoln. Whitman's was no hollow echoing of the romantic Love-and-Death motif, for he won his way through to solid personal knowledge. 'This Compost' starts with an instinctive revulsion from the thought that the earth is already crowded with corpses, that every continent is 'work'd over and over with sour dead.' But the poet then penetrates to the meaning of the cyclical rebirth of nature, and finds his first affirmation through the way that

> The resurrection of the wheat appears with pale visage out
>     of its graves.

He ends here with the reflection

> Now I am terrified at the Earth! it is that calm and patient,
> It grows such sweet things out of such corruptions.

Years later, after he had gone much farther in his facing and acceptance of death in his most mature poem, he turned back to 'This Compost,' and incorporated half a line, as though in recognition of where its affirmative knowledge had finally led him. Where he had previously written 'Out of its hill rises the yellow maize-stalk,' he now added—'the lilacs bloom in the dooryards.'

By 1860, with the addition of 'Out of the Cradle Endlessly Rocking' as well as the bulk of *Children of Adam* and the newly written *Calamus* section—which included his shyest and boldest poems—Whitman might well have seemed to reach the fullest emotional expression possible to his temperament. But the effect of the Civil War and its aftermath called out deeper resources and brought his work to a more heroic stature. From the climax of *Drum Taps* there was a gradual decline of creative energy, though Whitman himself believed that 'Passage to India' marked a further extension of both his political and spiritual themes. Nor was the tapering off during the nineteen years after his paralytic stroke anything like as great as the Van Doren selections would indicate.

Although he has been fairly representative of Whitman's career up to this point, he unaccountably gives only one poem after the mid-'seventies, and leaves out such characteristic later pieces as 'Prayer of Columbus,' 'To a Locomotive in Winter,' 'With Husky-Haughty Lips, O Sea,' and that small masterpiece, 'A Clear Midnight.' The chronological arrangement could also have thrown into poignant relief 'The Dismantled Ship' (1888), in which Whitman symbolizes his own disabled state; and the reader feels cheated when the poet is not allowed to end his 'Songs of Parting' with 'So Long!'

On looking back over Van Doren's arrangement, the one place where his abandonment of Whitman's classifications has been a conspicuous loss is in the case of *Drum Taps*. One important reason why that section stands out above the rest of *Leaves of Grass* lies in its thematic and dramatic ordering. And its entity is blurred, not by the loss of its covering title, but by the omission of 'First O Songs for a Prelude,' wherein Whitman struck his powerful opening note and by other links in the thematic progression. In particular, the absence of 'O Tan-Faced Prairie Boy' and 'As I Lay with My Head in Your Lap, Camerado' would argue that Van Doren tends to shy away from the more physical aspects of Whitman—an impression already suggested by his omission from *Children of Adam* of 'Spontaneous Me,' which contains Whitman's rankest exuberance in sexual pleasure.

Such matters of taste may, of course, be argued, but what cannot be argued and what unfortunately vitiates the general usefulness of this volume is the editor's haphazard handling of Whitman's text. He says that 'there has been no attempt to re-store the original text of any poem,' since 'Whitman's revisions were, after all, his own.' But he then proceeds to give, not Whitman's final revisions, but those of the intermediate edition of 1876, which have no sanction at all. How he fell into this is a puzzle, since to do so he would have had to neglect all recent editions. Whitman kept touching up his poems to the end, and to have, for instance, 'Out of the Cradle' and 'When Lilacs Last' each lacking ten or a dozen of their final, familiar phrases is no inconsiderable defect.

When we turn to the prose we are rewarded by finding the broad and simple choices—the first and last prefaces to the *Leaves*, all of *Democratic Vistas*, and a generous proportion of *Specimen Days*. It is particularly interesting now to look back to Whitman's intimate record of the progress and suffering of the Civil War, as solidified by his experiences as a volunteer nurse. But one could have wished for a more thorough discussion of Whitman's politics as a background for the issues handled in *Democratic Vistas*, where, at the outset of the post-Civil War period, the poet criticized so sharply the actual scene as contrasted with his earlier—and still enduring—hopes. Van Doren notes the importance of Whitman's Quaker heritage, but he does not mention that his father was a great admirer of Tom Paine. In fact no biographer has quite reckoned with the glowing patriotism of Walter Whitman, Sr., which carried him to the length of christening three of his sons George Washington, Thomas Jefferson, and Andrew Jackson.

*Democratic Vistas*, written first as two essays in response to

Carlyle's 'Shooting Niagara,' is very diffuse and could judiciously
be cut for the general reader in order to point up Whitman's
central conceptions of culture and such eloquent single passages
as that on 'the great word Solidarity.' Van Doren's introduction
hardly lets us sense the revolutionary strain in Whitman, and
*Democratic Vistas* is best prepared for by reading 'The Eighteenth Presidency,' the scathing campaign address that he prepared against Buchanan. And no comprehensive picture of the
poet's political development can be gained without reading his
account of 'The Strike Question' in 1879, when he realized that
the issue was no longer that of democracy in 'the abstract,' but
'of social and economic organization, the treatment of working
people by employers, and all that goes with it.' On such matters,
Sillen's selections, though hardly adequate for the scope of
Whitman's poetry, are much more challenging.

Ten years ago Van Doren wrote an essay called 'Walt Whitman, Stranger,' in which he discounted the validity of the poet's
'democratic dogmas' on the ground that they 'base themselves
upon the sentiment of "manly love."' He now seems to have
modified such a preposterous oversimplification, though without
yet perceiving the range of Whitman's concern with actual
American society. The figure that emerges from Van Doren's
introduction is a 'lonely' and 'fastidious' artist, filled with 'an
almost incurable sadness.' It is valuable to have those moods of
Whitman probed, but Van Doren hardly gives enough attention
to the Whitman of 'rapt satisfaction,' as William James described
him. Van Doren's Whitman could hardly have written *Leaves of
Grass* in its entirety; and the limitations of this editor's comprehension of the real Whitman are edged most sharply when he
pronounces that the poet's letters possess 'little or no literary
interest' and that the correspondence with Pete Doyle is 'silly.'

The reader can sample that correspondence for himself in
Emory Holloway's Random House collection of the *Complete
Poems and Selected Prose and Letters,* by far the most inclusive
of the one-volume editions. It is hard to see what is 'silly' about
Whitman's casual accounts to the young streetcar conductor of
how he was passing his time, about a political rally he had
watched in New York, or a railroad man he had been talking to

in a bar, or a miner out of work and run down. The easy colloquial pace—'a hot supper, a tip-top room . . . so you see, Pete,
your old man is in clover'—is what caused William James to
respond with delight, and Henry James to single them out for
their 'thousand images of patient, homely American life,' and for
'the beauty of the natural' in their 'flat, familiar, affectionate,
illiterate colloquy.' These letters are about as 'silly' as the com-
radeship between Ishmael and Queequeg, or as Melville's dedication of *Billy Budd* to his friend Jack Chase, the foretopman.
Van Doren's cool dismissal of them is significant in that it shows
how easily even one of the most sensitive of our poets and one
of the best of our liberal educators can withdraw from the
crude stuff of American existence.

Whitman's letters are of a piece with his most profound convictions about the language of poetry, which he voiced, characteristically, in his essay on 'Slang in America.' He believed
that language is 'not an abstract construction of the learn'd, or of
dictionary makers, but is something arising out of the work,
needs, ties, joys, affections, tastes of long generations of humanity, and has its bases broad and low, close to the ground. Its
final decisions are made by the masses, people nearest the concrete, having most to do with the actual land and sea.' Whitman's own poetic diction hardly lived up altogether to that ideal,
often being, as Emerson noted, 'a remarkable mixture of the
"Bhagavad-Gita" and The New York Herald.' Yet in each generation the writer has again to free himself from the limitations
of our genteel tradition if his language is to be at all commensurate with the amplitude of our life, and if Whitman's ideal
is to be further realized by adequate depiction of what he knew
to be 'the really heroic character of the common American.'

*The New York Times Book Review,* 1945

# Henry Adams: The Real Education

EVEN though it takes him only to the verge of his mature and lasting work, Ernest Samuels' study is the first adequate biography of Henry Adams. He has fully realized that the character presented in *The Education of Henry Adams* is one of its author's most subtle creations. He has consequently turned his back upon the old man's ironic evocation of his young self, and has made a fresh start. Out of the abundant record of Adams' early essays and the unceasing flow of his correspondence Samuels has revealed a quite different likeness.

Adams is not a figure many would study for the attractiveness of his personality. In the assessment he made of himself just after his graduation from college he noted two basic traits: 'One is a continual tendency towards politics; the other is family pride.' That combination could appear very charming to a circle of aristocratic intimates, but beyond that range Adams' mixture of conceit and self-distrust often chilled people into regarding him as simply an acute case of the Harvard man.

The center of Samuels' interest, therefore, is in the development of the mind that was to come to Indian-summer ripeness, as Adams approached seventy, in *Mont Saint Michel and Chartres* and the *Education,* two of the most remarkable books of our intellectual history. These books have played an immensely influential role in heightening our sense of the difference between medieval unity and modern multiplicity. Consequently, Samuels' detailed examination of the genesis and persistence of Adams' leading ideas constitutes a valuable chapter of our cultural background.

The conservative literary tastes which Adams formed at Har-

The Young Henry Adams by Ernest Samuels. Harvard University Press.

vard during the late eighteen-fifties remained with him throughout his life. He always admired Carlyle, and the quieter discipline of Burke upon his own style can be discerned even in his last writings. Guizot first challenged him to press beyond facts to establish the drift of history. But the young man whose Class Oration was permeated with the sense of the gulf between the moral order and the actual world had been permanently affected by a personality closer at hand. It was Agassiz who awakened his interest in science, Agassiz whose religious opposition to evolution was basically antirationalist. This influence was unfortunate for Adams' later attempt to establish analogies between science and history. It meant that he had never been compelled to reckon strictly with experimental method before passing on to cosmic generalizations. It may not be too much to attribute to Agassiz's tutelage the first seeds of Adams' final contempt for the intellect no less than for the world.

Despite his declared 'tendency towards politics,' the evidence shows that from the start the compulsive bias of his mind was inescapably literary. When he kept copies of his letters home from abroad, he was quite aware of the example of the young Horace Walpole. It is fascinating also to discover him responding to the symbolic attraction of the careers pursued by the heroes of Disraeli and Bulwer-Lytton. He aspired to be a Coningsby or a Pelham, as he wore the clothes of a dandy and yet, also like Pelham, pored over Mill's *Essay on Government*. During his years in London as his father's secretary we can see him also agreeing with Buckle that historians were needed of a stature comparable to Kepler or Newton.

It is fitting that the first important historical essay of such a distilled New Englander should have been devoted to undermining the Southern legend of the heroic John Smith, and to proving that the redoubtable captain was also a tall liar. From this point on, Samuels charts the course of Adams' varied essays on finance and science and current politics before he turned to his brief but brilliant career as a teacher of medieval history. Throughout his early writings one finds foreshadowed themes that were to become central for him later. None is more characteristic than the one he voiced to his brother during the Civil

War: 'Man has mounted science and is now run away with. I firmly believe that before many centuries more, science will be the master of man. The engines he will have invented will be beyond his strength to control. Some day science may have the existence of mankind in its power, and the human race commit suicide by blowing up the world.'

Notwithstanding such thought, Adams still aspired to be a political reformer up until 1876, when he and his family bolted the Republican Party only to find themselves defeated in a fluke election by 'a third-rate nonentity,' as Adams described Rutherford B. Hayes. That election also cost him his editorship of the *North American Review*, since his strong defense of the role of the independent voter outraged its Republican owners. He retired from the field of action still confirmed in the belief that the remedy for the abuse of economic power lay in private morality. As he was later to write to James Russell Lowell about his reading of Marx: 'I think I never struck a book which taught me so much, and with which I disagreed so radically in conclusion.'

The winter after Tilden's defeat, the son of Albert Gallatin, Jefferson's great Secretary of the Treasury, asked Adams to edit his father's papers. As he settled to that task at thirty-nine, Adams may not have realized that his real career was just beginning. But his biography of Gallatin was to lead him into his monumental nine-volume *History of the United States During the Administrations of Jefferson and Madison*. In that work—which lies beyond Samuels' present sphere—Adams was to demonstrate his central political belief: the force of the Constitution in making possible our continued national existence. This *History* took up nearly a dozen years of Adams' life, and then was greeted with the apathy that has been the withering reward of so many of our major works upon their first appearance.

Indeed, unlike Adams' two famous final books, his *History* has not even yet been accorded any close, detailed analysis. So conscious a writer as Adams could hardly have been unmindful of the analogy between his work and Gibbon's. But his subject was a rise, not a fall; he set himself to vindicate America against Europe. That is not the kind of subject associated with the popular image of Adams as the aged eagle appalled by democracy's degradation. His magnificent organization of that subject into one of the greatest achievements of American historiography still invites the critic.

*New Republic*, 1948

# Mark Twain at Work

I N three essays, which had previously served as a lecture and as prefaces to limited editions of *Tom Sawyer* and *Huck Finn*, Bernard DeVoto continues to present his findings from the Mark Twain manuscripts. As usual he throws his weight around. He tells us that he has seen no reason to revise any of his conclusions of a decade ago; that these essays might well be enlarged except that he is a writer 'who always has more books ahead of him than he will ever write'; and that even this fragment of a volume has involved for himself and his secretary 'a long, laborious, exhausting and fantastically minute study.' Despite all this pointless bluster and despite an equally unnecessary display of showy and rather amateur scholarship, the new material he offers us is of real interest. And whether he likes it or not, DeVoto's judgment has deepened since he wrote *Mark Twain's America* in 1932.

Familiarity with the manuscripts, which came into his hands four years ago, has enabled him to round out the story of Twain's impulsive and sporadic methods of composition. He prints for the first time a sketch written about 1870 which he believes to be its author's first attempt to go beyond casual anecdotes to the production of sustained fiction. Significantly this sketch be-

*Mark Twain at Work* by Bernard DeVoto. Harvard University Press.

gins to tap the material which was to be its author's one enduring source of creative vigor. It is told by Billy Rogers, who numbers among his friends a Tom Sawyer. It seems unquestionably the germ of the latter's adventures, and foreshadows both Twain's strength and weakness. Told in the first person, it has occasional passages in the firm native idiom that was to be Twain's great contribution to American style; but the mawkish story of Billy's hopeless love for Amy Johnson quickly breaks into the flat burlesque of his own characters that Twain could not entirely escape even in *Huck Finn*. Three series of fragmentary notes for that book throw quite a bit of light on the way Twain, after having left the manuscript lying around unfinished for half a dozen years, worked out its final structure. They also reveal, as DeVoto says, how Twain's creative improvisation was nearly always linked uncritically with extravaganza.

The manuscripts have also enabled DeVoto to write a definitive note on the subject that so outraged the 'twenties, the enforced expurgations. These all seem to have been small but significant concessions to a ludicrous propriety: 'as mild as Sunday school' had to become 'as mild as goose-milk,' such words as 'putrid,' 'rotten,' 'bowels' had to be blotted out, and the Duke's denunciation of the King had to sacrifice one thoroughly appropriate epithet, 'you unsatisfiable, tunnel-bellied old sewer.' Magazine standards and Livy's nerves were doubtless responsible for most of this weakening of the language, but DeVoto puts the question into new perspective by insisting that the 'sexual timidities' were Twain's own. No matter what his conversation may have been, when it came to writing for a general audience, he was demonstrably more prudish than Howells. DeVoto cites as evidence the whole range of Twain's work, the notable fact that only in *Pudd'nhead Wilson* are we aware of sexual desire as a human motive, and then it is in 'the forbidden world' of the Negro slaves. Elsewhere Twain could create the middle-aged women of the frontier, but his young heroines—not excepting Joan of Arc—are 'pasteboard.' It is revelatory also that in spite of his deep penetration into the fantasies of boyhood, he closed his eyes to anything that Huck knew about sex.

Such reflections show wherein DeVoto has extended his equipment. He now makes recurrent use of Freudian analysis, the validity of which for biographical studies he formerly found highly debatable. His final essay ends up where Van Wyck Brooks began, meditating on the symbols of Twain's despair. He still angrily denies that his work and Brooks' have anything in common, and, to be sure, he does not saddle Twain with Brooks' rigid thesis of the artist frustrated by society. But he experiments none the less with analytical technique, especially in probing the suffering of Twain's last years. His own thesis is that Twain was plunged into a compulsive anxiety by the series of family and financial disasters which overtook him in his middle fifties, and that he finally brought himself back to wholeness, after long years of frustration, by the therapeutic act of writing *The Mysterious Stranger*. This thesis, though supported by much interesting detail from unfinished manuscripts, seems hardly persuasive, since *The Mysterious Stranger* is itself such a truncated and immature work, and since DeVoto presents no evidence to show that Twain's despair was appreciably less after its completion.

Where DeVoto's psychological knowledge serves him in better stead is in his comprehension of the complex image of boyhood which Twain's best work presents us. This is an image compacted both of enchanted freedom and of haunted terror, and thus corresponds profoundly also to the environment which Huck knew. DeVoto is very shrewd in remarking that all of Twain's richest fiction springs from Hannibal, that it might all be grouped under the title which Twain gave to some autobiographical notes, 'Villagers of 1840–43.' But when he talks in social rather than psychological terms, DeVoto does not yet profit to the full from what he has learned of ambivalence. In his scorn for the detractors of frontier life, he sometimes talks as though the idyllic village of some of Twain's reveries had really existed, as though its remote serenity was really the historical fact 'of what we once were, of what it is now more than ever necessary to remember we once were.' Yet Twain, on nearly every page of Huck's epic procession, yields a more relevant image of social actuality by reminding us that the joy and freedom of the frontier were never long separate from the violence and the cruelty.

When DeVoto is not attempting to defend any thesis, either about Twain or the frontier or himself, he gives us some of the ripened insights that can come only through years of devoted attention to an author. Then he observes how much of the folk-mind itself is revealed through Huck's eyes, the folk-mind of a period that was shaped by 'the tremendous realities of conquering a hostile wilderness and yet shadowed by the unseen world.' Then, too, he stresses the democratic significance of the fact that Twain's most heroic character is Nigger Jim. We can be grateful for these insights, even though DeVoto seems determined to prove through his tub-thumping exaggerations that he possesses every temper except the critical temper.

*New Republic,* 1942

# Henry James

THE essence of Henry James' talent lies not in his short stories, nor even in his brilliant *nouvelles,* but in his longer novels. His art was primarily the art of preparation, of gradually building up his inner suspenses to the point where a single moment of revelation, even though it may be only Strether's glimpse of a lady and a gentleman in a boat on the Seine, will come with the shock of great drama. But his skills in the story were also abundant, and the reader can be very grateful that this medium-sized Random House volume has put back into circulation about a fifth of his production in this genre. Mr. Fadiman's selections are fairly representative, though one regrets the omission from James' middle period of 'Owen Wingrave,' the one story in which

*The Short Stories of Henry James,* selected and edited, with an introduction by Clifton Fadiman. Random House.

he dealt with the theme of militarism, and the complete neglect of James' last book of stories, *The Finer Grain,* the best single collection that he ever issued.

Mr. Fadiman's tone is unassuming, and he makes in passing several discriminating remarks, such as 'that, of all nineteenth-century novelists, Balzac and James knew women best—Balzac, the most "masculine" of men, and James, surely among the least.' He is perceptive of James' wit and humor, and speaks out of experience in deploring the standards of journalistic vulgarity that have often interfered with the appreciation of James' art. But in the short span of his introduction and notes, he makes a number of small mistakes and a few serious ones. Since the so-called James revival may easily degenerate into a fad, it may be useful to point out a few of these.

He is a little shaky on James' development. James did not start as 'a mediocre imitator of Hawthorne,' since even in his first published story he was striving for the realistic technique of Balzac. When James did experiment with the devices of allegory, as in 'The Last of the Valerii,' he is still separated from Hawthorne by the fact that he is also emulating the tightness of Mérimée's style. James' real closeness to Hawthorne (whom, incidentally, Mr. Fadiman would seem to underrate) consists in a spiritual kinship which is more deeply pervasive at the end of his career, in 'The Beast in the Jungle' and 'The Jolly Corner,' than at the beginning.

Still less was the young James 'a purveyor of genteel chit-chat,' since when his early stories fail, as they often do, it is owing rather to an excessive earnestness that his brother William warned him against, and that made him weigh down his brief form with more details than he yet knew how to develop. It is also misleading to say lightly that James 'never had to earn his own living.' When he first went to Europe he was helped by his father, but his letters reveal an uneasiness at being a drain on the family purse, and at every subsequent stage of his career we can see him reckoning with the double demands of economic necessity and artistic excellence.

One of the dangers of the present flurry about James is that he is now being praised for the wrong reasons, which will in the end lose him more readers than it will gain him. He did not reflect 'upon more ideas in the course of a single waking hour than is the lot of you or me in the course of a year,' and he is not, in any accurate use of the term, 'a philosophical novelist.' Philosophical novels would include such different works as *Wilhelm Meister, Moby Dick, Middlemarch, The Brothers Karamazov* and *The Magic Mountain.* They would also include many heavy and lugubrious attempts to be cosmic which quickly sink out of sight. James was not a thinker; his realm is consciousness and sensibility, not ideas. It seems equally unwise to exaggerate his claims as an 'anticipator' of modern psychiatry, since he deals with the superconscious, not with the subconscious, a point on which Gide has been very telling.

The present introducer is more in his element in his offhand conversational comments at the end of each story, and particularly good on the serious comedy in 'The Birthplace' and on the various levels of meaning in a masterpiece like 'The Beast in the Jungle.' But in at least three of these commentaries he shows up his very imperfect equipment for his present task. To use James' brief satiric sketch of a German pedant in the early 'Bundle of Letters' as an excuse for a tirade against the whole German people's 'War Against Mankind' may simply be a sign of the times. But James himself would have found it a shocking misrepresentation, since, with all his devotion to the British cause in 1914, his letters show that he never made the mistake of thinking that evil is ever merely external, something belonging solely to our enemies in which we are not implicated.

When Mr. Fadiman writes of 'The Great Good Place,' that 'like *The Pilgrim's Progress* or *The Divine Comedy*,' it 'is a criticism of a whole culture, though developed on a miniature scale,' and adds that to his mind it 'is, of the seventeen stories in this collection, the one most densely charged with contemporary application,' he makes clear the grounds on which he feels James' chief appeal. To other eyes this would seem one of James' unpleasantly soft stories, with the grave defect that, unlike Bunyan or Dante, for example, it projects its dream of a Utopian realm wholly in terms of the luxury products of this world.

But the distortion that will doubtless gain the widest popularity is that appearing in the note on 'The Jolly Corner' as well as in the introduction. Since it is nothing short of an effort to psychoanalyze James, it cannot be refuted briefly. Suffice it to say here that it oversimplifies a current thesis to the extent of seeing in the injury to James' back as a young man 'the first large event in his life.' That ignores all the evidence of James' autobiographies as to what an 'event' consisted in for his inward temperament. Nor did this sacroiliac strain cause 'a permanent disablement,' since James slowly, if painfully, regained his strength. But Mr. Fadiman's oversimplification will prove exciting, since it leads into the assumption that this strain rendered James sexually impotent. Before accepting that, it might be well to read the letters from William James to Henry, since William suffered from an even more severe and protracted strain in his back, and discussed with his brother his similar symptoms. Furthermore, since Henry James is one of the most objective of writers, whose work displays none of the specific anxieties or fantasies that are ordinarily traceable to the frustrations of sexual impotence, it is difficult to see what important insight we could gain into his work even if we could prove that assumption. But for the time being it will frequently be made.

*New Republic,* 1945

# Van Wyck Brooks

IN *The World of Washington Irving* Van Wyck Brooks has gone back to the era just previous to *The Flowering of New England* and has written the first volume of his literary history of the United States. Since this new book seems destined for the

*The World of Washington Irving* by Van Wyck Brooks. E. P. Dutton.

same kind of wide popularity that has greeted all his recent
work, and since, at the same time, that recent work has been
under sharp attack from many different critical quarters, it seems
appropriate now to scrutinize his method, to examine the image
of our past to which he is giving such wide currency, and to see
whether or not that method and that image are at all fairly open
to objection.

The method is easy to describe, since it follows the formula
that Mr. Brooks developed for his New England series. He proceeds, not by analyzing the writers' works or ideas, but by biographical sketches. This time he has a broader canvas. He cannot
depict the worthies of one region alone, but must move succes-
sively, in his opening chapters, from Philadelphia in 1800, to
New York, New England, the South, and the West. Such chapters would almost inevitably be somewhat diffuse. They become
far more so by Brooks' casual way of treating time. He does not
confine himself to an exact account of the country in 1800, such
as Henry Adams provided so brilliantly for his history of the
period of Jefferson and Madison. What Brooks does is to range
back and forth through the half century after the Revolution as
though it was a static entity. He conveys thereby little sense of
the exciting genetic development. When, at the close of the war,
someone pronounced it in Franklin's hearing as the War for
Independence, he retorted that the War for Independence remained yet to be fought. Brooks' negligence of chronology, his
repeated reliance on such loose phrases as 'during these years,'
'only the other day,' has deprived his narrative of most of the
dramatic tension of that cultural war.

His outlines are clearer when he comes to the biographies of
his chief figures, Jefferson, Audubon, Irving, Cooper, Bryant,
Simms, Poe, and N. P. Willis. As in his previous books he interweaves these careers as far as he can, and though that involves
a certain amount of repetition, it produces a sense of social
density. Since Parrington's method was also biographical in his
*Main Currents of American Thought,* and since he dealt with
nearly all of Brooks' leading figures, a comparison is relevant and
revelatory. Brooks of course makes no pretense to Parrington's
grasp of economic and political issues and therefore his surface

picture of 'brilliant and gay' Charleston naturally doesn't square
very well with the harshly aristocratic city in which Simms
nearly starved. Of greater moment is the fact that Parrington,
disciplined as he was by Sainte-Beuve and Taine, could give in
a dozen pages a more comprehensive and telling estimate of an
author's intellectual significance than Brooks can often do in
four or five times the space.

If Brooks is not writing social or intellectual history in any
strict sense, no more does his work belong with formal literary
history. He is not really placing works in their milieu, and he is
even less concerned with the genres to which they belong. Indeed, he frequently becomes so interested in the details of a
man's career that he hardly gets to his works at all. A reader
who had never heard of Freneau would reap here the picturesque
items of his trips to sea, but he would hardly realize the intense
imaginative quality of his best poems. For Brooks is almost
wholly indifferent to technical analysis. He sometimes gives a
free paraphrase of a book's contents, but he raises few issues
about structure or form. On the one or two occasions when he
faces himself with the merits of a poem, he is content with such
remarks as that Bryant, in 'To a Waterfowl,' 'for a moment entered the realm of magic,' or that Poe formed, in 'To Helen,' 'a
gem of purest ray serene.'

What all this points to is that Brooks' work belongs with the
kind of book that used to enjoy an immense popularity a century
ago, the kind of book indicated by such an old-fashioned title
as D'Israeli's *Curiosities of Literature, Consisting of Anecdotes,
Characters, Sketches, and Observations.* Brooks always steeps
himself in the letters and memoirs of a period and has a charming flair for the out-of-the-way anecdote. You can learn from him
as you can from nobody else that the ivy at Irving's Sunnyside
came from Melrose Abbey, that the gardenia was named for Dr.
Alexander Garden of Charleston, and that the author of 'The
Night Before Christmas' was a professor of Hebrew. Brooks has
a particular fondness for any literary association, such as that
Shelley's grandfather was born in Newark or that Keats' brother
lived in Louisville. And it is astonishing how many writers he
has managed to overtake on trips together, whether Brockden

Brown and the author of 'Home, Sweet Home' on a Hudson River sloop, or Simms declaiming the verses of Fitz-Greene Halleck to Bryant on the heights of Weehawken.

On a more serious level the chief service of Brooks' exploratory reading is the number of thumbnail introductions he can make to the general reader of half-forgotten figures. His very lack of strict categories allows him to present a glimpse of Matthew Maury, the oceanographer, or Andrew Jackson Downing, the landscape architect. Brooks is always happiest when he is describing nature, and in this period of the discovery of American scenery his best pages deal with the debt of Bryant and the Hudson River painters alike to Linnaeus' botanical accuracy, or with the magnificent achievements of Audubon and the other naturalists.

There is every reason why Brooks can be more adequate in dealing with the world of Washington Irving than with that of Hawthorne or of Henry James or of the present. Irving's New York was subject to none of the dynamic ideas which Brooks' concentration on personalities almost eliminated from the New England renaissance. Nor does Brooks have to reckon here with later intellectual movements which he has found so distasteful that it has caused him to renounce with one inaccurate phrase Joyce, Hemingway, O'Neill, Dreiser, and Eliot as all being 'bent on proving that life is a dark little pocket.' Moreover, Irving is an author whom Brooks can portray with real fondness, for he was genial, suave, and untroubled, with a genuine sweetness of sentiment and an antiquarian's taste for history and romance. The capacity of Brooks' imagination to feel at home in that world is testified by his chapter on Willis, the frothy essayist, to whom Brooks gives a much higher rating than he has enjoyed from any other twentieth-century critic.

When it comes to Poe, Brooks' biographical method works far better than it did, say, with Hawthorne. For Hawthorne's quality could hardly be reached by evoking the atmosphere of his largely uneventful existence, and as a result Brooks missed almost entirely the significance of his deeply tragic imagination. But in Poe's case the tragedy was on the surface as well, and the story of his shattered life corresponds in tone to the haunted realm of his fiction.

But the chief center of energy in this book is provided by the pivotal position which Brooks has given to Jefferson. He treats him first among his major figures, and though he hardly adds any new insights to Chinard's interpretation we can never have too many anecdotes about Jefferson. Furthermore, the most robust strain in Brooks' mind is his sympathy with the Jeffersonian tradition, and he takes great pleasure in stating that 'The left was the side of the American imagination.' When he tries to prove that contention in relation to Cooper, he writes all around the subject, since, again in contrast with Parrington, he fails even to mention *The American Democrat*, Cooper's most explicit statement of his particular mixture of democratic conviction and aristocratic leanings. But feeling through Cooper's career in his own circuitous way, Brooks comes out with one of his best formulations: that the vitality of Cooper's common men, Harvey Birch, Long Tom, and Natty Bumppo, as over against his stiff and stilted aristocrats, proves which side Cooper's 'genius loved.'

The generalization of this sector of our past with which Brooks ends his book is that its writers 'were emotionally uncomplicated and seemed singularly happy' in comparison with the writers of a later age. That generalization can be accomplished not merely by making a special exception for Poe; it demands also that you ignore the foreshadowing of Poe's dark compulsive fantasies in Freneau and Brockden Brown. The 'haunted mind' has been a pervasive strain in American writing from Cotton Mather through Hemingway and Faulkner, though Brooks apparently doesn't like to dwell on it. No more, apparently, in his present bland mood, does he like to entertain controversy. Otherwise he would scarcely have avoided turning Poe loose on Halleck's shallow substitution of fancy for imagination or have neglected to mention how unsatisfactory, for the needs of a major literature, Melville found Irving's 'studied avoidance of all topics but smooth ones.'

Before and after the last war Brooks was writing a series of books—read by a few hundred instead of by many thousands—

which took a wry view of our past, which harped on the thinness and starvation of our cultural life. I entirely disagree with Bernard DeVoto that the effect of such books was to depress the generation of the 'twenties with the futility of American possibilities. On the contrary, they served for the younger writers of that day as a challenge for reinvigoration. But Brooks himself now seems to agree with DeVoto. As the world tragedy of the last decade has deepened, Brooks has felt it increasingly urgent to provide American readers with an image of the nobility and assurance of our past. He seems to feel that what we need most now is a restored confidence. He may be right, although it could be argued that we will emerge from this war the most confident of all countries in the superiority of our ways, and that what we need more is an astringent antidote to shake us out of any complacent and fatuous dream of 'the American century.'

But, right or wrong, Brooks' feelings have little to do with the proper function of the historian or critic. Neither his earlier dejected image of our past nor his present glowing one is anything like an objective interpretation of the complex and warring forces that make up human life at any period. Brooks is not really a critic but a lyric poet *manqué*, who endows selected aspects of our history with the overtones of his own sensibility. A critic must meditate more profoundly on what Matthew Arnold meant by seeing the object as it really is; and, like Poe, he must be concerned with the first principles of the arts with which he is dealing.

*The New York Times Book Review*, 1944

# Instances of Critical Method

IN this case the publishers' blurbs are relevant. Van Wyck Brooks pronounces Nuhn a writer of 'real vision,' while Edmund Wilson gives his approval to Geismar. This makes an appropriate alignment, since *The Wind Blew from the East* is a kind of corn-fed *America's Coming of Age*, and *Writers in Crisis* uses a method certainly learned in part from *The Triple Thinkers*. It will be as instances of critical method and its application that these two books chiefly command our interest, as ambitious efforts to reorient and extend our living tradition.

Nuhn's study is the first installment of a projected trilogy. His leading assumption is that 'our main tradition is not "romantic," in any useful meaning of the word,' that Franklin and Jefferson, Emerson and Whitman, Twain and Garland and the later Middle Western novelists, have all been 'realistic' in their assimilation of experience. But these writers are not his subject here. He has reserved them for another volume, as he has also the treatment of the 'tragic strand' in our literature. Here he has concentrated on 'our minor "aristocratic tradition," ' more specifically on Henry James, Henry Adams, and Eliot, more generally on speculations of 'how to accommodate in our tradition the Atlantic Ocean'! He gives the first full-length literary account of a phenomenon which our historians have often noted, the so-called back-track movement. While our economic pioneers were driving ever more rapidly westward through the nineteenth century, our cultural current was often drawn eastward. We can note this as early as

*The Wind Blew from the East: A Study in the Orientation of American Culture* by Ferner Nuhn. Harper & Bros.
*Writers in Crisis: The American Novel Between Two Wars* by Maxwell Geismar. Houghton Mifflin Co.

239

Washington Irving and Longfellow, though the pilgrimages became more frequent after the Civil War. Howells and then Garland went reverently from the Middle West to Boston, while
James was just leaving Boston for Europe and leading the way
in turn for Eliot and the postwar expatriates of 1919. Nuhn's
mode of symbolizing this phenomenon is suggested by his chap-
ter-title, 'East Wind—Western Star,' and a characteristic instance
of his evocative style reveals his thesis: 'West for work and
money, back East for ease and grace. West for profanity, East
for piety. West for action, East for status. West for function,
East for ornament. West for democratic color, East for aristocratic form. That is what the East Wind says.'

When he descends to particulars, Nuhn's work is very uneven.
He makes the most extended application of his variegated thesis
to James, but seems betrayed by his dichotomizing when he goes
to the length of saying that for this novelist 'Europe is form without spirit, America spirit without form.' There are so many instances in which that vague contrast would not hold that it is
more profitable to consider Nuhn's handling of *The Golden
Bowl,* the one work of James to which he devotes a detailed
scrutiny. In dealing with 'the enchanted kingdom' of Maggie
Verver, he bears down hard upon the fairytale 'make-believe
ending,' and, to bring out the unreal element in the glowing aura
of Maggie's love, he writes a brilliantly ingenious passage on how
the story might have been told from Charlotte Stant's point of
view. That story would have brought to the surface realms of
the unconscious which James did not probe, and by revealing
aspects of unrecognized sexual pathology in the overly close
relations of Maggie and her father, it might well have ended by
turning 'the lovely princess' into 'the bad witch.'

It is too bad that Nuhn did not provide more such specific
analyses, since his wider generalizations about James are often
dubious. He is considerably less adequate on Adams, for here he
intrudes the fallacy which has so frequently distorted modern
criticism: that the man 'is more important than his work.' In the
case of an intellectual like Adams such a proposition is preposterous, inasmuch as the only relevant image we can have of him
is that which his writings provide. Nuhn further restricts the

value of this chapter by the device of substituting the part for
the whole, by concentrating upon—and overreading—the poem to
the Virgin of Chartres, as though it was Adams' central performance. He thereby symbolizes the main issue of Adams' life as a
choice 'between the Mothers and the Fathers.' The masterly
*History of the United States During the Administrations of
Jefferson and Madison* is hardly more than mentioned, though
this work alone would greatly modify the conception of Adams'
dependence upon Europe.

The most interesting point in the chapter on Eliot is Nuhn's
contention that *The Waste Land* 'is not tragic,' that it amounts to
being one of the long series of poetic 'descents into hell,' but that
there is no proper tragic resolution and release. This might raise
the absorbing question of why so many American writers have
possessed a tragic sense without having been able to write full
tragedy, of why our frequent structure has been an engulfing
descent into the maelstrom, even in the case of *Moby Dick*. Nuhn
almost entirely disqualifies himself as a commentator upon such
questions by another lapse in method, the most serious with
which his pages can be charged. He proceeds on the naive basis
that since a symbolist poem yields different levels of meaning, it
is fair game to find in it anything you choose. Consequently he
reads into Eliot's lines every stray association of his own. The
Dog Star means the ascendancy of naturalism or democracy, the
'fiery points' of the hair of the society woman in 'The Game of
Chess' suggest the nimbus of the Goddess of Liberty, Stetson
might 'on a chance' be Pound and the one-eyed merchant Joyce,
while the Elizabethan birdcall 'jug jug' connotes 'inspiration out
of jugs, or perhaps the jugular vein severed . . .'! These details
are only the beginning of the private poem which Nuhn sub-
stitutes for the original. He is even less disciplined in handling
Eliot's later work where he forces any line from its context to
prove what he will about the poet's retreat into faith.

If I have insisted upon Nuhn's defects and have not given due
credit to his range of 'stimulating' and 'challenging' ideas, it is
because I believe it our duty now to be on guard against the
modes of thought inaugurated in our criticism by Nuhn's master.
*America's Coming of Age* was salutary in making us aware of

the insufficiency of our cultural past; but by the time Brooks had reached middle age and was dissatisfied with his own earlier dissatisfaction, he substituted a quite different image. He sentimentalized our past and then went on to give a warped and mean-spirited view of our present. Nuhn is obviously a man of good intentions, with a more catholic and full-blooded taste than Brooks. But his method is wholly irresponsible. If we are to have adequate cultural history, we must begin by respecting the texts themselves. Nuhn's freehand renderings finally obliterate all essential distinctions even between Emerson and Dante, so that he doesn't grasp why Eliot should have felt it an issue to turn from Unitarianism to Catholicism. For Nuhn, or for any critic who so hypostatizes ideas, both 'visions' are equal.

The greater value of Geismar's book consists in the fact that he has hewed much closer to the pattern of what his authors have said. He has set himself explicitly to a study 'of the changing beliefs of the contemporary American novelist in our period of social crisis.' The solid foreground of his attention is occupied with the complete works to date of Lardner, Hemingway, Dos Passos, Faulkner, Wolfe, and Steinbeck. He examines these writers singly and in their relations with one another. He is particularly incisive, for instance, in showing what a similar verdict is pronounced upon the disintegrating millionaires' world of the 'twenties by Lardner's stories and by *To Have and Have Not*. He notes again how both Hemingway and Dos Passos were attracted to Spain for the pleasure, vitality, and dignity of its life, but with the contrast that *Death in the Afternoon* in 1932 was 'talking of the matador,' whereas *Rosinante* in 1922 was 'already discussing the masses.'

The limitations of Geismar's straightforward method are much simpler to pin down than Nuhn's. The most damaging one can be stated in the proposition that ideas are not novels. He says that 'ours is a particularly interesting time to study art,' but he hardly makes that study in any strict sense. As is sometimes the case with Wilson, he tends to take each novelist's form too much for granted and to range about in his content. The result is particularly apparent with Lardner. Geismar provides much the most thorough treatment yet in print of the implications of his frustrated satire, but sometimes, by taking Lardner's statements straight, he neglects the conventions of frozen-faced humor in which Lardner was dealing, and makes him seem serious in the wrong sense. Again Geismar is impressed with Wolfe's development, but he seems to assess it too much in Wolfe's own assertions, not enough through the evidence—the only cogent evidence —of a created work of art. And the vexed question of to what degree Faulkner is a writer with a genuine vision of social decadence rather than a synthetic Dostoevsky cannot be settled by the easy assumption that he is 'equal to any technic.' His technic must be scrutinized, his devices seen in their component parts, his dictions and rhythms alertly listened to, if we are to judge whether his effects are genuine or manipulated.

The chapter which shows Geismar's real strength within his limitations is naturally that on Dos Passos, since Dos Passos as a conscious social critic presents of all the group the most significant range of intellectual development. By considering everything the novelist has written, Geismar demonstrates how utterly the early Dos Passos hero, the aesthetic young man, was dissociated from American life. So too with this hero's creator: his concern with revolution in the postwar world was conditioned almost exclusively by European models—witness how much he seems to have learned, at the very start of his career, from the Spanish radical novelist Pío Baroja. In consequence of his lack of any living contact with the American past, a lack widely felt in his immediate generation, Dos Passos in his trilogy often seemed to equate democracy with finance capitalism, and to ignore our own revolutionary tradition. This restricted view caused him, as Geismar notes, to miss entirely the tragic significance of Woodrow Wilson at the climax of 1919, to see in him not the defeated hero of the older liberalism with his *hamartia* of pride, but a mere hollow gesturer, a marionette with his poppies at the tomb of the Unknown Soldier.

As evidence of Dos Passos' more recent growth, Geismar cites *The Ground We Stand On,* and though he does not exaggerate the value of that amateur history of the era from Roger Williams to Jefferson, he seems to press its implications for Dos Passos' reorientation pretty far. He finds that, as a result of that study, the novelist now seems to be on the verge 'of his own big American critique.' But the ground we stand on is no longer the brightly lighted terrain of the philosophers of the Enlightenment, and any effectual human freedom must obviously be won through the control of far more complex economic forces than our revolutionary fathers had to face.

It is to such complex forces that both Nuhn and Geismar devote their final chapters, and thus most clearly indicate the date line at which their critiques have been shaped. Geismar would seem to be in substantial agreement with Nuhn's statement that 'There is a new idea in the world, effective common choice in economic as well as political rule.' In his concern that our individualism should no longer be distorted into 'the superiority of one individual over another,' Geismar attempts to chart the most fertile lines of development for our social novel. He has by no means escaped the fashionable jargon of our journalistic criticism, which increasingly tends to categorize our literature in terms of rigid decades. Indeed, Geismar carries to its ludicrous extreme the tendency to regard the year '29 as a wall of fire separating the 'thirties from a Gomorrah given over entirely to 'rising stocks and rising skirts.' In so hypostatizing a decade and writing about it in a pastiche lingo imitated from Dos Passos' Newsreels, Geismar adds his own chapter to the willful oversimplifications of our past. For he quite neglects that, on the creative level with which he is dealing, the 'twenties were not primarily the realm of American Can & Can and Peaches Browning, but the period when more good poets were writing at their maturity than during any other decade in our history, and when the American theater first took on international stature. Fortunately Geismar does not indulge in the latest form of romanticism, now current in the liberal weeklies, where the view prevails that the next monolithic barrier is '39, and that since change is king, the one thing sure about the literature of the present decade is that it must have nothing in common with that of the last.

Both Nuhn and Geismar, in so far as he looks forward rather than back, are more serious critics than that. Both are occupied with our cultural continuity. They have further in common that both end up discussing our social structure. They are symptomatic of current politics in that though both seem committed to some form of socialism, they reject Marxist toughness. They both affirm their hopes with enheartening passion, even though Geismar sometimes breaks into merely excited rhetoric and Nuhn into folksy pep talk. They are both finally vague on how the transformation to their new societies is to be implemented. Nuhn doesn't get much more specific than that we must act through our tradition of 'good faith' rather than by compulsion. Geismar comes somewhat closer to social actuality by conjecturing that the popularity of *The Grapes of Wrath* might conceivably indicate that the United States will accomplish its sweeping economic changes 'as a new sort of popular fashion.' Both these writers bring new horizons to our criticism, though neither has mastered a method, and both write with the eloquence of innocence.

*Partisan Review,* 1942

# An Indispensable Resource

THE announced ending of *The Southern Review* could hardly have come at a worse time. For the war has inevitably accelerated that tendency of a mass society which Auden, among others, has observed, the tendency of the great majority to prefer opinion to knowledge. We can see the effects of that tendency almost everywhere in our journalistic criticism.

This piece, thus entitled and written in 1941 or 1942, is printed from a manuscript found among Matthiessen's papers. I have been unable to discover whether it was published.—ED.

With the death of Joyce following so near upon that of Yeats, and so near also to those of Freud and Frazer, of Trotsky and Bergson, we can realize, as Harry Levin has done in his incisive study of Joyce, how suddenly we are losing the landmarks of a whole cultural age. But the standardized way of manipulating opinion is to regard Joyce's death, in the manner of Van Wyck Brooks, as the end of an era when the artist was in willful isolation from society, and, therefore, as the harbinger of a more healthy day when the artist is to feel himself in accord with the aspirations of his nation. Such opinion involves a vicious perversion of the knowledge we might gain from Joyce's work. It involves the cardinal fallacy of identifying the writer's subject with his intention, of assuming that because Joyce portrayed a decaying Dublin he must himself have been decadent, instead of realizing that we have in *Ulysses* one of the most moving presentations of a debased stage of mechanized society. If the function of the artist is to give us the full knowledge that he has acquired of life, without suppressing anything, we can hardly blame Joyce for his subject. And if, through the integrity of Joyce's testimony, we see the dead end to which the isolated artist has come, we have there the kind of living evidence that art alone can present.

It will do no good—to move closer to our present crisis—for anyone to pretend that art serves society on the simplified level of a war poster. We may assume that the healthiest condition is when the artist speaks both *for* and *to* his society, since the great periods of the drama would reinforce that assumption. But we can make no single formula about the relation of the artist to war. In the circumstances of Athens, the function of Aristophanes was to satirize corrupt leadership and to work as hard for peace as he could. Charles Nordhoff, robbed now of his escape to the South Seas and filled with the right opinions about the war, finds it impossible, according to *Time*, to understand how Jane Austen could have written *Pride and Prejudice* during the Napoleonic wars—but the common reader would scarcely substitute her human knowledge for all the stanzas about Waterloo. Whitman, however, was brought to emotional maturity by the events of the Civil War, and wrote his profoundest lines on the theme of reconciliation, out of his rich sympathy for victor and vanquished alike. As a farther variant, we should remember that although Joyce's indifference to his age is now being symbolized by his having spent most of the last war in Switzerland writing about the single day of a Jew in Dublin, many far more 'normal' writers were doing comparable things. Our American poetic renaissance had just started in 1914, and the years between then and 1918 were marked, for example, by much of the best work of Frost and Sandburg, whose main attention was hardly deflected from their own regions, from north of Boston or from the lives of cornhuskers.

If this war is different from the last one, as even a lifelong pacifist like Karl Barth argues, it is so only in the sense that fascism in its violent denial of basic human rights is immeasurably worse than any of the capitalistic states of 1914. No more than the last is this a holy war, nor a war to determine our superiority over other peoples. The resistance to fascism can re-create the heroic sense, as Malraux proved in writing about China and Spain. But adequate resistance to fascism over a long period demands the continual renewal of the values for which we are fighting. It is not enough to keep open the channels of protest, to make sure that we preserve our right to discuss war aims and peace aims, and to prevent a democratic war against aggression from being perverted into a war for world empire. All these are major responsibilities, but what I am concerned with here is more impalpable, but no less important. It is nothing less than the necessity of the mind and spirit to preserve their health by the variety and scope of their action, by the free play, even the exuberance that only the arts can provide. These may seem strange attributes to argue for in a time of crisis, but we will be no better off for having lost our American humor, or our theater, or our music.

A great danger in our vigorously pragmatic national spirit is that now, even more than before, we will mistake essentials for inessentials and cut down on the arts as though they were sugar. We should not forget that even in peacetime our bias has been heavily toward the immediately instrumental. Almost any further push in that direction, either in our universities or our general thought, would so weaken the humane cultural traditions that in a few years we would be producing narrowly trained technicians whose state of mind was almost indistinguishable from the hard efficiency of the fascists. At such a time all modes of free communication should be encouraged, so that the artist will know that he continues to have an audience, and the critic that his responsibilities remain. The loss of *The Southern Review* is that of an indispensable resource, like a vitamin.

# VI.  THE BROKEN ARC

*When the Pacific called out the response of his [Melville's] united body and mind, he wrote the enduring signature of his age. He gave full expression to its abundance, to its energetic desire to master history by repossessing all the resources of a hidden past in a timeless and heroic present. But he did not avoid the darkness in that past, the perpetual suffering in the heart of man, the broken arc of his career which inevitably ends in death. He thus fulfilled what Coleridge held to be the major function of the artist: he brought 'the whole soul of man into activity.'*

'AMERICAN RENAISSANCE'

# *Credo, 1922*

H ERE at Yale we are inclined to take things rather too much for granted. We glibly talk of our traditions as something everlasting, and forget that most of them originated in the vague limbo of eighteen-ninety. We unconsciously consider the College of today to be the same as our fathers knew, and so it is astonishing to find in the musty pages of an old *Lit* an account of 'the more splendid entrances of Durfee, a building which is certainly ornamental and whose rooms are spacious and elegant.'

For, in general, we have accepted our surroundings as a permanent matter of fact, and have not stopped to analyze just why they are as they are. Most of us hardly know the reason of our being here at all. In our four years we are continually passing through a series of changes—πάντα ῥεῖ—everything is in a state of flux. Our ideas and ideals, our opinions and our minds are ever changing, developing, broadening. The Senior is the Freshman only in that he is the unifying body in which during the four-year span these many shifting thoughts have been welded together, and the instant has in truth been made eternity. For the Freshman is too engrossed with the business of becoming acclimatized, heeling some publication or other activity, and making friends to have much time for anything else. Towards the close of the spring term he looks forward to Sophomore year with a certain relish. Then is when he will do all that reading and extra study, that plain living and high thinking, which he has planned. But, curiously enough, Sophomore year brings with it new and unforeseen petty distractions which devour the time

This statement appeared as a 'Leader' editorial in the *Lit* in Matthiessen's senior year at Yale.—ED.

at an incredible rate, and leave no more room for contemplation than the year previous.

And so with the last half of the cycle: the two final years swing by confusedly and bring us to the precipice of graduation, a charm or two on our watch chain, a smattering of knowledge which we may or may not find comforting, nothing more.

Our development has been something of a hand-to-mouth affair. We have learned certain unrelated facts about this and that, and have sketchily attempted to piece them together. But ordinarily they have not fitted, because we have not devoted enough sheer intellectual effort to the analysis of our own ideas. We have not the slightest conception of what we *believe*. We may have learned to think with reasonable clarity, and our ideals may be rather high, but we have built up no scheme of life, nothing by which to live. Any philosophy or creed which we may possess is, at best, vague, inchoate, and fragmentary.

This, as I have said, is because we have never searched our souls with the cold, relentless light of reason in an attempt to understand every fiber of our make-up, we have taken things for granted, we have known only our exteriors, we have not known ourselves.

And living thus almost entirely on the surface, we have inevitably grown to think of a philosophy of life as hardly an essential. 'What need have I for all this truck about religion?' we ask frankly, for we have not yet been brought face to face with the Truth that in order to realize our highest possibilities we must be utterly dominated by an ideal. We wish to move the world, but we have not yet been impressed with the necessity of having a place to stand. We have not been convinced that we must believe in something.

The whole question has seemed to be something ethereal, something far removed from our own natural lives. Consequently we have been inclined to think of religion as little else but repression and that its followers knew nothing either of happiness or of life. They seemed to belong to a world apart—to a world that was drab and unreal.

So Christianity has become the most forbidding word in the language. Judging by its present fruits—by a decadent church

and by sweaty Y.M.C.A. gymnasiums—we have pronounced it
to be woefully lacking. We have not seen that these are in
reality not fruits at all, but abortions, that although the church
in its present form has outlived its usefulness, the spirit which
exists in each one of us is as dominating now as it ever was, if
only we will open our hearts to it. We have never stopped to
think these questions through to their conclusion. We take un-
truths and half-truths for granted, and allow misconceptions to
pass current without ever a sincere effort to get at the eternal
strength of things.

And so we hear men talk of humility, and we laugh at them.
We wish to assert ourselves, to express our own individuality,
and being humble seems to convey the very opposite. We look
upon it as something synonymous with servility, as a state of
groveling self-abasement in which a man must sacrifice both his
personality and his self-respect.

We hear men talk of brotherly love and it seems to us a
farce. How could anybody pretend to care for everyone equally,
to put his closest friend and the man in the street in the same
class? What could be more unnatural, more hypocritical?

And again we hear men talk of self-surrender and we hate
them for it. Why should I surrender myself? I am I. I possess
my ideas and ideals, and these are enough. Why should I not
strive to realize them without any external aid, any 'something
not myself'?

Thus we argue and thus we feel because we are repelled by
words whose meaning we do not fully understand. Our minds
have never pried deeply enough to find the Truth that humility
is nothing mean, nothing subservient, but rather the natural
consciousness of reverence before everything beautiful and
sacred in the universe. We have thought the ideal of brotherly
love to be futile because we have looked upon it only superficially. We have not realized that instead of a mere question of
surface like or dislike, it involves a tremendous tolerance and
sympathy with all of mankind, and that although difficult, if not
impossible, to attain in its fullness, it certainly is the antithesis
of hypocritical. We have loathed the very sound of self-surrender because we have taken the word in its cold and literal sense,

and have not understood that instead of sacrificing any trace of individuality in giving ourselves up to the spiritual and the ideal, we find instead a new fullness and depth to life. For self-surrender is actually a self-realization more compelling than our brightest dreams.

*Yale Literary Magazine,* 1922

# *Russell Cheney, 1881–1945*

RUSSELL Cheney, the eleventh and youngest child of Knight Dexter Cheney and Ednah Dow Smith, was born at South Manchester, Connecticut, on October 16, 1881, and died at Kittery, Maine, on July 12, 1945.

The Cheney family, originally of Norman stock, had come to this country from England in 1635, and had located first at Rowley, Massachusetts. By the beginning of the eighteenth century they were settled as prosperous farmers near Hartford, and in 1831 Cheney's grandfather and three brothers founded their mill for the manufacture of silk. Two of the painter's great-uncles, Seth and John Cheney, were notable steel-engravers.

Cheney attended the Hartford High School, and followed his four brothers to Yale, where his vivid nature began to unfold and made him many solid and lasting friends. He graduated in 1904, with no special scholastic distinction, though he did a great deal of reading on his own, particularly of French history. He also nourished himself on Emerson, who prepared him to find, some years later, Whitman as his poet. While at college he spoke of being an architect, but he had already secretly resolved to be a painter. Long afterwards he mentioned shyly how one eve-

The Introduction to *Russell Cheney, 1881–1945: A Record of His Work.*—ED.

ning, while by himself in the old studio where his great-uncles
had worked, he felt suddenly overcome by the beauty of a
replica of the Venus de Milo and knelt in adolescent dedication
at her knees. It was characteristic of him that in the midst of a
gregarious family he kept his inner life almost entirely unspoken.
But when he broached to his parents his desire to study art, he
encountered no opposition from his father, and from his mother
warm support.

He worked at the Art Students' League in New York for three
years, and then for another three years in Paris at the Académie
Julien, under Jean-Paul Laurens. He felt that he had an immense
amount to learn, since he had not started seriously to work until
he was twenty-three, an age at which most European painters
would already have been practiced in their craft. He realized
later that having been a student so long, he also had much to
unlearn. A wholly unself-conscious openness to new experience
remained with him throughout his life, and kept him young in
spirit to the end.

He was president of the Art Students' League in 1912, and
began to paint in the summers with the group surrounding
Charles H. Woodbury at Ogunquit, Maine. This book begins
with his Paris Salon portrait in 1911 and represents all phases
of his productive career. He painted in many different sections
of this country, as well as abroad, and the recent facile opposition between 'the American sceners' and 'the expatriates' breaks
down entirely in his case. He never thought of himself as anything
but an American, but he wanted to master great painting wherever it was to be found. As a student he made equally absorbed
copies of Manet's 'Girl with a Parrot' and Copley's 'Mrs. Seymour
Fort.' Like many other Americans he loved Paris, but he did not
find a strong taste for Racine incompatible with a lifelong devotion to Thoreau's *Walden*.

Cheney's work was exhibited extensively throughout the country, as well as at the Babcock, Montross, and Ferargil galleries
in New York. At the time of his death he was represented in
museums at San Francisco, Hartford, Newark, Boston, Portland,
Santa Fe, and Yale. He willed his remaining canvases and panels,
about two hundred altogether, to me as the friend most closely

in touch with his work. My aim in making this book of reproductions, in connection with a memorial exhibition, is to let his
pictures speak for themselves, as far as they can in black and
white. I have selected the pictures he regarded as the best from
all stages of his development. I have made no attempt to estimate
his achievement, since I can still hear his chuckle as he read:
'Writers on art as a rule know little of the actual problems of
painting, and the best they can do is deceive a public that knows
less.' That is not to say that he failed to respect a real expert like
Berenson or Roger Fry.

Fortunately Cheney himself furnished the best possible kind
of commentary on his work, in letters to friends, especially to
Phelps Putnam and to me. From a mass of material I have selected primarily the passages bearing upon the canvases repro-
duced. To an exceptionally uninhibited degree Cheney wrote as
he talked to his intimates. His handwriting was very rapid, 'hen-
tracks on eternity,' as he once called it, and corresponded both
to his lively mind and to his rich vibrant Connecticut voice. It
gave permanence to the most incisive and revelatory observations on the nature of art that it has been my privilege to hear.

*Russell Cheney: A Record of His Work*, 1947

# Phelps Putnam, 1894–1948

ALTHOUGH Phelps Putnam did not die until near the
end of the nineteen-forties, he was essentially a poet
of the nineteen-twenties. He belonged to the generation that
came of age with the First World War, and the world contemplated by his maturing thought was that of the postwar decade.
His first book, *Trinc* (1927), took its title from Rabelais' Oracle

of the Bottle, and its two sections were called, 'Green Wine' and
'Brandy.' This was Putnam's way of suggesting his conscious
shift in emphasis from his early lyrics to philosophical poems of
a headier concentration.

His 'Epistle to Mr. Manning and Mr. Walker,' both of whom
had been with him at Yale, is a vivid expression of that consciousness, and of the attitudes and temper of that period. Eliot's
epigraph for 'A Cooking Egg,' the Villon lines,

> En l'an trentiesme de mon aage
> Que toutes mes hontes j'ay beues,

served to condense a state of mind for many others, Putnam
among them. He envisaged his friends and himself as 'founder-
ing at twenty-nine,' after having 'been around' and having
earned their pay 'in mines and mills, in offices and wars.' But the
peculiarly American accent of that time comes in the poet's lines
voicing his attitude toward 'the brawl in Europe':

> We came away,
> Finding our pockets lined with bright exchange,
> To the clamor of our own remorseless mirth.
> And are we sad to see how nation after nation
> Sits crying in the acid light of change?
>
> We are not sad.
> We hear the rumor carelessly,
> It is the merest confirmation
> Of secrets whispered in our infant ears
> By change before we ever came to birth.

Europe might feel its cultural stability broken by the recent
vast destruction, and already menaced by further violence ahead,
but its losses were still three thousand miles away from us. As
Americans we had always been used to change, and at that
moment we were bursting with a new sense of untried vitality,
of an untold wealth of possibilities. This cocky awareness, as expressed by Putnam, with a reckless gusto even in its cynicism,
seems far closer to the quality of the nineteen-twenties as I remember them than the mood of empty disillusion often attributed
to them during the more socially conscious 'thirties.

Yet Putnam made no pompous assumption to wisdom. His
lines go on to sketch his haphazard search for some guidance
amid the crosscurrents of modern scientific cosmologies, particularly in the then newly popularized theory of relativity. But as
a poet, Joyce and Yeats and Eliot had made him more aware of
the need to repossess, at the heart of change, whatever cultural
continuity he could through a rediscovery of the use of myth.
Through myth a poet could affirm man's permanent nature beneath whatever superficially altered guises. It was again characteristic of Putnam that he felt his instinctive kinship with the
previous period in American history which had been most conscious of these very possibilities:

> Old Herman's Whale is blowing in our seas
> And Walt is roaring to the Whale
> Above the noise of guards and aeroplanes
> Down with the smugglers along the shore.

But the smugglers were there, it was the era of prohibition,
and Putnam's usual tones were those of defiance. As he looked
back over his spent youth for any clues to certitude, he found,
like Hemingway, his greatest assurance in his own body. The
central passage of affirmation in this 'Epistle' is in celebration of
the joys of food and drink and sexuality. All other stays may
fail man, all theories may die in his brain, but his blood and
spirit have known where to find their outrageous release. Yet as
he looked to the future, Putnam could end his poem only with
the ironic realization that even though he and his friends had
brought their 'pleasure home and paid no duty,' they could
hardly engage 'to meet for dinner on the spoil.' For they could
not foresee what rewards their age and land would yield them:

> Call it a foundling empire at our feet
> Sprawling undiapered and noisily,
> Or call it hell, but we,
> We shall not stand uncovered in the street
> To hear the tune the plaintive coroner sings;
> Our youths have met their quantum finally,
> We have moved away and given off their heat,
> And there is time to think of other things.

It was during the winter when he wrote this 'Epistle' that I began to know Putnam well. He had been at Yale half a dozen years before me, and I had first heard of him through *Parabalou*, the miscellany of verse issued in 1919 by several then recent Yale poets, including MacLeish and Stephen Benét as well as Putnam. The years just before and just after the war witnessed a more widespread flowering of poets at American colleges than at any previous time. At Harvard the generation of Cummings and Hillyer and Cowley had succeeded that of Eliot and Aiken. Edna Millay had been at Vassar and Leonie Adams at Barnard, John Peale Bishop and Edmund Wilson at Princeton, and in 1922 the *Fugitive* group gathered around Ransom at Vanderbilt.

Putnam had produced relatively little at college, but had gradually come to realize that the thing he wanted most to do was to write poetry. After graduation he had supported himself by various office jobs, including a brief period as assistant editor at The Atlantic Monthly Press. But his health was always uncertain since he already suffered from very bad asthma. By the mid-nineteen-twenties he was writing advertising copy for an insurance company, by which his father was also employed, and the poet and his wife were living in the Boston suburb of Jamaica Plain, in a top-floor apartment of his parents' home. It was there that he wrote the most matured poems of his first book.

These poems sprang into life from the kind of group interplay that has been more usual in France than in America. Nearly every Saturday evening Ruth Putnam would cook a superb dinner which we would supplement by whatever red wine or spurious gin we could lay our hands on, and then give most of the night to some of the best talk I have ever heard. Charles Walker, at that time a free-lance writer of left-wing sympathies, 'the swift confused American, the nervous alchemist' of Putnam's 'Epistle,' was often there. Russell Cheney, the painter, would come up for week ends from his Connecticut studio, and sometimes Fred Manning, whom Putnam had called 'bleak friend, my rare unswerving company,' from his position of teaching American history at Swarthmore. But the most frequent and most volatile spirits in the group were two of my Yale classmates,

Max Foster and Russell Davenport. Both of them had shared in 'the Yale Renaissance,' as we so uninhibitedly called it, and both continued in these years to be greatly concerned with poetry before finding their careers in law and political journalism. Indeed, Davenport had settled in Boston for a couple of years primarily to be near the group, and Foster, 'that youth bound laughing to his young despair' of one of Putnam's sonnets, hurled into these Saturday nights all the giddy exuberance and fantastic imagination otherwise pent up by the Harvard Law School.

These evenings kept alive for me the otherwise almost sterile winters of working for my doctor's degree at Harvard. I admired immensely the work in progress that Putnam, responding in turn to the stimulation from such an audience, was producing and would read to us from week to week. I admired also the attitude from which it came. Putnam had just been assimilating *The Waste Land*, which helped him realize that his own poetry grew from very different roots. He knew that he possessed nothing like Eliot's erudition. More importantly, he also knew that he felt little of Eliot's sense of the emptiness of life without belief. He did not want his poems to arise out of a density of literary reference, but more directly, like Whitman's, out of experience in which he had been personally immersed, out of the rich values he had discovered through that immersion.

What I admired most in that attitude was Putnam's unwavering self-reliance, his determination not to borrow uncritically from even the best models, but to find out what was right for him. He detected the delusion in setting out to be a Poet with a capital letter as a means to gaining acclaim. He knew that such careerism, all too rife in America, was particularly destructive in the arts, since it could only result in work turned out for the career's sake, work factitiously pumped up. He hoped to write some good poems, but he knew that these could not be manufactured to order. If he did not have something that he was compelled to say, he hoped that he would keep quiet. The first poem he had read at Exeter which left him with the feeling of wanting to write was 'The Scholar Gypsy,' and much of that elusive indolent spirit, relaxed and waiting for its rare moments of inspiration, stayed with him in his maturity.

He was aware that the artist was peculiarly naked and de-
fenseless in America, since his values were inescapably opposed
to the ruthless competitive drives of our society. Whether consciously or not, he took his stand closest to that of an earlier New
England intransigent. He was most like Thoreau in the quality
of his philosophical anarchism. The objects of Putnam's affection
were, to be sure, quite different, but both worshipped at the
shrine of Pan. What Putnam found to celebrate constituted the
poems of 'Green Wine.'

The sonnet sequence proved to be the most successful form
for his early utterance, which was already more meditative than
purely lyric. One of these series affirmed the resources of 'strong
drink,' another explored the manifold possibilities of 'the cynic
mind.' Still another was inscribed 'To the Memory of Yale
College,' and that sequence especially marks Putnam's work off
from the self-consciously intellectualist verse of the imitators of
Eliot. Putnam always held a low view of the education that had
been officially offered him. He claimed that the only useful function of his courses at Yale had been to compel him to develop
his skeptical intelligence, in reaction to the conventional absurdities which they expounded. But the experience of being at
college was something else. Its essence was an intellectual companionship that you created with your contemporaries. This kind
of education, this sense of living on a grand scale, has been described more frequently in connection with Cambridge or Oxford than with American colleges, but it was as absorbing as
anything Putnam ever knew:

> Where was despair a swift and careless joke,
> And where was melancholy sweet and green?
> Where was remorse a thin and lovely smoke,
> And where was sin still arrogant and keen?
>
> Where was unseemly chance a playful child,
> And indolence the aim of death and birth,
> And where was drunkenness still bright and wild,
> And where was everything the food of mirth?
>
> There in the college all these things were so—
> The throat of thirsty youth drank our despair,

A gorgeous wine which made our senses glow
So that derisive laughter echoed there.

And even now with thin and clarion strains
That laughter sweeps across our pompous brains.

It is hard to know how this kind of poetry now strikes readers without a comparable experience, since it is not at all in the dominant idioms of our time. It is unashamedly romantic in its recapture of qualities more alive in youth than afterwards. Its margin of affirmation is a very narrow one since it deploys through paradoxes the equilibrium of which is almost inevitably destroyed by the severer tensions of later existence. Putnam was well aware of that fact in the retrospect with which he framed such poems. His delight in tearing away illusions had led him to the resolute conclusion that

> a nothingness
> Engulfs our wisdom any way we guess.

And yet, in the most dramatic transition of his early work, he went on:

A nothingness, and coolly from the waste
Now slender beauty rises strong and harsh,
And with it comes a salt ironic taste,
A tang of evening floating on the marsh.

That beauty is not delicate nor weak,
It can withstand all mockery and doubt,
It is the very words the mockers speak,
And only hardy fools can find it out.

The contrasting epithets fill out the range of Putnam's values, as he set himself to be one of those hardy fools. It should also be remarked that the poet's language here, rising to his theme, is at its most released and limpid. It bears authentic evidence of one of Putnam's chief ancestors in its echo both of the gnomic quality of Emerson's 'Brahma' and of its purling eloquence.

The last of Putnam's sonnet sequences commemorated his friends under the title, 'Seven Against Chance,' but he had begun to be very dissatisfied that his utterance was too personal. He set himself deliberately to master a more 'objective mode.' He was affected strongly by Yeats' doctrine of the mask or anti-self, as it voiced the need for the artist to undergo the discipline of taking for his model an artist whose style was the most difficult opposite from his own. For Putnam, who described himself in his 'Epistle' as

> drunk, sick, and over-kissed,
> Full of the sleepy romance of disdain,
> But favored by the snobbery of chance,

the most exacting mask could be no other than that of Dante. That anti-self could not only help him advance from lyric to philosophic expression. It could also help him explore the possibilities of suitable structures for the longer narratives that he now wanted to try.

He began to set down in his notebooks descriptions of a group of characters, as he searched for legends to contain their modern adventures. He conceived of a hero called Bill Williams, an American wanderer, who should encounter many varieties of experience and thereby gradually encompass our growing national complexity. Bill was to be the observer even more than the participant, and two of Bill's friends, Smollet Smith and Bigelow Hasbrouck, were among the characters whom Putnam was to realize most thoroughly in his poems. They actually corresponded to two sides of his own nature, as Prufrock and Sweeney corresponded to the poles of Eliot's distaste and fascinated revulsion. Smith was a young lyric poet, with disheveled clothes and impulsive gestures. Hasbrouck was somewhat more complex, an embodiment of the seasoned skeptical mind. As Putnam described him, with his 'finely etched white face,' his 'snug black coat and unruffled linen,' his black fedora and gold-topped cane, you became aware that here was the portrait of a dandy, in the direct line from Baudelaire.

These characters now started to figure in Putnam's narratives, in somewhat bewildering juxtaposition with some of his own friends. Partly in emulation of Dante, perhaps, but more surely as a means of projecting his own satire of contemporary bour-

geois society, Putnam launched Bill Williams on a passage
through Hell. It was a realm that Putnam knew well:

> The hero Bill was wandering around;
> He was no doubt in Hell, without a guide.
> He saw himself and all his brothers drowned
> In pools of crowded flesh and swarms of flies
> Buzzing about the ears and mouth and eyes
> Finding always a path to creep inside
> The brain and lay their vulgar eggs, and feed.
> He saw the smarter eunuchs learn the trick
> Of emulating minor anthropoids,
> To pick up dollars for the organ-man,
> And in their eyes he saw that they were sick.
> He saw the net of shimmering nerves unfurled
> And flayed to the teasing whine of rubber tires. . . .

This mood of seeing the modern world itself as an Inferno was
conditioned no doubt by Eliot's inheritance from Flaubert and
the symbolist poets. But Putnam's realistic observations were
sharply individual, as they were also in the other poems that
concluded *Trinc*, 'Hasbrouck and the Rose' and 'Bill Gets Burned.'
He called the poem, of which the above lines formed the opening, 'Bill and *Les Enfants Pendus*.' The children 'hung up' by
life were Foster and Davenport and Putnam himself. The poet
warns his hero to 'avoid those ropes which strangulate the will.'
He also reassures Bill: 'The acreage of Hell is not your home.'

The further contours of Bill's travels were shadowed forth in
the structure that Putnam devised for his second book, *The Five
Seasons* (1931). All of the ten poems collected here either involve Bill or provide a background for him. The opening poem,
'Words of an Old Woman,' conceives of the American continent
itself as a woman's body, as Hart Crane also did at this time, and
as MacLeish was to echo in his *Frescoes for Mr. Rockefeller's
City*. Putnam's harsh theme is the alienation of the land from
its succession of despoiling ravishers. He has by now endowed
Bill with mythic proportions in calling him 'a bastard child' of
the Sun by an earthly mother. In his desire to have his poems
move thus on two levels at once, both the realistic and the symbolic, Putnam was again sharing in one of the major tendencies

of that time. He gained thereby both imaginative density and amplitude.

In the central long poem in this book, 'Daughters of the Sun,' Bill—as the brief prose introduction notes—'having been abandoned to that darkness which was his Hell, at last met with his father.' The poem which Bill then recites is a hymn of celebration of the loves given to him by the Sun, varied loves of 'honor and innocence and lust,' which reached their joyous light-drenched climax in the perfect sensual companion of his blood. But such love was too ecstatic to endure, and, at the end of this poem, the hero is asking his father to release him at last from the body, 'into the energy of solitude.'

The title-poem carries Bill from summer in New York, autumn in New Mexico, and winter in New England to spring in a 'new world,' and—with the extensions always dear to Putnam's heart— at last beyond 'the unjust sequences of time,' where

> we, deploying always on the ridge
> Of hearts which meet the fire hardily,
> Shall take a season which we do not know.

The concluding poem finds Bill at the top of a mountain pass, 'on the knees of Chance,' where he suddenly hears the voices of millions of people singing a hymn to Chance, the only God within their experience.

The loose scaffolding provided for this volume implied a further structure in Putnam's mind, and he filled several notebooks with outlines that envisaged his hero as a kind of American Faust in his thirst for experience. The plot for the sustained narrative would sketch in some background from our geography and history. It would take Bill through successive stages of his education, both in the country and in cities. It would display the munificent gifts of nature to us, and then the consequences of our violent quests for power. Sickened by some of our more brutal exploitations, Bill would search again for the roots of freedom. He would realize that he no longer had a Church, but that he must reckon with the modern State 'as Institute and as Fact.'

Bill was to be peculiarly American in his 'concept of himself as the first man, as if he started all over, with no regard for the experience or opinions of parents, fathers of the state, dignitaries of religion, or of teachers of other than factual realities.' He was to conceive of himself too 'as the absolute in democratic feeling and action . . . Equality of any kind is no moral overturn or illumination to him, as it wouldn't be to any American who felt himself an American . . . He chooses anarchy as the actual, the real. He does not choose it as good or bad.'

Yet the poem was to witness a development in the hero's conceptions. He was to move from purely private loves to a more adequate 'love of his neighbor as himself.' He was to see that a too exclusive preoccupation with individualism could mean the loss of the individual. He was to gain 'a feeling of solidarity' with his fellow men, for, precarious as that might be to come by and to maintain, such feeling opened the only door to life.

Allen Tate and Paul Rosenfeld and Morton Zabel, in their appreciative reviews of *The Five Seasons,* all looked forward to the larger work. But though Putnam lived for almost twenty years after first outlining his intentions, *The Earthly Comedy* was not written. The only other poems he printed were a few jagged fragments.

What happened? The question was often asked by his friends, and the many partial answers yield another record of the problems of the artist in our time. The most obvious barrier to sustained composition was Putnam's health. Among his undated manuscripts is a page headed 'Asthma':

Invisible enemy—unseen fingers at my throat . . .

Down there the meadow sloping to the brook—under the willows where I lay. And I upon the bed gasping, having taken poison from the grasses of the field.

How shall I live who do not know when this will strike—yes even in the arms of women strike and turn a lover to a shrivelled, wheezing aged man with centuries of death piled on his chest.

In two minutes to change a man to a strangling beast, choking for life, to dissolve a soul into an ailing sore of flesh . . . But only we, my brothers, know the ecstasy of drawing natural breath.

But I remember the old man [Carl Eitel] who was penniless and

never drew a breath without hard struggle. How he lived lonely in
far valleys in the desert and went on, painting when he could stand,
rare pictures. He was more sick and more courageous than I am.

This devil to which one can only yield—and fight by supine cunning
in despair.

And I will not yield an inch. I will not give up the places I must
see, nor the women I must love, nor the work that I must do. I will
only concentrate upon these noble things because I must waste so
much energy in trying to make a half dead corpse into a man.

Asthma was finally to kill him by weakening his heart and
bringing on a stroke. But his clear-eyed knowledge that other
artists—like Proust—had carried through their work in its despite,
generally preserved him from the worse disease of self-pity.

Confronting his problem within the issues of his art, it can
be said that Putnam was a prime example of the split that Emerson recognized as so often fatal to his contemporaries, the split
between genius and talent. Tate was, I believe, the first to call
Putnam 'a New England romantic,' and he was in no respect
more bound up with his heritage than in his reliance upon moments of vision, and in his all too apparent helplessness when
those moments failed. He never possessed any great range of
technical resource. He passed beyond the sonnet sequence to
loose couplets and to a limber-cadenced primarily blank verse.
But in the case of nearly all his successful poems he depended
far more upon an initial *élan* than upon the gradual accruals of
craftsmanship. In one of his fragments he said:

> I swore my talent should not turn
> Into another penny getting black,

but he could not seem to prevent it. His language, so swift and
firm at its best, often grew constricted when he labored over it.
And when he tried for intensification by deliberately abandoning what he called the 'long fulsome lines' of his 'Daughters of
the Sun,' the resulting unrhymed tetrameters were merely bare
and harsh.

How much the lessening of his inspiration was due to the
group's breaking up is hard to say. But their own careers dis-
persed them, and when Putnam separated from his first wife

and moved away himself for some years, those ebullient evenings were over. Also, it must be added, that along with the
corrosion of several of his other young values, drunkenness no
longer remained 'bright and wild.' As Putnam himself said, it
often released our tongues only into 'dull and sodden' clanging.
But a worse delusion than alcohol may have lurked in the pitfall
that has betrayed so many other Americans: the bottomless hole
into which they have disappeared in determining to produce the
great American novel or the monumental epic. One of the most
promising features in Putnam's first outlines for his long poem
was his refusal to adopt any arbitrary structure such as he came
to feel had badly handicapped Crane in *The Bridge,* in that
poet's effort to make too much depend on his central symbol as
a span between past and future. But as the notes for *The Earthly
Comedy* began to pile up, as he tried to fit in episodes long before his hero's birth and to involve him in every possible rami-
fication of the unfolding consciousness of our age, Putnam unwittingly became a prey to the opposite mistake of refusing to
accept any formal limitations whatever. He sketched a poem
too vast ever to be able to shoulder the weight of writing it.

   It's easy enough now for someone like myself, whose tastes
are more for classic than for romantic art and thought, to point
out where Putnam went wrong. But he spent many sleepless
nights sweating over the confusions inherent in his values. Like
his hero he had trusted his instincts unfalteringly, but he came
to the painful recognition that the ego may be the most blinding
of traps.

   In his 'Hymn to Chance' his voices sang: 'Make us tough and
mystical.' Both those oddly-associated adjectives were freighted
for him beyond their usual connotations. The 'toughness' that he
invoked was what has made the Hemingway hero such a pervasive register for our time. It was really a shield for the sensitive mind that had cast away the protective Victorian conventions, and had found itself rawly exposed to experience. It was
another kind of Yeatsian mask. Putnam put it on when he said:
'I am a hobo with a low repute.' That may sound like a pose,
but when you think it over, you realize that it is a strictly accurate description of the status of the artist in America. 'Mystical'

is a word one might not have expected to be valued at all by Putnam, who had seemed to find himself at ease in Hasbrouck's 'enchanted cynicism.' But Bill Williams in Hell had asked: 'What guidance in this mess?' And one of Putnam's notes reflected: 'If Bill should go so far as to have a Vergil, he would have old Walt Whitman—the Whitman of *Democratic Vistas*, who would indeed think himself in Hell if he were with us now.'

If we are in Hell, where is our Heaven? What kind of deity was invoked as Lord Chance? Putnam's 'Hymn' addressed him under many different guises. As Lord Gardener, for his gifts of the blossoming earth. As Lord Prince of Hell, for his gift of thought, 'which coils insistently through our too sensate dust.' As Lord Costumer, for his seductive gifts of blood and spirit. The poet himself recognized that such a protean conception, beyond 'the tiny names of gods,' was also beyond exact formulation. Indeed, he believed that fact to be the essence of Chance's immeasurable power. Yet only through the acceptance of that power, under his basic title of Lord Anarch, did Bill—and Putnam—believe that they could stand erect and free.

'Chance' is unquestionably the 'key-word' in Putnam's poetry. A young man who had had all the opportunities of our wide-open 'twenties, he had known himself, in his 'Epistle,' to have been favored by chance's 'snobbery.' But he had also apostrophized Manning as

> My reckless brother, gleaming furious
> To kill the chance inimical to us.

As he advanced into the darkly menaced years of the depression, he realized that 'unseemly' chance was not the 'playful child' that it could appear at college. He saw it as 'gray hands enfolding all our lives.'

What then was Bill, even under the mystical guidance of Whitman, to affirm? Putnam was hardly in revolt against formal religion. As was the case for so many of his immediate contemporaries, that war had been won so long ago that it no longer engaged him. He was exposed to Unitarianism in his home, but from adolescence on he was an atheist. As we have seen, he believed that the State was the one great living institution with

which his hero was inescapably confronted. In his first notes for
his 'general scheme,' written before 1930, he put it this way:
'The Modern State which is the decadent counterpart of the
Medieval Cathedral. Into it the bourgeois put their money, and
on it the disinherited rest their hopes, as in Russia—a Modern
Astarte, a blowsy whore.' That fits in with the formulation that
he was soon to develop in his 'Hymn': 'Bill finds freedom when
he finds Chance—and freedom only exists in anarchy.'

But even before he published *The Five Seasons*, Putnam's own
politics had begun to change. He had become a close friend of
Bronson Cutting, the New Mexican senator who was to decline
the offer to be Roosevelt's Secretary of the Interior, since, among
other reasons, his own quiet acceptance of the necessity of socialization had already gone farther than anything that was contemplated by the New Deal. Putnam grew to realize that the artist
and the intellectual could hardly stand any longer in isolation.
He had always thought of himself as a rebel, but now the
grounds of his rebellion gradually shifted into a more frontal attack against modern capitalism. Many of the fragmentary poems
that he wrote during the last seven or eight years of his life
deal with political subjects: a tribute to Carlo Tresca, a mocking
satire of Colonel McCormick, some lines to a young soldier
voicing the hope that this war into which the boy was entering
so innocently might prove really to be a people's war for liberation.

It may be that Putnam's shifting political convictions were
another handicap to the completion of his narrative, but only, I
believe, in the sense that any work risks such blurring transformation if it remains unachieved too long. Despite the frustrations of his illness and his inability to do prolonged work, Putnam's central beliefs in the nineteen-forties took on a fighting
confidence that they had not had before. Equality was no longer
something to be lightly taken for granted, even in America, but
to be constantly re-won against native fascists, north or south.
He had read sporadically in Marxist theory, and reached the
conclusion that the continual development of industrial techniques for distribution as well as production meant that no people or class in the world could long be barred from their share

in the common wealth. He still believed it was his function to be 'solid in rebellious life':

> Because rebellion was the core of sanity
> In the time and country I was living in.

But in a new postwar America which seemed to be forgetting with terrifying rapidity the necessity of holding to the conception of 'one world,' if there were to be any world at all, Putnam felt that rebellion was no longer a function of the individual alone. His concern with solidarity deepened, and, despite all risks involved in transforming theory into practice, he began to speak of himself as a communist. Instead of accepting the blind determination of Chance, he now conceived freedom in Engels' terms, as the recognition of necessity.

His final scale of values can be suggested in an outline for two unwritten poems:

### Ballad of Lost Pleasures

First, I lost the riding of horses (Hay fever).

Second, I lost the delight of full-blooming fields, the excess of bloom.

Third, I lost the company of cats, dogs, and all furred animals. (And I did not like snakes well enough to take up with them.)

Fourth, I lost the pleasure of thinking I was the only rebellious guy.

Fifth, I lost my irritated mind.

Sixth, my body lost its resiliency, in the endeavor to breathe.

Seventh, O Venus, having served you in all ways, I lost the urgency of love.

### Ballad of Gained Pleasures

First, I gained the company of men and women, too.

Second, the race seemed kind to me.

Third, money and power slipped out of my hands. (I did not have the gift.)

Fourth, I began to see myself as without self.

Fifth, I began, before I died, to live and act in the new world, thinking of others rather than myself.

Sixth, being old and hardened, I did not connect this with the Christian myth, nor any other myth.

In the mass of his other fragments there is much anguish bordering on despair as he knew himself dying with his work undone. Occasionally a line soared out of his suffering:

> This falcon has brought down no game today.

But as that line knew, most of these fragments did not leave the ground:

> I have worn the white carnation,
> Seen it shrivel into brown,
> And my talent wilting down . . .

In a will dated two summers before his death, from his parents' home to which he had returned once more, he left his manuscripts in charge of his brother-in-law Stephen Fritchman and myself, with the expressed feeling that most of the unprinted did not warrant publication, and with the characteristic addition: 'Don't disgrace me, boys.' On the back of the page he wrote:

### Melancholy Lyric

> There is an old serious male living
> In a small room, but with loud thoughts.
> He is sick and this feller cannot travel.
>
> There is the great world turning around his room,
> The whole world turning, and there he is
> Getting all the reports, in print, over the air,
> In the more learned books, in pamphlets,
> And kindlier friends bringing life to him.
>
> The poor bastard detests his doom.
> Who would not with the smell of life
> And the stir along the streets, in the shops,
> And the live occurrences happening
> Far from his small, serious room?

Yeats found that the artist's life, even at its best, is an endless 'preparation for something that never happens.' Emerson kept coming back to the metaphor that on the very edge of the river of life he felt himself to be parched and miserably dying. Putnam enacted that metaphor to its bitter conclusion. But though

he felt that he had ended in defeat, his best passages, both those
of lyric delicacy and those of realistic acidness, still look as good
as they did twenty years ago. They convey the sharp-eyed intensity suggested in Cheney's masterful portrait of Putnam,
painted in the fall that *Trinc* appeared. The high point of his
eloquence was reached in his passage to the chief daughter of
the Sun. But, again like Emerson, Putnam's eloquence was that
of the rhapsode, so cloudily full that it inescapably deliquesced
after lines whose magnificence defied the lightning.

The two poems by which he will probably continue to be
most frequently represented in anthologies, 'Hasbrouck and the
Rose' and 'Ballad of a Strange Thing,' are his most achieved. The
first of these is a remarkable piece of concentration, a whole
dramatic episode in forty lines. It is set at a drinking party of
Bill's friends, and the drama consists in an interchange between
Smollet Smith and Hasbrouck that reveals a devastating contrast
between their philosophies. Smollet, after many drinks, flourishing his glass in the air, says:

> 'Drink with me, Bill, drink up to the Rose.'
> But Hasbrouck laughed like old men in a myth,
> Inquiring, 'Smollet, are you drunk? What rose?'
> And Smollet said, 'I drunk? It may be so;
> Which comes from brooding on the flower, the flower
> I mean toward which mad hour by hour
> I travel brokenly; and I shall know,
> With Hermes and the alchemists—but, hell,
> What use is it talking that way to you?
> Hard-boiled, unbroken egg, what can you care
> For the enfolded passion of the Rose?'
>
> Then Hasbrouck's voice rang like an icy bell:
> 'Arcane romantic flower, meaning what?'

And what follows corresponds to the contrast between the ideal-
ization in Guillaume de Lorris' opening sections of the *Roman
de la Rose* and its cynical worldly conclusion by Jean de Meun.
For Hasbrouck has known the Rose, 'the glowing bath / Of
ecstasy and clear forgetfulness.' He has known her for two nights

and a day of exquisite debauchery as she lay beside him in a
hotel room 'in Springfield, Massachusetts.'

> 'And that is all I know about the flower;
> I have eaten it—it has disappeared.
> There is no Rose.'

> Young Smollet Smith let fall his glass; he said
> 'Oh Jesus, Hasbrouck, am I drunk or dead?'

Hasbrouck's single speech takes up half the poem. His own
kind of rhapsody is well expressed through brokenly irregular
verse; and this central passage is effectively framed between the
rhymes in the opening description which carry into Smollet's
speech and the single couplet of Smollet's dismayed conclusion.
The conversational language is that of the place and period. We
exulted in a new sense of escaping from the then conventional
restrictions in mixing complex discourse with profanity and the
latest slang. We believed that Donne had done the same. But
the danger was that a poet like Putnam would follow Hemingway so far in throwing over the worn-out abstractions that his
speech would later be reduced to the catch-all words of his
friends, 'the poor bastards,' 'the swell guys,' a far too impoverished vocabulary for the usages of a poet.

In retrospect Putnam's outstanding work would now seem to
be his 'Ballad of a Strange Thing.' It is ironic that this should be
so, since it was the first poem he wrote in his transition from
'Green Wine' to 'Brandy.' He staked much more himself on the
poems dealing with Bill, but this two-hundred line narrative,
composed just as his myth-making faculty was beginning to
swing into play and before he had settled on his later characters,
possesses both freshness and completeness. One of the most
saddening risks that an artist runs is that the first ore he strikes
in a new vein may be its richest.

In this poem are lines giving Putnam's ripe evocation of the
New England countryside where he had lived as a boy:

> And then the days moved gravely by,
> Time drowned in fluent clarity
> Flowing between him and me,
> Who only lay along the walls

Unshamed of indolence, and heard
The dusty harvesters' harsh calls
To sweating teams, loading the sheaves
On the steep withered fields—their care
Was none of ours; or reasoned there
Where the mill-pond burned with leaves
And rustled at the dam, on those
Stark thoughts that rose
Out of cool spoken words, or we
Loafing in the arbor ate
Slowly the warm grapes, the rusty
Creaking swallows skimmed
The long ridgepoles, the day grew late
Easily, and dimmed.

The poet's companion here in this idyll of autumn is a wanderer named Jack Chance. Their ease of relaxation hums through
these lines. Here Putnam's handling of his prevailing tetrameter
may be occasionally clumsy, but it is not at all constricted, even
when his eight syllables contract to a condensed four. The sequence of rhymes is skillfully varied, especially when 'me,' seemingly left unrhymed, is finally matched with 'we,' thus helping
to bind the poet with his new friend. The sense breaks across the
lines in loose-fingered chords; and the syntax, though also loose,
holds the pattern of the poet's thoughts. The final lines in this
passage carry the skimming of the swallows into a comparable
skimming and dipping of the light. The falling of both the
adverb 'easily' and the verb 'dimmed' is as graceful and as firm
as Putnam could have wanted to write.

Jack is the hero. It is he who recites tall tales and bawdy songs
to the village group drinking their cider around the fire, spinning
them out with the corrosive cunning of a sorcerer. But on Hal-
lowe'en night he outdoes himself with the ballad stanzas that
rise fluently to his lips and out of Putnam's structure. His story is
about how he once saw a man chasing a girl along a brook.
When he finally caught up with her, she turned in defiance and
then plunged into the stream, and all the man held in his embrace were some spiked reeds that cut his hands. But then he
stooped and made a whistle of one of the reeds and saying,

'Sometimes there's music in these girls,' he 'blew five even notes and stopped.'

> 'And then there came along the bank
> A black majestic goat
> With yellow eyes and gilded horns
> And a white beard at its throat.
>
> The goat lay down before his feet
> Respectfully, dipping its head,
> And the man laughed and, "Can this be
> A messenger?" he said.
>
> And played again and now more wild
> And cloudily intricate,
> And the goat arose and danced like one
> Hieratic and sedate.
>
> And that is all,' said Chance, and then
> He said, 'So long,' and walked away
> Casually, as if the night were day.
> And we jumped up calling, and then
> Stood silent for over us coldly fell
> Five piercing notes, each like a spark;
> We stood there stiffly and immersed,
> Hearing laughter in the dark,
> Until I spoke, being the first,
> 'We had better go home now to bed;
> We have drunk too much,' I said.

Jack Chance is seen no more in Pollard Mill. Instead the rains beat down the autumn leaves, and after the winter, in a brief concluding passage, comes the war in Europe. The spell of Jack's world is broken, but in Putnam's season of possession of it, he had laid hold upon a folk-myth that he could reincarnate on his own native soil with fantasy and robustness. Jack is also Putnam's version of the scholar gypsy. As he becomes Pan wooing Syrinx, Chance is fused with the god of fertility, the happiest embodiment that Putnam's otherwise bleak deity was to find.

*Kenyon Review,* 1949

# Theodore Spencer, 1902–1949

## I

THEODORE Spencer, Boylston Professor of Rhetoric and Oratory and Tutor in the Department of English, died of a sudden heart attack on January 18, 1949.

Born at Villanova, Pennsylvania, on July 4, 1902, he was the only son of Theodore Spencer and Helena Carroll Frazier. His father, vice-president and general manager of the Bell Telephone Company in Philadelphia, died when his son was three. The boy grew up with his mother and sister at Haverford, where he attended the Haverford Academy. Extremely tall, blond, and thin, he entered Princeton with the class of 1923. He plunged eagerly into the literary life of the college as an editor of the undergraduate magazine. He was also very active in the dramatic club, and once remarked that if he had only been six inches shorter, he would have tried to go on the professional stage. But as his tastes developed, he became more concerned with writing, and, upon graduating, accepted an opportunity for further study of literature at Trinity College, Cambridge. There he took the first part of the English Tripos. He also continued to write verse, and he is still remembered in the role of the Duke in the Marlowe Society production of *The Duchess of Malfi*.

Elizabethan drama continued to be one of his central interests when he enrolled in the Harvard Graduate School in the fall of

The first of these two pieces on Spencer was published as a 'faculty minute' in the *Harvard University Gazette;* the original draft was written by Matthiessen, subject to revision by the other signatory members of the committee: I. A. Richards, Kenneth B. Murdock, John H. Finley, Jr., Harry Levin, and W. J. Bate. The second piece was written for the magazine *Contemporary Poetry*. From each account I have deleted material which was treated more fully in the other.—ED.

1925. His thesis, which grew—ten years later—into his first book, *Death and Elizabethan Tragedy* (1936), was written under Kittredge. But its subtitle, 'A Study of Convention and Opinion,' suggests also the kinship he felt with Lowes. And although he was never formally enrolled in any of Babbitt's courses, he came to realize that his debt to them was the greatest of any formed during his years as a graduate student. For Babbitt strengthened his belief in the cardinal importance of ideas.

Spencer became a tutor in 1927, the year before he received his doctor's degree. He was to remain convinced that the tutorial system was the most valuable aspect of Harvard undergraduate education. One of the original group of tutors in Eliot House, he contributed richly to the life there. He was one of those most responsible for the Eliot performances of Elizabethan comedies at Christmas time. His concern with the tutorial system was to deepen through his later chairmanship of the Board of Tutors in English, and through his long association with the Committee on Degrees in History and Literature.

His first lectures were given in 1928, in Lowes' graduate course on Chaucer. These led the next year to his own course in Comparative Literature, 'Studies in the Transition from Medieval to Modern Culture.' This course, which he was to offer frequently thereafter, indicated his method and range in teaching. It moved from Dante to Montaigne and the Elizabethans, and drew also upon philosophy and the fine arts. But Spencer's first publication in book form rose from another center of his interests. This was *A Garland for John Donne*, which he edited in 1931. Opening with an essay by T. S. Eliot, this collection helped clarify why the generation of poets and critics after the First World War had felt such a close kinship with the seventeenth-century metaphysical poets. When Eliot returned to Harvard as Norton Professor of Poetry in 1932–33, Spencer was delighted to assist him in a course on contemporary literature. This was to develop, a few years later, into a comparable course of his own, in which Spencer was to introduce many Harvard students to the leading writers of our time. He was also to edit *Stephen Hero*, the first draft of Joyce's *Portrait of the Artist as a Young Man*.

But at the time his appointment as an assistant professor ran out in 1939, Harvard had not yet fully appreciated Spencer's quality. He was not promoted, but within a few weeks after that news, he was the first American ever to have been elected as a permanent lecturer in English literature at Cambridge, England. The outbreak of the Second World War prevented him from taking up that post, and Harvard had a rare opportunity for second thought. Spencer became an associate professor in 1940, and was promoted to the Boylston chair in 1946.

During these years, his powers ripened. *Shakespeare and the Nature of Man* (1942) grew naturally from his big undergraduate course on Shakespeare, as well as from a series of Lowell lectures. In his earlier book he had been occupied with the conflicting attitudes towards life from which Elizabethan tragedy had sprung. Now he broadened his survey to outline the Renaissance world-view, and to describe the tension which is resolved in Shakespeare's tragedies, the tension between the forces of order and the forces making for chaos.

After his appointment as Boyston professor, he gave for the first time courses in advanced composition. He offered one of the first courses under the new heading of General Education, a course dealing with the New Testament, Dante, and Shakespeare. He was particularly active, as chairman of the Morris Gray Committee, in bringing to Harvard a long list of distinguished poets for readings from their work. His interests also continued to expand outside the university. He served as president of the College English Association, became a Fellow in American Letters at the Library of Congress, a trustee of the Boston Athenaeum, of the New England Conservatory of Music, and of Wellesley College. His first marriage, to Anna Murray, ended in divorce. Their son John is now a senior at Andover. He was married to Eloise Bergland Worcester last spring.

It is impossible to convey, in a faculty minute, the gaiety and resilience of Ted Spencer's spirit. He had mastered the disciplines of scholarship, but he was not the conventional scholar. His stylish clothes and bright bow ties, the lifelong fondness for playing the piano as a delight to himself and his friends, the eager knowledge of birds which can be seen also in his poems, the verve with which he read Shakespeare aloud, the capacity for throwing himself into each new enthusiasm—all these things had seemed to keep him younger than middle age. Most characteristically winning was a certain humorous, half-deprecating grace, natural perhaps to a man of his height who forever bent in conversation, but which reflected at bottom his modesty and even tenderness of feeling. His junior colleagues have spoken of how he went out of his way to welcome newcomers to Harvard. W. H. Auden has stated his value as a critic of the manuscripts of fellow poets. His great function for his generation in American teaching lay in his refusal to admit any false separation between present and past, in his quiet insistence that the study of literature must always bear directly upon our own lives.

As long ago as his first book, Spencer knew that an acceptance of life involves an acceptance of death. This knowledge was woven into one of his best poems:

> The day was a year at first
> When children ran in the garden;
> The day shrank down to a month
> When the boys played ball.
>
> The day was a week thereafter
> When young men walked in the garden;
> The day was itself a day
> When love grew tall.
>
> The day shrank down to an hour
> When old men limped in the garden;
> The day will last forever
> When it is nothing at all.

*Harvard University Gazette,* 1949

## II

When one's life has been interwoven with another's for twenty-five years, it is hard to isolate a few memories since each one ripples out into an ever widening circle of associations. Theodore Spencer and myself came to Harvard as graduate students in the same fall, and from then on many of my best hours were spent in his company.

Spencer was continually ranging out of the university in his contacts. He loved to meet people, and had a particular flair in bringing his lions together to act like lambs with one another. With his quick and always boyish charm he was an unfailing host. One of the memorable annual occasions was the way, decked out in fancy vest and bright bow tie, he greeted a house full of visitors to celebrate Shakespeare's birthday with his own concoction of Fish House punch.

Among all his varied activities the writing of verse continued constant. *The Waste Land* had appeared during Spencer's senior year at Princeton, and through Eliot, like all of our generation, he had been drawn to Donne. But Spencer was also a musician, and his sensitive ear found some of its keenest delights in the later style of Yeats.

His own poetry betrayed for many years the special problem of having responded so generously to the chief modern masters. For a decade he was writing 'metaphysical' poetry as refracted by the nineteen-twenties, and he called one unpublished collection 'Ixion's Children.' But the mood of disillusion suggested by this title, that we were those who having embraced merely a cloud were now bound on an endlessly revolving wheel, really did not fit his essentially light spirit. Nor did the harsh contrasts and sudden breaks in style which brought into poetry some of the dissonances of modern music. For Spencer's natural feeling was for the melodic line, and he was to find his way out of too close imitation of the early Eliot by more tradition rather than less. It was in the course of an essay about Yeats that he praised the steady harmony of Samuel Daniel; and in one of his latest and best pieces of criticism he found in Sidney a closer kinship with his own aims than had existed in Donne.

This is to say that Spencer's real gift was for the short lyric. When he brought to his use of the Yeatsian refrain all the delicacies and subtleties of his own response to rhythm, he wrote, in *The Paradox in the Circle*, some of his very best poems. This collection, not made until he was nearing forty, shows how hard it often is really to live up to Spencer's basic conviction that poetry can be nourished only on life. For not until these poems did an unexpected access of rich and ecstatic love lift him out of the class of the too facile disciple to find a mature voice of his own. This was both a speaking and a singing voice, gay and witty as well as tender and poignant, delighting in the cadences of the light-footed dancing dandy, and yet asking too: 'What terrible thing is time?'

Thereafter he was to try several longer philosophical structures, and he always disagreed with my view that these were not his métier. But he also kept on experimenting with new lyric forms, and his pleasure in virtuosity led him into the exacting discipline of making a whole series of six-line poems. The best of these, whatever their apparent subject, are variations on the single theme of the new-found happiness of his second marriage. But within eight months after that marriage his heart suddenly stopped.

A remark he made several years ago expressed his enduring belief about art. He had brought home from England a picture he liked by a young and unknown painter. As we looked at it together, Spencer said: 'I don't suppose this man will ever be a major artist. But he's completely devoted to his craft. And that devotion is the chief thing, isn't it, in keeping the arts alive?'

*Contemporary Poetry,* 1950

Indiana University
Gary Center Library